OXFORD READINGS IN PH

Series Editor **G. J. Warnock**

THE PHILOSOPHY OF HISTORY

Also published in this series

Other volumes are in preparation

THE PHILOSOPHY
OF HISTORY

Edited by
PATRICK GARDINER

OXFORD UNIVERSITY PRESS

1974

Oxford University Press, Ely House London W. 1

GLASGOW NEW YORK TORONTO MELBOURNE WELLINGTON
CAPE TOWN IBADAN NAIROBI DAR ES SALAAM LUSAKA ADDIS ABABA
DELHI BOMBAY CALCUTTA MADRAS KARACHI LAHORE DACCA
KUALA LUMPUR SINGAPORE HONG KONG TOKYO

ISBN 0 19 875031 5

© OXFORD UNIVERSITY PRESS 1974

PRINTED IN GREAT BRITAIN
BY RICHARD CLAY (THE CHAUCER PRESS) LTD
BUNGAY, SUFFOLK

CONTENTS

INTRODUCTION

UNTIL comparatively recently the function of the philosophy of history was largely envisaged as being one of determining the nature and significance of the human past. So regarded, it has enjoyed a long career, stretching back to Graeco-Roman times and reaching its culmination in the imposing theories elaborated during the eighteenth and nineteenth centuries by such men as Vico, Hegel, Comte, and Marx. According to this traditional view, philosophers of history were concerned (broadly speaking) with the same subject-matter as historians in the conventional sense; they approached it, however, from a position far removed from that occupied by their less adventurous colleagues. For they were thought of as being engaged, not upon limited and piecemeal inquiries of the sort found in ordinary historical work, but upon the more ambitious and dramatic undertaking of providing an all-embracing interpretation of the historical process as a whole. Admittedly, those who embarked on this enterprise often conceived of the past in strikingly divergent terms. By some, for instance, it was seen as exhibiting a unilinear progression towards a prospective and intrinsically desirable future state, by others as taking a cyclical course that involved the continual recurrence of identifiable patterns of growth and decay; some considered it to be governed by causal or mechanistic principles analogous to those elicited by the physical sciences, while others by contrast invoked rational or purposive notions and professed to discern in history the unfolding of a pervasive 'logic' or the shapes of a unitary design; to some the sequence of events appeared to conform to a necessary or deterministic order, while others understood it as allowing for the play of an element of irreducible contingency or freedom. But, whatever differences of outlook and emphasis there may have been, there was general agreement that they were committed to a substantive or factual branch of study, one that dealt directly—albeit from an Olympian vantage-point—with happenings in the realm of human affairs.

During the present century this classical conception of philosophy of history has suffered a heavy loss of prestige. It has not been denied that, in the course of evolving their comprehensive systems, historical theorists sometimes threw off seminal ideas and insights which were subsequently absorbed within the structure of professional historiography; this is especially evident in the case of the Marxian scheme, and further examples could be cited. Moreover, it has been allowed that their writings often acted as a spur to the development of inquiries in other domains, anticipating lines of investigation which have since been pursued, at the level of detailed empirical research, within the fields of sociology and anthropology. But the central aspiration to afford a total explanatory account of the past has been less sympathetically regarded, and the critical reception given by historians and philosophers alike to A. J. Toynbee's *A Study of History* some years ago was symptomatic of a widespread disenchantment with the entire genre to which the book belonged.[1] It was not merely that the authors of such works often seemed prepared to override or disregard facts that conflicted with the tenets of cherished doctrine; they were also accused of conceptual imprecision and of formulating hypotheses which turned out on inspection to be either hopelessly vague or else to be no more than the tautological consequences of definitions arbitrarily determined in advance. More generally, it was objected that they tended to rely upon unexamined *a priori* assumptions, regarding both the methods they employed and the nature of the material with which they were dealing. Even where (as was frequently the case) they claimed to conform to canons of reasoning accepted in the natural sciences, it was far from obvious that they possessed an accurate conception of what these were or that their actual procedures bore a convincing resemblance to the models they professed to follow. And did not such a programme in any case raise a fundamental issue of principle—the problem, namely, of whether it was justifiable to regard the historical studies as amenable to a scientifically orientated methodology, however this might be conceived?

To pose a question like the one just mentioned is to introduce considerations that relate to the status of history as a particular type of knowledge or mode of thought. And it is, in fact, to such considerations, as opposed to substantive ones concerning the over-all character and tenor of the historical process, that contemporary philosophical attention has been chiefly directed. The shift of standpoint involved has far-

---

[1] For one historian's comments, see P. Geyl, *Debates with Historians* (The Hague, 1955), especially Chs. 5–8. A highly influential philosophical critique of historical speculation is to be found in K. R. Popper's *The Open Society and its Enemies* (London, 1945) and the same author's *The Poverty of Historicism* (London, 1957); for a careful philosophical examination of Toynbee, see also W. H. Dray, 'Toynbee's Search for Historical Laws' (*History and Theory*, 1960).

reaching implications. For, unlike their speculative predecessors, most present-day contributors to the philosophy of history take it to be a second-order form of inquiry with the aim, not of trying to elucidate and assess the human past itself, but rather of seeking to elucidate and assess the ways in which historians typically describe or comprehend that past. It is treated, in other words, as having to do with such matters as the presuppositions underlying historical narratives, the categories implicit in historical judgement and explanation, and the modes of argument whereby historical conclusions are supported or established. Hence, as currently practised, it can be said to accord with the analytical and conceptually self-conscious temper that now prevails among philosophers of the English-speaking world.

The writings included in the present anthology will be found in general to reflect this altered perspective. Yet, in acknowledging the extent and importance of the change, it should not be supposed that there are no significant continuities between traditional views of the subject and the modern notion of it as a predominantly critical discipline. As has already been implied, classical theorists were by no means at one in their opinion of the kind of interpretation to which historical phenomena are susceptible. Alongside those who, like Comte and Buckle, were inspired by the example set by the natural sciences, there were others who insisted that the scientific paradigm was not appropriate to history and who claimed that an altogether different framework was called for if historical evolution and development were to be rendered intelligible. Thus men like Vico, Herder, and Hegel tended to stress the contrasts rather than the similarities between the sphere of natural events and processes and the sphere of human thought and action, rejecting the assumption that, because natural scientists had been conspicuously successful in applying generalizing principles and abstract quantitative categories to the former, it followed that the latter could be tidily fitted into the same theoretical mould. From this point of view their attempts to explain the past in its entirety appeared to have a distinguishable methodological aspect and to embody specific claims about the actual character and scope of historical thought. It is worth noting, moreover, that a number of the procedural suggestions they advanced within an overridingly speculative setting later re-emerged, at the turn of the present century, in the work of certain Continental writers who expressly eschewed speculative ambitions in favour of purely epistemological concerns. Foremost among such thinkers were Wilhelm Dilthey and Benedetto Croce; and it was to their pioneering conceptions, together with those propounded in England by their influential follower,

R. G. Collingwood, that philosophy of history in the contemporary critical sense owed much of its initial impetus By challenging the belief that the study of human affairs is essentially continuous with the scientific investigation of natural phenomena and by insisting that the historian's approach to his subject-matter must, in the nature of the case, radically diverge from that adopted in other domains of inquiry, they helped to place the problem of historical knowledge and understanding in a fresh light. The effect was to throw into sharp relief a range of issues that have since become focal points of controversy.

Some of the issues in question are to be found, forcefully raised, in the British Academy lecture by Collingwood with which this collection opens. It is not without significance that Collingwood's original philosophical affiliations, like those of Dilthey and Croce, lay with the tradition of post-Kantian German idealism. Adherents to that tradition, by contrast with exponents of classical British empiricism, tended to portray the human mind in predominantly active terms: they treated it, in other words, as creative and self-determining, playing a constructive role in life and experience rather than passively responding, in mechanical fashion, to the promptings of external or internal stimuli. The special importance that Collingwood ascribed to history, and his conviction that its character had been disastrously misconstrued by empiricist philosophers, can be seen to reflect this underlying picture of man as an autonomous purposive agent. As the essay included here shows, he considered the Humean, or 'positivistic', ambition to formulate a theory of human nature in accordance with principles borrowed from the physical sciences to be infected by cardinal errors. To subscribe to it is to assume that human behaviour is subject to universal regularities, invariant from age to age, and that in this sphere, as elsewhere, explanation necessarily consists in subsuming what occurs beneath 'a general formula or law of nature'. Against such a view Collingwood claims that human nature is involved in a constant process of reflective self-transformation, in the sense that men are to be found continually modifying, revising, and supplementing the inheritance of skills, attitudes, and modes of experiencing the world which they receive from their predecessors and hand on to their successors; it follows that the notion of a fixed human character, conforming to a set of unchanging principles valid for men at all times and places, is a myth. Furthermore, Collingwood maintains that the position he wishes to reject in any case presupposes the adoption of an external or 'spectatorial' standpoint that is wholly inappropriate to the context of human affairs. For the phenomena with which we are there concerned must be

conceived under the category of agency, and to comprehend an event
as an action, as opposed to a mere natural happening, is to see it as the
expression of human thought and volition. It has (to employ his
metaphor) an 'outside' and an 'inside'; less picturesquely, it is the embodiment at the level of observable physical reality of that developing
rationality which is man's distinctive attribute. Interpreting what men
do is thus a matter of eliciting the processes of thought that inform
their perceivable behaviour and are intrinsic to its correct identification
and description. But such interpretation is the business of the historical,
not the scientific, understanding. For the historian, unlike the natural
scientist, does not seek to explain events by correlating them with other
events in the light of some well-attested uniformity or general law; his
aim is rather to uncover their inner rationale, and this can only be
done—Collingwood argues—by 're-enacting' within his own mind the
thoughts of the person or persons with whose activities he is dealing.
Hence historical knowledge is irreducibly different from scientific knowledge: moreover, it is only by historical inquiry so conceived that man
can ever acquire an acceptable understanding of himself, a true grasp
of his diverse and changing powers as an agent in the world.

The initial attitude adopted by analytical philosophers to such attempts to vindicate the autonomy of history was a sceptical one. By
some, for instance, Collingwood's 'inner–outer' conception of historical
events was regarded as incorporating the relics of a discredited Cartesian dualism; it was also treated as encouraging the unplausible view
that the historian possesses a mysterious power of empathetic identification with the minds of historical agents which sets his interpretations of
their behaviour beyond the reach of empirical appraisal or criticism.[2]
Others were content simply to argue that Collingwood's account of
historical understanding, like the associated *Verstehen* doctrines of Dilthey and Max Weber, was in fact irrelevant to the main question at
issue. For to claim that such understanding required the re-enactment of
past thinking was merely to direct attention to the method, admittedly
familiar among historians, of imaginatively putting oneself in another's
position in order to arrive at an explanatory hypothesis. But that was
not to show that the explanations historians actually provide differ in
logical structure from those put forward in other areas of investigation;
in particular, it did not demonstrate that explaining historical actions

[2] This is a judgement to which I myself at one time subscribed: see my *The Nature of Historical Explanation* (Oxford, 1952). A later, and more sympathetic, treatment of Collingwood's aims is to be found in my article 'Historical Under-standing and the Empiricist Tradition', in *British Analytical Philosophy*, ed. B. Williams and A. Montefiore (London, 1965).

by reference to motivational factors was possible without assuming the truth of relevant psychological generalizations.[3] The majority of critics of this type were of an empiricist and scientifically orientated persuasion, and they tended to treat the so-called 'covering law' model of analysis—according to which explanation ideally consists in showing that a statement affirming the occurrence of the event to be explained is deducible from a set of premises comprising both statements of antecedent conditions and general laws—as the only serious candidate in the field.

This somewhat dismissive reaction has, however, by no means been the sole response, much of the interest of more recent work lying in the challenges it has provoked. One objection has taken the form of claiming that any attempt to specify the laws assumed to be implicit in the explanations given by historians breaks down; the general statements cited by proponents of the covering-law model are either too vague and loose for them to serve the purpose assigned to them or else prove to be so highly particularized as to deprive them of explanatory force. It is with such alleged difficulties that the article by Professor Mandelbaum is concerned. He admits that, in so far as covering-law theorists wish to maintain that explaining a complex historical event is a matter of subsuming it directly beneath a law asserting a simple uniformity between events of that type and certain regular accompaniments or antecedents, the above criticism of their position is hard to meet. Hence it is natural to suppose that some different account is needed. An alternative suggestion is one that represents the historian as committed to undertaking a detailed causal analysis of the event to be explained, whereby particular aspects or components are distinguished and shown to be connected with the presence of other factors. Mandelbaum allows that this kind of inquiry, understood as requiring close attention to the intricacies of the individual case, may be correctly identified as central to explanation in history. But it is not true that it is confined to the historical and social studies; it is characteristically employed in scientific contexts as well. Moreover—and more crucially—it is difficult to see how the various connections in question could be established, and relevant considerations be separated from irrelevant, without appealing to certain laws or empirical uniformities which may be presumed to hold at this level of selective analysis. His conclusion seems therefore to be, not that general laws play no part in historical explanation and understanding, but rather that the nature of the role they perform has commonly been misunderstood.

[3] See, e.g., C. G. Hempel's article, 'The Function of General Laws in History', *Journal of Philosophy*, 1942.

Even so, and despite its attractions, Mandelbaum's proposal would hardly satisfy all critics of the covering-law model, many of whom have expressed sympathy with Collingwood's belief that the interpretation of human action raises quite special difficulties for standard empiricist accounts of explanation. It is, indeed, noticeable that a revival of interest in Collingwood and the tradition to which he belonged has developed alongside a more general philosophical preoccupation with the notion of agency and the system of concepts in which it is embedded. Thus stress has been laid upon the distinction between behaviour regarded as a mere succession of bodily movements and behaviour understood as something attributable to a person in his capacity as a conscious purposive being. Although human activity in general comprises physical movement, it does not follow that the characterization of what someone does as an agent can be replaced without loss by a description that is confined—in however detailed a fashion—to registering bodily happenings. For in the former case, unlike the latter, we are committed to placing the individual's behaviour within an explanatory framework that has no apparent analogue at the merely physical level. Here the central concern is one of eliciting the sense or point of what is done, and this (it may be argued) can only be achieved in so far as we show it to be intelligible in terms of reasons, motives, or beliefs ascribable to the agent in question. Hence to understand an action is primarily to comprehend it, not as a causal consequence of antecedent events to which it stands in a purely contingent relation, but rather as an expression or vehicle of meaning whereby it is conceptually tied to some underlying pattern of thought or intention; moreover, such a pattern itself presupposes a background structure of established rules or practices of the sort that is integral to human life and experience as we know them. With these considerations in mind, it has been maintained by some recent philosophers that fruitful comparisons can be made between understanding what people do and understanding what they say. Not only may linguistic communication itself be viewed as a specific instance of rule-governed interaction between persons; it is also evident that the use of language enters indispensably into those other, non-linguistic, activities in which men typically engage as social beings with shared ideas and attitudes and with a common attachment to institutions.

A position of this kind, which draws upon themes implicit in the later writings of Wittgenstein, has been persuasively presented in the work of Professor Winch. In his view, explanation in the social sphere essentially consists in elucidating the significance of behaviour in terms acceptable to the agents concerned. Among other things, it involves a grasp of the concepts and conventions that govern their actions; these supply the relevant standards or criteria according to which what they do can be seen to be appropriate within a given context and thereby shown to be, in the requisite sense, intelligible. Furthermore, as he intimates throughout his book *The Idea of a Social Science*, Winch regards his approach as having implications for the analysis of historical procedures as well as sociological ones. In the concluding chapter of that essay—which is reproduced in the present volume—he explicitly contrasts his own conception of historical understanding with the positivist notion of it as 'the application of generalizations and theories to particular instances'; he contends that such understanding, which rests on an appreciation of 'humanly followed rules' rather than on a covert reference to 'causal laws', differs fundamentally from anything that is to be found exemplified in the natural sciences. And this is an opinion that has been to some extent echoed in Professor Dray's influential discussions of what he terms 'rational explanation' in history,[4] where stress is laid upon the role played by norms and principles—'the categories and concepts of *practice*'—in determining the reasonableness or appropriateness of specific historical actions.

The article by Dray included here, and Professor Hempel's reply which follows it, can, indeed, be said to be illustrative of a continuing philosophical debate. It is true that Dray does not suppose that providing a rational explanation necessarily rules out the possibility of giving one that conforms to the covering-law model; as he makes clear, he dissociates his position from Winch's in this respect. Nevertheless, he is insistent that there are two distinct types of explanation involved and that they belong to quite separate 'conceptual networks'. He implies, moreover, that it was a valid recognition of this logical difference, and not merely a confused appeal to metaphysical or psychological considerations, that originally prompted idealist theorists to emphasize notions like 'empathy' and 're-enactment' in their accounts of historical inquiry; however much positivist criticism may have sought to minimize the significance of such claims, they in fact pointed to a distinctive and irreducible aspect of historical interpretation, central to the status of history as a humanistically conceived discipline. Hempel, on his side, respects Dray's desire to offer an analysis which accords with historical practice and which does not attempt to force the explanations historians customarily provide into a rigid preselected mould. At the same time, he draws attention to an apparent difficulty in Dray's treatment of the subject which others have noted, namely, that to exhibit a historical agent's behaviour as having been appropriate or 'rationally required' in the light of certain aims and beliefs is not, as such, to explain why the action was in fact performed. Not only must the reasons in question be justifiably attributable to the agent concerned; they must further be understood to have been connected with what he did in the sense of determining or influencing him to do it. But this presupposes a conception of what it is to be a rational agent and of how such agents are normally disposed to respond to considerations or circumstances of various kinds. Hence it is argued that, even in the favoured cases where a person's conduct invites a rational interpretation, a tacit reference to assumptions of a general or law-like character is still essential from an explanatory standpoint. And similar arguments apply in the far-from-uncommon cases where the behaviour to be accounted for does not measure up to rational standards or where it has not been accompanied by any process of reflective deliberation. According to this view, then, explanation in terms of reasons for action does not in the end demand the postulation of an alternative analytical model, and for Hempel at least the claim that the covering-law theory affords an overall schema, capable of accommodating such explanation within its scope, remains substantially unshaken. Even so, scepticism regarding its adequacy persists. Thus—as Hempel himself notes—it has been urged that the general statements cited as underlying rational explanation do not in fact constitute empirical laws of the type required by the theory: to refer to what a rational agent would do under specified conditions is not so much to appeal to a falsifiable empirical generalization as to invoke an analytic truth which is elucidatory of the criteria that govern our notion of rational action.[5] Moreover, while recognizing that an account must be given of the actual connection between an agent's behaviour and the objectives and beliefs held to explain it, other critics have gone on to insist that this does not necessitate a retraction of the claim that such connections are in an important way conceptual in nature, rather than being straightforwardly causal in the sense posited by the covering-law thesis. Discussion here has chiefly centred upon the alleged interdependence of motivational and behavioural concepts, particular attention being paid to the conditions of application of terms like 'intention' and 'purpose' and to the logical implications of their use in contexts involving practical reasoning.[6] Much clearly turns on

---

[5] An objection on these lines is raised by Dray in his *Philosophy of History* (Englewood Cliffs, N.J., 1964), pp. 14–15.

[6] An interesting and rigorous presentation of the case for accepting a distinctive

such intricate questions as the relations between explanation and description in characterizing human activity and the extent to which it is
legitimate to distinguish the manner in which wants or desires account
for behaviour from the ways in which intentions or resolves may be
said to do so. It is with an aspect of these problems, seen as impinging
upon highly controversial issues in the contemporary analysis of speech
and action, that Mr. Skinner's article is in part concerned.

Skinner also touches upon a further matter that tends to arise in this
area. As has been seen, a basic theme in the work of philosophers of
history in the anti-positivist tradition, from Dilthey and Collingwood
on, has been the need to interpret historical events in a fashion that
would have been natural and acceptable to those who participated in
them. It is pre-eminently this (it is often argued) that marks off the approach of the physical scientist from that of the historical or social
investigator. For the former comprehends and orders his material by
means of categories and theories that are constructed by himself and his
fellow scientists, these being imposed on an externally conceived reality;
the latter, on the other hand, only achieves understanding in so far as
he interprets his human subject-matter in terms logically tied to, or
rooted in, the ideas and norms by reference to which the persons concerned would themselves conceptualize or explain what was going on.
On the face of it, such a position has the merit of being apparently consonant with established historical methodology, correctly stressing the
importance of avoiding anachronism and of exercising the kind of
imagination presupposed by the possession of a historical sense or
vision. Pressed to extremes, however, it has been felt to have more controversial consequences.

One problem that presents itself here is that of whether the beliefs
and practices of other periods can be treated as constituting relatively
self-contained systems, embodying their own independent standards of
intelligibility and rationality in a manner that makes criticism or assessment in the light of more recent criteria inappropriate. By some writers
this possibility has been viewed as carrying sceptical implications; the
limitations of the intellectual framework which the historian derives
from his particular cultural milieu would be liable to render his interpretations of previous ages inherently problematic, thus raising

---

model of teleological explanation in the historical and social spheres, based on the
'schema' of practical inference, is to be found in G. H. von Wright, *Explanation
and Understanding* (London, 1971). For an earlier treatment of related issues, see
also A. Donagan, 'Historical Explanation: The Popper–Hempel Model Reconsidered' (*History and Theory*, 1964).

general doubts concerning the status and reliability of much historical inquiry. More frequently, though, a less radical moral—reminiscent in certain respects of Herder—has been drawn, according to which it must be illegitimate for the historian to import into his accounts of the past notions of significance that are foreign to, or go beyond, the outlooks of those with whom he is dealing. Such a claim can be understood in more than one way; but, however taken, it seems open to the objection that it places unrealistically narrow restrictions upon historical procedure. Thus it is one thing to emphasize the historian's obligation to try to grasp, imaginatively and 'from within', the fashion in which his subjects conceived of their behaviour, the point or meaning they ascribed to it, the beliefs upon which it was founded: it is another to contend that this is all he is entitled to do. Should we wish, for example, to disqualify those analyses—quite commonly encountered in modern historiography—which question the agents' own conceptions of themselves and their doings and which suggest that, for reasons perhaps beyond the horizon of their understanding, they were in some way fundamentally confused or even the victims of an ideological illusion? Nor it this all. As Professor Walsh points out in his essay, history is commonly presumed to have aims that reach further than the explanation of why men behaved as they did, the eliciting of their intentions, policies, or principles. It also typically concerns itself with the outcome —whether anticipated by them or not—of their actions and (more generally) with such things as processes of development or collective movements to which they often contributed without being aware of so doing. There is, in other words, a clear sense in which the historian's retrospective vantage-point enables him to discriminate pervasive patterns or themes in the past and thereby to accord to events a significance not the less real for having been unenvisaged, and possibly unenvisageable, by contemporary participants or observers. The characteristic employment by historians of comprehensive categories and frameworks, which Walsh refers to as 'colligation', has precisely the function of illuminating the data in this way, highlighting continuities or connections in what might otherwise have given the impression of being an inchoate mass of disparate happenings. In general, it is fair to say that these aspects of historical understanding, together with those revealed by an examination of the role of narrative in history,[7] have only

---

[7] A discussion which focuses upon the nature and function of narrative in historiography is provided by W. B. Gallie in his *Philosophy and the Historical Understanding* (London, 1964). For another account which stresses, although from a different standpoint, narrative considerations, see A. C. Danto, *Analytical Philosophy of History* (Cambridge, 1965).

quite recently begun to receive from philosophers the scrutiny they deserve.

The availability of such modes of organizing and interpreting his material does not, of course, mean that the historian is entitled to neglect, override, or misconstrue the evidence at his disposal. Yet their presence in historical writing may, even so, call attention to a wider issue which has been a source of considerable theoretical dispute, if not disquiet. For it is hard—in many cases at least—not to regard their use as presupposing certain fundamental criteria of relevance or importance, criteria which in turn might seem to reflect personal attitudes and practical concerns. How far, though, is the admission of such a 'subjective' dimension into historical description compatible with the notion of history as a factual and objective discipline, concerned to provide a faithful account of what happened that is uncoloured by the preoccupations and interests of the present? It was partly with this difficulty in mind that the American historian of ideas, A. O. Lovejoy, gave an eloquent defence of the view that historical selection should be determined, not by what seems relevant or important to the historian or his own contemporaries, but solely by what seemed to be so in the eyes of the historical persons with whom he is concerned.[8] This proposal, however, once again invites the rejoinder that it sets implausible limits to historical practice which, if strictly observed, might issue in highly eccentric results. And it may further be challenged on the grounds that it offers to remedy a largely imaginary complaint, since the considerations presumed to impugn historical objectivity spring from an initially mistaken notion of what primarily governs the historian's criteria of selection. An approach along these lines is indicated in Professor Passmore's contribution to the subject. While in history—as elsewhere—selection is necessary and unavoidable, it does not follow that judgements of relevance and importance in the context of particular historical inquiries must be understood to derive from the arbitrary preferences or subjective interests of the historian. For, in so far as historical work takes as its starting-point specific problems, it is these —rather than factors of the sort just mentioned—which essentially determine what is worthy of inclusion or emphasis in the stories and accounts the historian provides. It may well be true that in choosing topics for investigation he is apt to be affected by contemporary preoccupations, with the consequence that histories written at one time are liable to show striking variations when compared with those written

[8] See his article, 'Present Standpoints and Past History', reprinted in *The Philosophy of History in our Time*, ed. H. Meyerhoff (New York, 1959).

at a different one. But to say that his choice of problems bears the mark of current concerns is not to say that the solutions he produces must be similarly influenced or infected; nor is there any justification on this score for distinguishing history from a host of other accredited forms of inquiry.

Generally speaking, Passmore is wary of attempts to differentiate sharply between history's claims to be objective and those made on behalf of other branches of knowledge. Further, as he rightly points out, it is easy to forget that the sciences themselves constitute a somewhat heterogeneous array. Nevertheless, if the question at issue is more narrowly interpreted to be one of whether it is a distinctive feature of the historical studies that an element of evaluation, moral or otherwise, enters of necessity into the actual structure and texture of the historian's thought about the past, the position is less clear. Much descriptive history of the period type, for instance, appears to involve singling out items or tendencies for attention in the light of over-all standards to which the historian subscribes and which he broadly expects his readers to share. And even in the case of narrative or explanatory history it would seem that conceptions of what is intrinsically important or interesting, and not merely of what is instrumentally or relatively so in respect of some particular outcome, often help to determine the stress that is laid upon certain factors and themes. Apart from these considerations, moreover, a further point is sometimes emphasized. Thus it has been maintained that the actual language the historian employs, bound up as it is with the delineation of human character and motivation, invariably incorporates a grasp of, and commitment to, a complex network of values and norms. To suggest that it might be suitably purged or 'purified' of such connotations by radical terminological reform is to propose an undertaking of almost unthinkable magnitude and one that would be ultimately destructive of history as we know it.

The latter argument figures prominently in Sir Isaiah Berlin's essay, *Historical Inevitability*,[9] where it is considered in the context of a comprehensive critique of theories which purport to portray the historical process as a unitary system, governed throughout by 'forces' or laws that preclude the possibility of events having taken a course different from the one they in fact followed. It was indicated at the beginning

[9] Other discussions of this much-debated topic include the following: L. Strauss, 'The Social Science of Max Weber' (*Measure*, Vol. 2, 1951); E. Nagel, *The Structure of Science* (London, 1961), Ch. 13; E. H. Carr, *What is History?* (New York, 1962), Ch. 3.

of this Introduction that philosophy of history in the speculative sense typically addressed itself to the formulation of such theories, and Berlin is partly concerned to expose the emptiness of its pretensions in this regard. But—as the extract from his essay which is included in the present volume shows—he also raises a problem with more general implications. For the notion that all human behaviour is susceptible to a deterministic interpretation can be entertained without necessarily embracing extravagant historical hypotheses of the kind he selects for attack. And if it is entertained, how far is such a supposition consonant with the assumptions that underlie history as this is customarily studied and written? It may, for example, be urged that the evaluative aspects of historical discourse and judgement cannot in the end be dissociated from certain basic ideas that pervade ordinary thought and are integral to our moral experience; and it may further be argued that these ideas are only applicable in so far as it is accepted that human beings are endowed with a measure of freedom of choice. According to Berlin, however, freedom in the requisite sense is excluded on determinist premises; concepts involving praise or blame, for instance, would either become otiose or else undergo a radical transformation if it were generally believed that every human choice is a necessary outcome of antecedent causal conditions ultimately beyond the individual's control. Thus, while he disclaims the intention of seeking to offer a refutation of deterministic interpretations of human behaviour, Berlin none the less contends that a consistent upholder of the determinist position is in fact committed to a drastic revision of categories which are as deeply entrenched in historical thought and language as they are in those of everyday life; moreover, he considers that the far-reaching and ramifying consequences of such a revision for historical practice have seldom, if ever, been realistically appreciated by those philosophers and historians who have given theoretical endorsement to the determinist thesis. Berlin's argument depends, as he himself points out, upon an interpretation of notions like free choice and responsibility which has often been contested—especially among empiricist thinkers—and which continues to meet resistance. As will be seen, it is questioned by Professor Nagel in the course of his careful examination of the status of determinism in both scientific and historical contexts. Whether his objections provide a convincing answer to the challenge Berlin presents is something the reader must judge for himself.[10]

Discussions of historical determinism in fact echo, once again, a

[10] For Berlin's own answer to these and related criticisms, see his *Four Essays on Liberty* (London, 1969), Introduction, pp. x–xxxvii.

theme which has been observed to recur throughout the career of philosophy of history, in its traditional as well as in its more modern manifestations. When, towards the end of his article, Nagel claims that to abandon determinism as a 'regulative principle' would be to 'withdraw from the enterprise of science', he at the same time issues a warning against the dangers of setting 'premature limits' to the scope of inquiry in its 'search for explanations'. Though the injunction is cautiously phrased, it is plain that he has the human studies partly in mind; yet this salutary reminder touches on points which—at least so far as history is concerned—remain contentious. For, while the attribution of explanatory aims to the historian is hardly in doubt, disagreement may still arise as to the nature of these. Are they logically continuous with those of the scientist and, if not, to what extent would a rejection of determinist principles in the field of human behaviour constitute an unacceptable restriction on the possibilities of historical understanding? It has, for example, been claimed on behalf of the 'rational' model of historical explanation that its acceptance is wholly consistent with the adoption of an indeterminist or 'libertarian' view of human action. Thus the problem returns of deciding where the actual limits upon historical inquiry may legitimately be placed, and this in turn is connected with the wider task of defining, and possibly redrawing, the boundaries of the natural sciences and the humanistic disciplines. To embark on such undertakings is to enter an area fraught with difficulties—conceptual, methodological, and ideological—which extend over a very broad range of philosophical concerns. Many of the questions posed in the contemporary analysis of history lie close to the centre of this strongly, and at times passionately, disputed territory.

I

HUMAN NATURE AND HUMAN HISTORY

R. G. COLLINGWOOD

I. THE SCIENCE OF HUMAN NATURE

MAN, who desires to know everything, desires to know himself. Nor is he only one (even if, to himself, perhaps the most interesting) among the things he desires to know. Without some knowledge of himself, his knowledge of other things is imperfect: for to know something without knowing that one knows it is only a half-knowing, and to know that one knows is to know oneself. Self-knowledge is desirable and important to man, not only for its own sake, but as a condition without which no other knowledge can be critically justified and securely based.

Self-knowledge, here, means not knowledge of man's bodily nature, his anatomy and physiology; nor even a knowledge of his mind, so far as that consists of feeling, sensation, and emotion; but a knowledge of his knowing faculties, his thought or understanding or reason. How is such knowledge to be attained? It seems an easy matter until we think seriously about it; and then it seems so difficult that we are tempted to think it impossible. Some have even reinforced this temptation by argument, urging that the mind, whose business it is to know other things, has for that very reason no power of knowing itself. But this is open sophistry: first you say what the mind's nature is, and then you say that because it has this nature no one can know that it has it. Actually, the argument is a counsel of despair, based on recognizing that a certain attempted method of studying the mind has broken down, and on failure to envisage the possibility of any other.

It seems a fair enough proposal that, in setting out to understand the nature of our own mind, we should proceed in the same way as when we try to understand the world about us. In studying the world of nature, we begin by getting acquainted with the particular things and particular events that exist and go on there; then we proceed to understand them, by seeing how they fall into general types and how these general types are interrelated. These interrelations we call laws of nature; and it is by ascertaining such laws that we understand the things

From *The Idea of History* (Oxford: Carendon Press, 1946), pp. 205–31. First published in *Proceedings of the British Academy*, 22 (1936), 97–127. Reprinted by permission of The Clarendon Press, Oxford.

and events to which they apply. The same method, it might seem, is applicable to the problem of understanding mind. Let us begin by observing, as carefully as possible, the ways in which our own minds and those of others behave under given circumstances; then, having become acquainted with these facts of the mental world, let us try to establish the laws which govern them.

Here is a proposal for a 'science of human nature' whose principles and methods are conceived on the analogy of those used in the natural sciences. It is an old proposal, put forward especially in the seventeenth and eighteenth centuries, when the principles and methods of natural science had been lately perfected and were being triumphantly applied to the investigation of the physical world. When Locke undertook his inquiry into that faculty of understanding which 'sets Man above the rest of sensible Beings, and gives him all the Advantage and Dominion which he has over them', the novelty of his project lay not in his desire for a knowledge of the human mind, but in his attempt to gain it by methods analogous to those of natural science: the collection of observed facts and their arrangement in classificatory schemes. His own description of his method as a 'historical, plain Method' is perhaps ambiguous; but his follower Hume was at pains to make it clear that the method to be followed by the science of human nature was identical with the method of physical science as he conceived it: its 'only solid foundation', he wrote, 'must be laid on experience and observation'. Reid, in his *Inquiry into the Human Mind*, was if possible even more explicit. 'All that we know of the body, is owing to anatomical dissection and observation, and it must be by an anatomy of the mind that we can discover its powers and principles.' And from these pioneers the whole English and Scottish tradition of 'philosophy of the human mind' was derived.

Even Kant did not take an essentially different view. He certainly claimed that his own study of the understanding was something more than empirical; it was to be a demonstrative science; but then he held the same view concerning the science of nature; for that also, according to him, has in it an *a priori* or demonstrative element, and is not based merely on experience.

It is evident that such a science of human nature, if it could attain even a tolerable approximation to the truth, could hope for results of extreme importance. As applied to the problems of moral and political life, for example, its results would certainly be no less spectacular than were the results of seventeenth-century physics when applied to the mechanical arts in the eighteenth century. This was fully realized by its promoters. Locke thought that by its means he could 'prevail with the busy Mind of Man, to be more cautious in meddling with things exceeding its Comprehension; to stop, when it is at the utmost of its Tether; and to sit down in a quiet Ignorance of those Things, which, upon Examination, are found to be beyond the reach of our Capacities'. At the same time, he was convinced that the powers of our understanding are sufficient for our needs 'in this state', and can give us all the knowledge we require for 'the comfortable provision for this life, and the way that leads to a better'. 'If [he concludes] we can find out those Measures, whereby a Rational creature, put in the state which Man is in this World, may and ought to govern his Opinions and Actions depending thereon, we need not be troubled that some other things escape our knowledge.'

Hume is even bolder. ' 'Tis evident', he writes, 'that all the sciences have a relation, more or less, to human nature ... since they lie under the cognizance of men, and are judged of by their powers and faculties. 'Tis impossible to tell what changes and improvements we might make in these sciences were we thoroughly acquainted with the extent and force of human understanding.' And in sciences directly concerned with human nature, like morals and politics, his hopes of a beneficent revolution are proportionately higher. 'In pretending, therefore, to explain the principles of human nature, we in effect propose a complete system of the sciences, built on a foundation almost entirely new, and the only one upon which they can stand with any security.' Kant, for all his habitual caution, claimed no less when he said that his new science would put an end to all the debates of the philosophical schools, and make it possible to solve all the problems of metaphysics at once and for ever.

It need not imply any underestimate of what these men actually achieved if we admit that these hopes were in the main unfulfilled, and that the science of human nature, from Locke to the present day, has failed to solve the problem of understanding what understanding is, and thus giving the human mind knowledge of itself. It was not through any lack of sympathy with its objects that so judicious a critic as John Grote found himself obliged to treat the 'philosophy of the human mind' as a blind alley out of which it was the duty of thought to escape.

What was the reason for this failure? Some might say that it was because the undertaking was in principle a mistake: mind cannot know itself. This objection we have already considered. Others, notably the representatives of psychology, would say that the science of these thinkers was not sufficiently scientific: psychology was still in its infancy. But if we ask these same men to produce here and now the practical results for which those early students hoped, they excuse themselves by saying that psychology is still in its infancy. Here I think they wrong themselves and their own science. Claiming for it a sphere which it cannot effectively occupy, they belittle the work it has done and is doing in its proper field. What that field is, I shall suggest in the sequel.

There remains a third explanation: that the 'science of human nature' broke down because its method was distorted by the analogy of the natural sciences. This I believe to be the right one.

It was no doubt inevitable that in the seventeenth and eighteenth centuries, dominated as they were by the new birth of physical science, the eternal problem of self-knowledge should take shape as the problem of constructing a science of human nature. To anyone reviewing the field of human research, it was evident that physics stood out as a type of inquiry which had discovered the right method of investigating its proper object, and it was right that the experiment should be made of extending this method to every kind of problem. But since then a great change has come over the intellectual atmosphere of our civilization. The dominant factor in this change has not been the development of other natural sciences like chemistry and biology, or the transformation of physics itself since more began to be known about electricity, or the progressive application of all these new ideas to manufacture and industry, important though these have been; for in principle they have done nothing that might not have been foreseen as implicit in seventeenth-century physics itself. The really new element in the thought of today as compared with that of three centuries ago is the rise of history. It is true that the same Cartesian spirit which did so much for physics was already laying the foundations of critical method in history before the seventeenth century was out;[1] but the modern conception of history as a study at once critical and constructive, whose field is the human past in its entirety, and whose method is the reconstruction of that past from documents written and unwritten, critically analysed and interpreted, was not established until the nineteenth, and is even yet not fully worked out in all its implications. Thus history occupies in the world of today a position analogous to that occupied by physics in the time of Locke: it is recognized as a special

[1] 'Historical criticism was born in the seventeenth century from the same intellectual movement as the philosophy of Descartes.' E. Bréhier, in *Philosophy and History: Essays presented to Ernst Cassirer* (Oxford, 1936), p. 160.

and autonomous form of thought, lately established, whose possibilities have not yet been completely explored. And just as in the seventeenth and eighteenth centuries there were materialists, who argued from the success of physics in its own sphere that all reality was physical, so among ourselves the success of history has led some people to suggest that its methods are applicable to all the problems of knowledge, in other words, that all reality is historical.

This I believe to be an error. I think that those who assert it are making a mistake of the same kind which the materialists made in the seventeenth century. But I believe, and in these pages I shall try to show, that there is at least one important element of truth in what they say. The thesis which I shall maintain is that the science of human nature was a false attempt—falsified by the analogy of natural science —to understand the mind itself, and that, whereas the right way of investigating nature is by the methods called scientific, the right way of investigating mind is by the methods of history. I shall contend that the work which was to be done by the science of human nature is actually done, and can only be done, by history: that history is what the science of human nature professed to be, and that Locke was right when he said (however little he understood what he was saying) that the right method for such an inquiry is the historical, plain method.

II. THE FIELD OF HISTORICAL THOUGHT[2]

I must begin by attempting to delimit the proper sphere of historical knowledge as against those who, maintaining the historicity of all things, would resolve all knowledge into historical knowledge. Their argument runs in some such way as this.

The methods of historical research have, no doubt, been developed in application to the history of human affairs: but is that the limit of their applicability? They have already before now undergone important extensions: for example, at one time historians had worked out their methods of critical interpretation only as applied to written sources containing narrative material, and it was a new thing when they learnt to apply them to the unwritten data provided by archae-

---

[2] In the argument of this section I owe much to Mr. Alexander's admirable essay on 'The Historicity of Things', in the volume on *Philosophy and History* already quoted. If I seem to be controverting his main thesis, that is not because I disagree with his argument or any part of it, but only because I mean more than he does by the word historicity. For him, to say that the world is 'a world of events' is to say that 'the world and everything in it is historical'. For me, the two things are not at all the same.

ology. Might not a similar but even more revolutionary extension sweep into the historian's net the entire world of nature? In other words, are not natural processes really historical processes, and is not the being of nature a historical being?

Since the time of Heraclitus and Plato, it has been a commonplace that things natural, no less than things human, are in constant change, and that the entire world of nature is a world of 'process' or 'becoming'. But this is not what is meant by the historicity of things; for change and history are not at all the same. According to this old-established conception, the specific forms of natural things constitute a changeless repertory of fixed types, and the process of nature is a process by which instances of these forms (or quasi-instances of them, things approximating to the embodiment of them) come into existence and pass out of it again. Now in human affairs, as historical research had clearly demonstrated by the eighteenth century, there is no such fixed repertory of specific forms. Here, the process of becoming was already by that time recognized as involving not only the instances or quasi-instances of the forms, but the forms themselves. The political philosophy of Plato and Aristotle teaches in effect that city-states come and go, but the idea of the city-state remains for ever as the one social and political form towards whose realization human intellect, so far as it is really intelligent, strives. According to modern ideas, the city-state itself is as transitory a thing as Miletus or Sybaris. It is not an eternal ideal, it was merely the political ideal of the ancient Greeks. Other civilizations have had before them other political ideals, and human history shows a change not only in the individual cases in which these ideals are realized or partially realized, but in the ideals themselves. Specific types of human organization, the city-state, the feudal system, representative government, capitalistic industry, are characteristic of certain historical ages.

At first, this transience of specific forms was imagined to be a peculiarity of human life. When Hegel said that nature has no history, he meant that whereas the specific forms of human organization change as time goes on, the forms of natural organization do not. There is, he grants, a distinction of higher and lower in the specific forms of nature, and the higher forms are a development out of the lower; but this development is only a logical one, not a temporal, and in time all the 'strata' of nature exist simultaneously.[3] But this view of nature has been overthrown by the doctrine of evolution. Biology has decided

---

[3] *Naturphilosophie: Einleitung: System der Philosophie*, § 249, *Zusatz* (*Werke*, Glockner's edition, vol. 9, p. 59).

that living organisms are not divided into kinds each permanently distinct from the rest, but have developed their present specific forms through a process of evolution in time. Nor is this conception limited to the field of biology. It appeared simultaneously, the two applications being closely connected through the study of fossils, in geology. Today even the stars are divided into kinds which can be described as older and younger; and the specific forms of matter, no longer conceived in the Daltonian manner, as elements eternally distinct like the living species of pre-Darwinian biology, are regarded as subject to a similar change, so that the chemical constitution of our present world is only a phase in a process leading from a very different past to a very different future.

This evolutionary conception of nature, whose implications have been impressively worked out by philosophers like M. Bergson, Mr. Alexander, and Mr. Whitehead, might seem at first sight to have abolished the difference between natural process and historical process, and to have resolved nature into history. And if a further step in the same resolution were needed, it might seem to be provided by Mr. Whitehead's doctrine that the very possession of its attributes by a natural thing takes time. Just as Aristotle argued that a man cannot be happy at an instant, but that the possession of happiness takes a lifetime, so Mr. Whitehead argues that to be an atom of hydrogen takes time—the time necessary for establishing the peculiar rhythm of movements which distinguishes it from other atoms—so that there is no such thing as 'nature at an instant'.

These modern views of nature do, no doubt, 'take time seriously'. But just as history is not the same thing as change, so it is not the same thing as 'timefulness', whether that means evolution or an existence which takes time. Such views have certainly narrowed the gulf between nature and history of which early nineteenth-century thinkers were so conscious; they have made it impossible to state the distinction any longer in the way in which Hegel stated it; but in order to decide whether the gulf has been really closed and the distinction annulled, we must turn to the conception of history and see whether it coincides in essentials with this modern conception of nature.

If we put this question to the ordinary historian, he will answer it in the negative. According to him, all history properly so called is the history of human affairs. His special technique, depending as it does on the interpretation of documents in which human beings of the past have expressed or betrayed their thoughts, cannot be applied just as it stands to the study of natural processes; and the more this technique is elaborated in its details, the further it is from being so applicable. There is a certain analogy between the archaeologist's interpretation of a stratified site and the geologist's interpretation of rock-horizons with their associated fossils; but the difference is no less clear than the similarity. The archaeologist's use of his stratified relics depends on his conceiving them as artifacts serving human purposes and thus expressing a particular way in which men have thought about their own life; and from his point of view the palaeontologist, arranging his fossils in a time-series, is not working as a historian, but only as a scientist thinking in a way which can at most be described as quasi-historical.

Upholders of the doctrine under examination would say that here the historian is making an arbitrary distinction between things that are really the same, and that his conception of history is an unphilosophically narrow one, restricted by the imperfect development of his technique; very much as some historians, because their equipment was inadequate to studying the history of art or science or economic life, have mistakenly restricted the field of historical thought to the history of politics. The question must therefore be raised, why do historians habitually identify history with the history of human affairs? In order to answer this question, it is not enough to consider the characteristics of historical method as it actually exists, for the question at issue is whether, as it actually exists, it covers the whole field which properly belongs to it. We must ask what is the general nature of the problems which this method is designed to solve. When we have done so, it will appear that the special problem of the historian is one which does not arise in the case of natural science.

The historian, investigating any event in the past, makes a distinction between what may be called the outside and the inside of an event. By the outside of the event I mean everything belonging to it which can be described in terms of bodies and their movements: the passage of Caesar, accompanied by certain men, across a river called the Rubicon at one date, or the spilling of his blood on the floor of the senate-house at another. By the inside of the event I mean that in it which can only be described in terms of thought: Caesar's defiance of Republican law, or the clash of constitutional policy between himself and his assassins. The historian is never concerned with either of these to the exclusion of the other. He is investigating not mere events (where by a mere event I mean one which has only an outside and no inside) but actions, and an action is the unity of the outside and inside of an event. He is interested in the crossing of the Rubicon only in its relation to Republican law, and in the spilling of Caesar's blood only in its

relation to a constitutional conflict. His work may begin by discovering
the outside of an event, but it can never end there; he must always
remember that the event was an action, and that his main task is to
think himself into this action, to discern the thought of its agent.

In the case of nature, this distinction between the outside and the inside of an event does not arise. The events of nature are mere events,
not the acts of agents whose thought the scientist endeavours to trace.
It is true that the scientist, like the historian, has to go beyond the mere
discovery of events; but the direction in which he moves is very different. Instead of conceiving the event as an action and attempting to
rediscover the thought of its agent, penetrating from the outside of the
event to its inside, the scientist goes beyond the event, observes its relation to others, and thus brings it under a general formula or law of
nature. To the scientist, nature is always and merely a 'phenomenon',
not in the sense of being defective in reality, but in the sense of being a
spectacle presented to his intelligent observation; whereas the events of
history are never mere phenomena, never mere spectacles for contem-
plation, but things which the historian looks, not at, but through, to
discern the thought within them.

In thus penetrating to the inside of events and detecting the thought
which they express, the historian is doing something which the scientist
need not and cannot do. In this way the task of the historian is more
complex than that of the scientist. In another way it is simpler: the
historian need not and cannot (without ceasing to be a historian)
emulate the scientist in searching for the causes or laws of events. For
science, the event is discovered by perceiving it, and the further search
for its cause is conducted by assigning it to its class and determining
the relation between that class and others. For history, the object to be
discovered is not the mere event, but the thought expressed in it. To
discover that thought is already to understand it. After the historian has
ascertained the facts, there is no further process of inquiring into their
causes. When he knows what happened, he already knows why it happened.

This does not mean that words like cause are necessarily out of place
in reference to history; it only means that they are used there in a special
sense. When a scientist asks, 'why did that piece of litmus paper turn
pink?' he means 'on what kinds of occasions do pieces of litmus paper
turn pink?' When a historian asks 'why did Brutus stab Caesar?'
he means 'what did Brutus think, which made him decide to stab
Caesar?' The cause of the event, for him, means the thought in the
mind of the person by whose agency the event came about: and this

is not something other than the event, it is the inside of the event itself.

The processes of nature can therefore be properly described as sequences of mere events, but those of history cannot. They are not processes of mere events but processes of actions, which have an inner side, consisting of processes of thought; and what the historian is looking for is these processes of thought. All history is the history of thought.

But how does the historian discern the thoughts which he is trying to discover? There is only one way in which it can be done: by re-thinking them in his own mind. The historian of philosophy, reading Plato, is trying to know what Plato thought when he expressed himself in certain words. The only way in which he can do this is by thinking it for himself. This, in fact, is what we mean when we speak of 'understanding' the words. So the historian of politics or warfare, presented with an account of certain actions done by Julius Caesar, tries to understand these actions, that is, to discover what thoughts in Caesar's mind determined him to do them. This implies envisaging for himself the situation in which Caesar stood, and thinking for himself what Caesar thought about the situation and the possible ways of dealing with it. The history of thought, and therefore all history, is the re-enactment of past thought in the historian's own mind.

This re-enactment is only accomplished, in the case of Plato and Caesar respectively, so far as the historian brings to bear on the problem all the powers of his own mind and all his knowledge of philosophy and politics. It is not a passive surrender to the spell of another's mind; it is a labour of active and therefore critical thinking. The historian not only re-enacts past thought, he re-enacts it in the context of his own knowledge and therefore, in re-enacting it, criticizes it, forms his own judgement of its value, corrects whatever errors he can discern in it. This criticism of the thought whose history he traces is not something secondary to tracing the history of it. It is an indispensable condition of the historical knowledge itself. Nothing could be a completer error concerning the history of thought than to suppose that the historian as such merely ascertains 'what so-an-so thought', leaving it to someone else to decide 'whether it was true'. All thinking is critical thinking; the thought which re-enacts past thoughts, therefore, criticizes them in re-enacting them.

It is now clear why historians habitually restrict the field of historical knowledge to human affairs. A natural process is a process of events, a historical process is a process of thoughts. Man is regarded as the only subject of historical process, because man is regarded as the only animal that thinks, or thinks enough, and clearly enough, to render his actions the expressions of his thoughts. The belief that man is the only animal that thinks at all is no doubt a superstition; but the belief that man thinks more, and more continuously and effectively, than any other animal, and is the only animal whose conduct is to any great extent determined by thought instead of by mere impulse and appetite, is probably well enough founded to justify the historian's rule of thumb.

It does not follow that all human actions are subject-matter for history; and indeed historians are agreed that they are not. But when they are asked how the distinction is to be made between historical and non-historical human actions, they are somewhat at a loss how to reply. From our present point of view we can offer an answer: so far as man's conduct is determined by what may be called his animal nature, his impulses and appetites, it is non-historical; the process of those activities is a natural process. Thus, the historian is not interested in the fact that men eat and sleep and make love and thus satisfy their natural appetites; but he is interested in the social customs which they create by their thought as a framework within which these appetites find satisfaction in ways sanctioned by convention and morality.

Consequently, although the conception of evolution has revolutionalized our idea of nature by substituting for the old conception of natural process as a change within the limits of a fixed system of specific forms the new conception of that process as involving a change in these forms themselves, it has by no means identified the idea of natural process with that of historical process; and the fashion, current not long ago, of using the word evolution in a historical context, and talking of the evolution of parliament or the like, though natural in an age when the science of nature was regarded as the only true form of knowledge, and when other forms of knowledge, in order to justify their existence, felt bound to assimilate themselves to that model, was the result of confused thinking and a source of further confusions.

There is only one hypothesis on which natural processes could be regarded as ultimately historical in character: namely, that these processes are in reality processes of action determined by a thought which is their own inner side. This would imply that natural events are expressions of thoughts, whether the thoughts of God, or of angelic or demonic finite intelligences, or of minds somewhat like our own inhabiting the organic and inorganic bodies of nature as our minds inhabit our bodies. Setting aside mere flights of metaphysical fancy, such a hypothesis could claim our serious attention only if it led to a better understanding of the natural world. In fact, however, the scientist can reasonably say of it 'je n'ai pas eu besoin de cette hypothèse', and the theologian will recoil from any suggestion that God's action in the natural world resembles the action of a finite human mind under the conditions of historical life. This at least is certain: that, so far as our scientific and historical knowledge goes, the processes of events which constitute the world of nature are altogether different in kind from the processes of thought which constitute the world of history.

III. HISTORY AS KNOWLEDGE OF MIND

History, then, is not, as it has so often been misdescribed, a story of successive events or an account of change. Unlike the natural scientist, the historian is not concerned with events as such at all. He is only concerned with those events which are the outward expression of thoughts, and is only concerned with these so far as they express thoughts. At bottom, he is concerned with thoughts alone; with their outward expression in events he is concerned only by the way, in so far as these reveal to him the thoughts of which he is in search.

In a sense, these thoughts are no doubt themselves events happening in time; but since the only way in which the historian can discern them is by rethinking them for himself, there is another sense, and one very important to the historian, in which they are not in time at all. If the discovery of Pythagoras concerning the square on the hypotenuse is a thought which we today can think for ourselves, a thought that constitutes a permanent addition to mathematical knowledge, the discovery of Augustus, that a monarchy could be grafted upon the Republican constitution of Rome by developing the implications of *proconsulare imperium* and *tribunicia potestas*, is equally a thought which the student of Roman history can think for himself, a permanent addition to political ideas. If Mr. Whitehead is justified in calling the right-angled triangle an eternal object, the same phrase is applicable to the Roman constitution and the Augustan modification of it. This is an eternal object because it can be apprehended by historical thought at any time; time makes no difference to it in this respect, just as it makes no difference to the triangle. The peculiarity which makes it historical is not the fact of its happening in time, but the fact of its becoming known to us by our rethinking the same thought which created the situation we are investigating, and thus coming to understand that situation.

Historical knowledge is the knowledge of what mind has done in the past, and at the same time it is the redoing of this, the perpetuation of past acts in the present. Its object is therefore not a mere object, something outside the mind which knows it; it is an activity of thought, which can be known only in so far as the knowing mind re-enacts it and knows itself as so doing. To the historian, the activities whose history he is studying are not spectacles to be watched, but experiences to be lived through in his own mind; they are objective, or known to him, only because they are also subjective, or activities of his own.

It may thus be said that historical inquiry reveals to the historian the powers of his own mind. Since all he can know historically is thoughts that he can rethink for himself, the fact of his coming to know them shows him that his mind is able (or by the very effort of studying them has become able) to think in these ways. And conversely, whenever he finds certain historical matters unintelligible, he has discovered a limitation of his own mind; he has discovered that there are certain ways in which he is not, or no longer, or not yet, able to think. Certain historians, sometimes whole generations of historians, find in certain periods of history nothing intelligible, and call them dark ages; but such phrases tell us nothing about those ages themselves, though they tell us a great deal about the persons who use them, namely that they are unable to rethink the thoughts which were fundamental to their life. It has been said that *die Weltgeschichte ist das Weltgericht*; and it is true, but in a sense not always recognized. It is the historian himself who stands at the bar of judgement, and there reveals his own mind in its strength and weakness, its virtues and its vices.

But historical knowledge is not concerned only with a remote past. If it is by historical thinking that we rethink and so rediscover the thought of Hammurabi or Solon, it is in the same way that we discover the thought of a friend who writes us a letter, or a stranger who crosses the street. Nor is it necessary that the historian should be one person and the subject of his inquiry another. It is only by historical thinking that I can discover what I thought ten years ago, by reading what I then wrote or what I thought five minutes ago, by reflecting on an action that I then did, which surprised me when I realized what I had done. In this sense, all knowledge of mind is historical. The only way in which I can know my own mind is by performing some mental act or other and then considering what the act is that I have performed. If I want to know what I think about on a certain subject, I try to put my ideas about it in order, on paper or otherwise; and then, having thus arranged and formulated them, I can study the result as a historical document and see what my ideas were when I did that piece of thinking: if I am dissatisfied with them, I can do it over again. If I want to know what powers my mind possesses as yet unexplored, for example, whether I can write poetry, I must try to write some, and see whether it strikes me and others as being the real thing. If I want to know whether I am as good a man as I hope, or as bad as I fear, I must examine acts that I have done, and understand what they really were: or else go and do some fresh acts and then examine those. All these inquiries are historical. They proceed by studying accomplished facts, ideas that I have thought out and expressed, acts that I have done. On what I have only begun and am still doing, no judgement can as yet be passed.

The same historical method is the only one by which I can know the mind of another, or the corporate mind (whatever exactly that phrase means) of a community or an age. To study the mind of the Victorian age or the English political spirit is simply to study the history of Victorian thought or English political activity. Here we come back to Locke and his 'historical, plain Method'. Mind not only declares, but also enjoys or possesses, its nature, both as mind in general and as this particular sort of mind with these particular dispositions and faculties, by thinking and acting, doing individual actions which express individual thoughts. If historical thinking is the way in which these thoughts are detected as expressed in these actions, it would seem that Locke's phrase hit the truth, and that historical knowledge is the only knowledge that the human mind can have of itself. The so-called science of human nature or of the human mind resolves itself into history.

It will certainly be thought (if those who think in this way have had patience to follow me thus far) that in saying this I am claiming more for history than it can ever give. The false view of history as a story of successive events or a spectacle of changes has been so often and so authoritatively taught in late years, especially in this country, that the very meaning of the word has become debauched through the assimilation of historical process to natural process. Against misunderstandings arising from this source I am bound to protest, even if I protest in vain. But there is one sense in which I should agree that the resolution of a science of mind into history means renouncing part of what a science of mind commonly claims, and, I think, claims falsely. The mental scientist, believing in the universal and therefore unalterable truth of his conclusions, thinks that the account he gives of mind holds good of all future stages in mind's history: he thinks that his science shows what mind will always be, not only what it has been in the past and is now. The historian has no gift of prophecy, and knows it; the historical study of mind, therefore, can neither foretell the future developments of human thought nor legislate for them, except so far as they must proceed—though in what direction we cannot tell—from the present as their starting-point. Not the least of the errors contained in the science of human nature is its claim to establish a framework to which all future history must conform, to close the gates of the future and bind posterity within limits due not to nature of things (limits of that kind are real, and are easily accepted) but to the supposed laws of the mind itself.

Another type of objection deserves longer consideration. It may be granted that mind is the proper and only object of historical knowledge, but it may still be contended that historical knowledge is not the only way in which mind can be known. There might be a distinction between two ways of knowing mind. Historical thought studies mind as acting in certain determinate ways in certain determinate situations. Might there not be another way of studying mind, investigating its general characteristics in abstraction from any particular situation or particular action? If so, this would be a scientific, as opposed to a historical, knowledge of mind: not history, but mental science, psychology, or the philosophy of mind.

If such a science of mind is to be distinguished from history, how is the relation between the two to be conceived? It seems to me that two alternative views of this relation are possible.

One way of conceiving it would be to distinguish between what mind is and what it does: and to entrust the study of what it does, its particular actions, to history, and reserve the study of what it is for mental science. To use a familiar distinction, its functions depend on its structure, and behind its functions or particular activities as revealed in history there lies a structure which determines these functions, and must be studied not by history but by another kind of thought.

This conception, however, is very confused. In the case of a machine, we distinguish structure from function, and think of the latter as depending on the former. But we can do this only because the machine is equally perceptible to us in motion or at rest, and we can therefore study it in either state indifferently. But any study of mind is a study of its activities; if we try to think of a mind absolutely at rest, we are compelled to admit that if it existed at all (which is more than doubtful) at least we should be quite unable to study it. Psychologists speak of mental mechanisms; but they are speaking not of structures but of functions. They do not profess ability to observe these so-called mechanisms when they are not functioning. And if we look closer at the original distinction we shall see that it does not mean quite what it seems to mean. In the case of a machine, what we call function is really only that part of the machine's total functioning which serves the purpose of its maker or user. Bicycles are made not in order that there may be bicycles, but in order that people may travel in a certain way. Relatively to that purpose, a bicycle is functioning only when someone is riding it. But a bicycle at rest in a shed is not ceasing to function: its parts are not inactive, they are holding themselves together in a particular order; and what we call possession of its structure is nothing but this functioning of holding itself thus together. In this sense, whatever is called structure is in reality a way of functioning. In any other sense, mind has no function at all; it has no value, to itself or to anyone else, except to be a mind, to perform those activities which constitute it a mind. Hume was therefore right to maintain that there is no such thing as 'spiritual substance', nothing that a mind is, distinct from and underlying what it does.

This idea of mental science would be, to use Comte's famous distinction, 'metaphysical', depending on the conception of an occult substance underlying the facts of historical activity; the alternative idea would be 'positive', depending on the conception of similarities or uniformities among those facts themselves. According to this idea, the task of mental science would be to detect types or patterns of activity, repeated over and over again in history itself.

That such a science is possible is beyond question. But two observations must be made about it.

First, any estimate of the value of such a science, based on the analogy of natural science, is wholly misleading. The value of generalization in natural science depends on the fact that the data of physical science are given by perception, and perceiving is not understanding. The raw material of natural science is therefore 'mere particulars', observed but not understood, and, taken in their perceived particularity, unintelligible. It is therefore a genuine advance in knowledge to discover something intelligible in the relations between general types of them. What they are in themselves, as scientists are never tired of reminding us, remains unknown: but we can at least know something about the patterns of facts into which they enter.

A science which generalizes from historical facts is in a very different position. Here the facts, in order to serve as data, must first be historically known; and historical knowledge is not perception, it is the discerning of the thought which is the inner side of the event. The historian, when he is ready to hand over such a fact to the mental scientist as a datum for generalization, has already understood it in this way from within. If he has not done so, the fact is being used as a datum for generalization before it has been properly 'ascertained'. But if he has done so, nothing of value is left for generalization to do. If, by historical thinking, we already understand how and why Napoleon established his ascendancy in revolutionary France, nothing is added to our understanding of that process by the statement (however true) that similar things have happened elsewhere. It is only when the particular fact cannot be understood by itself that such statements are of value.

Hence the idea that such a science is valuable depends on a tacit and false assumption that the 'historical data', 'phenomena of conscious-ness', or the like upon which it is based are merely perceived and not historically known. To think that they can be thus merely perceived is to think of them not as mind but as nature; and consequently sciences of this type tend systematically to dementalize mind and convert it into nature. Modern examples are the pseudo-history of Spengler, where the individual historical facts which he calls 'cultures' are frankly con-ceived as natural products, growing and perishing, 'with the same superb aimlessness as the flowers of the field', and the many psycho-logical theories now fashionable, which conceive virtues and vices, knowledge and illusion, in the same way.

Secondly, if we ask how far the generalizations of such a science hold good, we shall see that its claim to transcend the sphere of history is baseless. Types of behaviour do, no doubt, recur, so long as minds of the same kind are placed in the same kind of situations. The be-haviour-patterns characteristic of a feudal baron were no doubt fairly constant so long as there were feudal barons living in a feudal society. But they will be sought in vain (except by an inquirer content with the loosest and most fanciful analogies) in a world whose social structure is of another kind. In order that behaviour-patterns may be constant, there must be in existence a social order which recurrently produces situations of a certain kind. But social orders are historical facts, and subject to inevitable changes, fast or slow. A positive science of mind will, no doubt, be able to establish uniformities and recurrences, but it can have no guarantee that the laws it establishes will hold good beyond the historical period from which its facts are drawn. Such a science (as we have lately been taught with regard to what is called classical econ-omics) can do no more than describe in a general way certain charac-teristics of the historical age in which it is constructed. If it tries to overcome this limitation by drawing on a wider field, relying on ancient history, modern anthropology, and so on for a larger basis of facts, it will still never be more than a generalized description of certain phases in human history. It will never be a non-historical science of mind.

To regard such a positive mental science as rising above the sphere of history, and establishing the permanent and unchanging laws of human nature, is therefore possible only to a person who mistakes the transient conditions of a certain historical age for the permanent conditions of human life. It was easy for men of the eighteenth century to make this mistake, because their historical perspective was so short, and their knowledge of cultures other than their own so limited, that they could cheerfully identify the intellectual habits of a western European in their own day with the intellectual faculties bestowed by God upon Adam and all his progeny. Hume, in his account of human nature, never attempted to go beyond observing that in point of fact 'we' think in certain ways, and left undiscussed the question what he meant by the word we. Even Kant, in his attempt to go beyond the 'question of fact' and settle the 'question of right', only showed that we must think in these ways if we are to possess the kind of science which we actually possess. When he asks how experience is possible, he means by experience the kind of experience enjoyed by men of his own age and civilizations. He was, of course, not aware of this. No one in his time had done enough work on the history of thought to know that both the science and the experience of an eighteenth-century European were highly peculiar historical facts, very different from those of other peoples and other times. Nor was it yet realized that, even apart from the evidence of history, men must have thought in very different ways when as yet they were hardly emerged from the ape. The idea of a science of human nature, as entertained in the eighteenth century, belonged to a time when it was still believed that the human species, like every other, was a special creation with unalterable characteristics.

The fallacy inherent in the very idea of a science of human nature is not removed by pointing out that human nature, like every kind of nature, must according to the principles of modern thought be conceived as subject to evolution. Indeed, such a modification of the idea only leads to worse consequences. Evolution, after all, is a natural process, a process of change; and as such it abolishes one specific form in creating another. The trilobites of the Silurian age may be the ancestors of the mammals of today, including ourselves; but a human being is not a kind of wood-louse. The past, in a natural process, is a past superseded and dead. Now suppose the historical process of human thought were in this sense an evolutionary process. It would follow that

the ways of thinking characteristic of any given historical period are
ways in which people must think then, but in which others, cast at
different times in a different mental mould, cannot think at all. If that
were the case, there would be no such thing as truth: according to the
inference correctly drawn by Herbert Spencer, what we take for knowledge is merely the fashion of present-day thought, not true but at the
most useful in our struggle for existence. The same evolutionary view
of the history of thought is implied by Mr. Santayana, when he de-
nounces history as fostering 'the learned illusion of living again the life
of the dead', a subject fit only for 'minds fundamentally without loyal-
ties and incapable or fearful of knowing themselves'; persons interested
not in 'the rediscovery of an essence formerly discovered or prized',
but only in 'the fact that people once entertained some such idea'.[4]

The fallacy common to these views is the confusion between a natural
process, in which the past dies in being replaced by the present, and a
historical process, in which the past, so far as it is historically known,
survives in the present. Oswald Spengler, vividly realizing the difference
between modern mathematics and that of the Greeks, and knowing that
each is a function of its own historical age, correctly argues from his
false identification of historical with natural process that to us Greek
mathematics must be not only strange but unintelligible. But in fact,
not only do we understand Greek mathematics easily enough, it is
actually the foundation of our own. It is not the dead past of a mathematical thought once entertained by persons whose names and dates we
can give, it is the living past of our own present mathematical inquiries,
a past which, so far as we take any interest in mathematics, we still
enjoy as an actual possession. Because the historical past, unlike the
natural past, is a living past, kept alive by the act of historical thinking
itself, the historical change from one way of thinking to another is not
the death of the first, but its survival integrated in a new context involving the development and criticism of its own ideas. Mr. Santayana,
like so many others, first wrongly identifies historical process with
natural process, and then blames history for being what he falsely
thinks it to be. Spencer's theory of the evolution of human ideas embodies the error in its crudest form.

Man has been defined as an animal capable of profiting by the experience of others. Of his bodily life this would be wholly untrue: he
is not nourished because another has eaten, or refreshed because another has slept. But as regards his mental life it is true; and the way in
which this profit is realized is by historical knowledge. The body of

4 *The Realm of Essence*, p. 69.

human thought or mental activity is a corporate possession and almost all the operations which our minds perform are operations which we learned to perform from others who have performed them already. Since mind is what it does, and human nature, if it is a name for anything real, is only a name for human activities, this acquisition of ability to perform determinate operations is the acquisition of a determinate human nature. Thus the historical process is a process in which man creates for himself this or that kind of human nature by recreating in his own thought the past to which he is heir.

This inheritance is not transmitted by any natural process. To be possessed, it must be grasped by the mind that possesses it, and historical knowledge is the way in which we enter upon the possession of it. There is not, first, a special kind of process, the historical process, and then a special way of knowing this, namely historical thought. The historical process is itself a process of thought, and it exists only in so far as the minds which are parts of it know themselves for parts of it. By historical thinking, the mind whose self-knowledge is history not only discovers within itself those powers of which historical thought reveals the possession, but actually develops those powers from a latent to an actual state, brings them into effective existence.

It would therefore be sophistical to argue that, since the historical process is a process of thought, there must be thought already present, as its presupposition, at the beginning of it, and that an account of what thought is, originally and in itself, must be a non-historical account. History does not presuppose mind; it is the life of mind itself, which is not mind except so far as it both lives in historical process and knows itself as so living.

The idea that man, apart from his self-conscious historical life, is different from the rest of creation in being a rational animal is a mere superstition. It is only by fits and starts, in a flickering and dubious manner, that human beings are rational at all. In quality, as well as in amount, their rationality is a matter of degree: some are oftener rational than others, some rational in a more intense way. But a flickering and dubious rationality can certainly not be denied to animals other than men. Their minds may be inferior in range and power to those of the lowest savages, but by the same standards the lowest savages are inferior to civilized men, and those whom we call civilized differ among themselves hardly less. There are even among non-human animals the beginnings of historical life: for example, among cats, which do not wash by instinct but are taught by their mothers. Such rudiments of education are something not essentially different from a historic culture.

Historicity, too, is a matter of degree. The historicity of very primitive societies is not easily distinguishable from the merely instinctive life of societies in which rationality is at vanishing-point. When the occasions on which thinking is done, and the kinds of things about which it is done, become more frequent and more essential to the life of society, the historic inheritance of thought, preserved by historical knowledge of what has been thought before, becomes more considerable, and with its development the development of a specifically rational life begins.

Thought is therefore not the presupposition of a historical process which is in turn the presupposition of historical knowledge. It is only in the historical process, the process of thoughts, that thought exists at all; and it is only in so far as this process is known for a process of thoughts that it is one. The self-knowledge of reason is not an accident; it belongs to its essence. This is why historical knowledge is no luxury, or mere amusement of a mind at leisure from more pressing occupations, but a prime duty, whose discharge is essential to the maintenance, not only of any particular form or type of reason, but of reason itself.

IV. CONCLUSIONS

It remains to draw a few conclusions from the thesis I have tried to maintain.

First, as regards history itself. The methods of modern historical inquiry have grown up under the shadow of their elder sister, the method of natural science; in some ways helped by its example, in other ways hindered. Throughout this essay it has been necessary to engage in a running fight with what may be called a positivistic conception, or rather misconception, of history, as the study of successive events lying in a dead past, events to be understood as the scientist understands natural events, by classifying them and establishing relations between the classes thus defined. This misconception is not only an endemic error in modern philosophical thought about history, it is also a constant peril to historical thought itself. So far as historians yield to it, they neglect their proper task of penetrating to the thought of the agents whose act they are studying, and content themselves with determining the externals of these acts, the kind of things about them which can be studied statistically. Statistical research is for the historian a good servant but a bad master. It profits him nothing to make statistical generalizations, unless he can thereby detect the thought behind the facts about which he is generalizing. At the present day, historical thought is almost everywhere disentangling itself from the toils of the positivistic fallacy, and recognizing that in itself history is nothing but the re-enactment of past thoughts in the historian's mind; but much still needs to be done if the full fruits of this recognition are to be reaped. All kinds of historical fallacies are still current, due to confusion between historical process and natural process: not only the cruder fallacies of mistaking historical facts of culture and tradition for functions of biological facts like race and pedigree, but subtler fallacies affecting methods of research and the organization of historical inquiry, which it would take too long to enumerate here. It is not until these have been eradicated that we can see how far historical thought, attaining at last its proper shape and stature, is able to make good the claims long ago put forward on behalf of the science of human nature.

Secondly, with regard to past attempts to construct such a science.

The positive function of so-called sciences of the human mind, whether total or partial (I refer to such studies as those on the theory of knowledge, of morals, of politics, of economics, and so forth), has always tended to be misconceived. Ideally, they are designed as accounts of one unchanging subject-matter, the mind of man as it always has been and always will be. Little acquaintance with them is demanded in order to see that they are nothing of the sort, but only inventories of the wealth achieved by the human mind at a certain stage in its history. The *Republic* of Plato is an account, not of the unchanging ideal of political life, but of the Greek ideal as Plato received it and reinterpreted it. The *Ethics* of Aristotle describes not an eternal morality but the morality of the Greek gentleman. Hobbes's *Leviathan* expounds the political ideas of seventeenth-century absolutism in their English form. Kant's ethical theory expresses the moral convictions of German pietism; his *Critique of Pure Reason* analyses the conceptions and principles of Newtonian science, in their relation to the philosophical problems of the day. These limitations are often taken for defects, as if a more powerful thinker than Plato would have lifted himself clear out of the atmosphere of Greek politics, or as if Aristotle ought to have anticipated the moral conceptions of Christianity or the modern world. So far from being a defect, they are a sign of merit; they are most clearly to be seen in those works whose quality is of the best. The reason is that in those works the authors are doing best the only thing that can be done when an attempt is made to construct a science of the human mind. They are expounding the position reached by the human mind in its historical development down to their own time. When they try to justify that position, all they can do is to exhibit it as a logical one, a coherent whole of ideas. If, realizing that any such justification is circular, they try to make the whole depend on something outside itself, they fail, as indeed they must; for since the historical present includes in itself its own past, the real ground on which the whole rests, namely the past out of which it has grown, is not outside it but is included within it.

If these systems remain valuable to posterity, that is not in spite of their strictly historical character but because of it. To us, the ideas expressed in them are ideas belonging to the past; but it is not a dead past; by understanding it historically we incorporate it into our present thought, and enable ourselves by developing and criticizing it to use that heritage for our own advancement.

But a mere inventory of our intellectual possessions at the present time can never show by what right we enjoy them. To do this there is only one way: by analysing them instead of merely describing them, and showing how they have been built up in the historical development of thought. What Kant, for example, wanted to do when he set out to justify our use of a category like causation, can in a sense be done; but it cannot be done on Kant's method, which yields a merely circular argument, proving that such a category can be used, and must be used if we are to have Newtonian science; it can be done by research into the history of scientific thought. All Kant could show was that eighteenth-century scientists did think in terms of that category; the question why they so thought can be answered by investigating the history of the idea of causation. If more than this is required; if a proof is needed that the idea is true, that people are right to think in that way; then a demand is being made which in the nature of things can never be satisfied. How can we ever satisfy ourselves that the principles on which we think are true, except by going on thinking according to those principles, and seeing whether unanswerable criticisms of them emerge as we work? To criticize the conceptions of science is the work of science itself as it proceeds; to demand that such criticism should be anticipated by the theory of knowledge is to demand that such a theory should anticipate the history of thought.

Finally, there is the question what function can be assigned to the science of psychology. At first sight its position appears equivocal. On the one hand, it claims to be a science of mind; but if so, its apparatus of scientific method is merely the fruit of a false analogy, and it must pass over into history and, as such, disappear. And this is certainly what ought to happen so far as psychology claims to deal with the functions of reason itself. To speak of the psychology of reasoning, or the psychology of the moral self (to quote the titles of two well-known books), is to misuse words and confuse issues, ascribing to a quasi-naturalistic science a subject-matter whose being and development are not natural but historical. But if psychology avoids this danger and re-nounces interference with what is properly the subject-matter of history, it is likely to fall back into a pure science of nature and to become a mere branch of physiology, dealing with muscular and nervous movements.

But there is a third alternative. In realizing its own rationality, mind also realizes the presence in itself of elements that are not rational. They are not body; they are mind, but not rational mind or thought. To use an old distinction, they are psyche or soul as distinct from spirit. These irrational elements are the subject-matter of psychology. They are the blind forces and activities in us which are part of human life as it consciously experiences itself, but are not parts of the historical process: sensation as distinct from thought, feelings as distinct from conceptions, appetite as distinct from will. Their importance to us consists in the fact that they form the proximate environment in which our reason lives, as our physiological organism is the proximate environment in which they live. They are the basis of our rational life, though no part of it. Our reason discovers them, but in studying them it is not studying itself. By learning to know them, it finds out how it can help them to live in health, so that they can feed and support it while it pursues its own proper task, the self-conscious creation of its own historical life.

II

CONCEPTS AND ACTIONS

PETER WINCH

I. THE INTERNALITY OF SOCIAL RELATIONS

To illustrate what is meant by saying that the social relations between
men and the ideas which men's actions embody are really the same
thing considered from different points of view, I want ... to consider
the general nature of what happens when the ideas current in a
society change: when new ideas come into the language and old ideas
go out of it. In speaking of 'new ideas' I will make a distinction. Imagine
a biochemist making certain observations and experiments as a result
of which he discovers a new germ which is responsible for a certain
disease. In one sense we might say that the name he gives to this new
germ expresses a new idea, but I prefer to say in this context that he
has made a discovery within the existing framework of ideas. I am
assuming that the germ theory of disease is already well established in
the scientific language he speaks. Now compare with this discovery the
impact made by the first formulation of that theory, the first introduction of the concept of a germ into the language of medicine. This was a
much more radically new departure, involving not merely a new factual
discovery within an existing way of looking at things, but a completely
new way of looking at the whole problem of the causation of diseases,
the adoption of new diagnostic techniques, the asking of new kinds of
question about illnesses, and so on. In short it involved the adoption of
new ways of doing things by people involved, in one way or another, in
medical practice. An account of the way in which social relations in the
medical profession had been influenced by this new concept would include an account of what that concept was. Conversely, the concept itself is unintelligible apart from its relation to medical practice. A doctor
who (i) claimed to accept the germ theory of disease, (ii) claimed to aim
at reducing the incidence of disease, and (iii) completely ignored the
necessity for isolating infectious patients, would be behaving in a self-
contradictory and unintelligible manner.

From *The Idea of a Social Science* by Peter Winch (London: Routledge and
Kegan Paul, 1958), Ch. 5, pp. 121–36. Reprinted with minor deletions by permission
of the publishers.

Again, imagine a society which has no concept of proper names, as we know them. People are known by general descriptive phrases, say, or by numbers. This would carry with it a great many other differences from our own social life as well. The whole structure of personal relationships would be affected. (Consider the importance of numbers in prison or military life. Imagine how different it would be to fall in love with a girl known only by a number rather than by a name; and what the effect of that might be, for instance, on the poetry of love.) The development of the use of proper names in such a society would certainly count as the introduction of a new idea, whereas the mere introduction of a *particular* new proper name, within the existing framework, would not.

I have wanted to show by these examples that a new way of talking sufficiently important to rank as a new idea implies a new set of social relationships. Similarly with the dying out of a way of speaking. Take the notion of friendship: we read, in Penelope Hall's book, *The Social Services of Modern England* (Routledge), that it is the duty of a social worker to establish a relationship of friendship with her clients; but that she must never forget that her first duty is to the policy of the agency by which she is employed. Now that is a debasement of the notion of friendship as it has been understood, which has excluded this sort of divided loyalty, not to say double-dealing. To the extent to which the old idea gives way to this new one social relationships are impoverished (or, if anyone objects to the interpolation of personal moral attitudes, at least they are *changed*). It will not do, either, to say that the mere change in the meaning of a word need not prevent people from having the relations to each other they want to have; for this is to overlook the fact that our language and our social relations are just two different sides of the same coin. To give an account of the meaning of a word is to describe how it is used; and to describe how it is used is to describe the social intercourse into which it enters.

If social relations between men exist only in and through their ideas, then, since the relations between ideas are internal relations, social relations must be a species of internal relation too. This brings me into conflict with a widely accepted principle of Hume's: 'There is no object, which implies the existence of any other if we consider these objects in themselves, and never look beyond the ideas which we form of them.' There is no doubt that Hume intended this to apply to human actions and social life as well as to the phenomena of nature. Now to start with, Hume's principle is not unqualifiedly true even of our knowledge of natural phenomena. If I hear a sound and recognize it as a clap of thunder, I already commit myself to believing in the occurrence of a number of other events—e.g. electrical discharges in the atmosphere— even in calling what I have heard 'thunder'. That is, from 'the idea which I have formed' of what I heard I *can* legitimately infer 'the existence of other objects'. If I subsequently find that there was no electrical storm in the vicinity at the time I heard the sound I shall have to retract my claim that what I heard was thunder. To use a phrase of Gilbert Ryle's, the word 'thunder' is theory-impregnated; statements affirming the occurrence of thunder have logical connections with statements affirming the occurrence of other events. To say this, of course, is not to reintroduce any mysterious causal nexus *in rebus*, of a sort to which Hume could legitimately object. It is simply to point out that Hume overlooked the fact that 'the idea we form of an object' does not just consist of elements drawn from our observation of that object in isolation, but includes the idea of connections between it and other objects. (And one could scarcely form a conception of a language in which this was not so.)

Consider now a very simple paradigm case of a relation between actions in a human society: that between an act of command and an act of obedience to that command. A sergeant calls 'Eyes right!' and his men all turn their eyes to the right. Now, in describing the men's act in terms of the notion of obedience to a command, one is of course committing oneself to saying that a command has been issued. So far the situation looks precisely parallel to the relation between thunder and electrical storms. But now one needs to draw a distinction. An event's character as an act of obedience is *intrinsic* to it in a way which is not true of an event's character as a clap of thunder; and this is in general true of human acts as opposed to natural events. In the case of the latter, although human beings can think of the occurrences in question only in terms of the concepts they do in fact have of them, yet the events themselves have an existence independent of those concepts. There existed electrical storms and thunder long before there were human beings to form concepts of them or establish that there was any connection between them. But it does not make sense to suppose that human beings might have been issuing commands and obeying them before they came to form the concept of command and obedience. For their performance of such acts is itself the chief manifestation of their possession of those concepts. An act of obedience itself contains, as an essential element, a recognition of what went before as an order. But it would of course be senseless to suppose that a clap of thunder contained any recognition of what went before as an electrical storm; it is our recognition of the sound, rather than the sound itself, which contains that recognition of what went before.

Part of the opposition one feels to the idea that men can be related to each other through their actions in at all the same kind of way as can propositions be related to each other is probably due to an inadequate conception of what logical relations between propositions themselves are. One is inclined to think of the laws of logic as forming a *given* rigid structure to which men try, with greater or less (but never complete) success, to make what they say in their actual linguistic and social intercourse conform. One thinks of propositions as something ethereal, which just because of their ethereal, non-physical nature, can fit together more tightly than can be conceived in the case of anything so grossly material as flesh-and-blood men and their actions. In a sense one is right in this; for to treat of logical relations in a formal systematic way is to think at a very high level of abstraction, at which all the anomalies, imperfections, and crudities which characterize men's actual intercourse with each other in society have been removed. But, like any abstraction not recognized as such, this can be misleading. It may make one forget that it is only from their roots in this actual flesh-and-blood intercourse that those formal systems draw such life as they have; for the whole idea of a logical relation is only possible by virtue of the sort of agreement between men and their actions which is discussed by Wittgenstein in the *Philosophical Investigations*. Collingwood's remark on formal grammer is apposite: 'I likened the grammarian to a butcher; but if so, he is a butcher of a curious kind. Travellers say that certain African peoples will cut a steak from a living animal and cook it for dinner, the animal being not much the worse. This may serve to amend the original comparison.'[1] It will seem less strange that social relations should be like logical relations between propositions once it is seen that logical relations between propositions themselves depend on social relations between men.

What I have been saying conflicts, of course, with Karl Popper's 'postulate of methodological individualism' and appears to commit the sin of what he calls 'methodological essentialism'. Popper maintains that the theories of the social sciences apply to theoretical constructions or models which are formulated by the investigator in order to explain certain experiences, a method which he explicitly compares to the construction of theoretical models in the natural sciences.

This use of models explains and at the same time destroys the claims of methodological essentialism ... It explains them, for the model is of an

[1] R. G. Collingwood, *The Principles of Art* (Oxford, 1938), p. 259.

abstract or theoretical character, and we are liable to believe that we see it, either within or behind the changing observable events, as a kind of observable ghost or essence. And it destroys them because our task is to analyse our sociological models carefully in descriptive or nominalist terms, viz. *in terms in individuals*, their attitudes, expectations, relations, etc.—a postulate which may be called 'methodological individualism'.[2]

Popper's statement that social institutions are just explanatory models introduced by the social scientist for his own purposes is palpably untrue. The ways of thinking embodied in institutions govern the way the members of the societies studied by the social scientist behave. The idea of war, for instance, which is one of Popper's examples, was not simply invented by people who wanted to *explain* what happens when societies come into armed conflict. It is an idea which provides the criteria of what is appropriate in the behaviour of members of the conflicting societies. Because my country is at war there are certain things which I must and certain things which I must not do. My behaviour is governed, one could say, by my concept of myself as a member of a belligerent country. The concept of war belongs *essentially* to my behaviour. But the concept of gravity does not belong essentially to the behaviour of a falling apple in the same way: it belongs rather to the physicist's *explanation* of the apple's behaviour. To recognize this has, *pace* Popper, nothing to do with a belief in ghosts behind the phenomena. Further, it is impossible to go far in specifying the attitudes, expectations, and relations of individuals without referring to concepts which enter into those attitudes, etc., and the meaning of which certainly cannot be explained in terms of the actions of any individual persons.[3]

II. DISCURSIVE AND NON-DISCURSIVE 'IDEAS'

In the course of this argument I have linked the assertion that social relations are internal with the assertion that men's mutual interaction 'embodies ideas', suggesting that social interaction can more profitably be compared to the exchange of ideas in a conversation than to the interaction of forces in a physical system. This may seem to put me in danger of over-intellectualizing social life, especially since the examples I have so far discussed have all been examples of behaviour which expresses *discursive* ideas, that is, ideas which also have a straightforward linguistic expression. It is because the use of language is so intimately, so inseparably, bound up with the other, non-linguistic, activities which

[2] K. R. Popper, *The Poverty of Historicism* (London, 1957), Section 29.
[3] Cf. M. Mandelbaum, 'Social Facts', *British Journal of Sociology*, 6, 4 (1955).

men perform, that it is possible to speak of their non-linguistic behaviour also as expressing discursive ideas. Apart from the examples of this which I have already given in other connections, one needs only to recall the enormous extent to which the learning of any characteristically human activity normally involves talking as well: in connection, e.g. with discussions of alternative ways of doing things, the inculcation of standards of good work, the giving of reasons, and so on. But there is no sharp break between behaviour which expresses discursive ideas and that which does not; and that which does not is sufficiently like that which does to make it necessary to regard it as analogous to the other. So, even where it would be unnatural to say that a given kind of social relation expresses any ideas of a discursive nature, still it is closer to that general category than it is to that of the interaction of physical forces.

Collingwood provides a striking illustration of this in his discussion of the analogy between language and dress.[4] Again, consider the following scene from the film *Shane*. A lone horseman arrives at the isolated homestead of a small farmer on the American prairies who is suffering from the depredations of the rising class of big cattle-owners. Although they hardly exchange a word, a bond of sympathy springs up between the stranger and the homesteader. The stranger silently joins the other in uprooting, with great effort, the stump of a tree in the yard; in pausing for breath, they happen to catch each other's eye and smile shyly at each other. Now any explicit account that one tried to give of the kind of understanding that had sprung between these two, and which was expressed in that glance, would no doubt be very complicated and inadequate. We understand it, however, as we may understand the meaning of a pregnant pause (consider what it is that makes a pause *pregnant*), or as we may understand the meaning of a gesture that completes a statement. 'There is a story that Buddha once, at the climax of a philosophical discussion ... took a flower in his hand, and looked at it; one of his disciples smiled, and the master said to him, "You have understood me." '[5] And what I want to insist on is that, just as in a conversation the point of a remark (or of a pause) depends on its internal relation to what has gone before, so in the scene from the film the interchange of glances derives its full meaning from its internal relation to the situation in which it occurs: the loneliness, the threat of danger, the sharing of a common life in difficult circumstances, the satisfaction in physical effort, and so on.

It may be thought that there are certain kinds of social relation,

[4] R. G. Collingwood, *The Principles of Art*, p. 244.
[5] Ibid., p. 243.

particularly important for sociology and history, of which the fore-going considerations are not true: as for instance wars in which the issue between the combatants is not even remotely of an intellectual nature (as one might say, e.g. that the crusades were), but purely a struggle for physical survival (as in a war between hunger migrants and the possessors of the land on which they are encroaching).[6] But even here, although the issue is in a sense a purely material one, the form which the struggle takes will still involve internal relations in a sense which will not apply to, say, a fight between two wild animals over a piece of meat. For the belligerents are *societies* in which much goes on besides eating, seeking shelter, and reproducing; in which life is carried on in terms of symbolic ideas which express certain attitudes as be-tween man and man. These symbolic relationships, incidentally, will affect the character even of those basic 'biological' activities: one does not throw much light on the particular form which the latter may take in a given society by speaking of them in Malinowski's neo-Marxist terminology as performing the 'function' of providing for the satisfaction of the basic biological needs. Now of course, 'out-group attitudes' between the members of my hypothetical warring societies will not be the same as 'in-group attitudes' (if I may be forgiven the momentary lapse into the jargon of social psychology). Nevertheless, the fact that the enemies are *men*, with their own ideas and institutions, and with whom it would be possible to communicate, will affect the attitudes of members of the other society to them—even if its only effect is to make them the more ferocious. Human war, like all other human activities, is governed by conventions; and where one is dealing with conventions, one is dealing with internal relations.

III. THE SOCIAL SCIENCES AND HISTORY

This view of the matter may make possible a new appreciation of Collingwood's conception of all human history as the history of thought. That is no doubt an exaggeration and the notion that the task of the historian is to rethink the thoughts of the historical participants is to some extent an intellectualistic distortion. But Collingwood is right if he is taken to mean that the way to understand events in human history, even those which cannot naturally be represented as conflicts between or developments of discursive ideas, is more closely analogous to the way in which we understand expressions of ideas than it is to the way we understand physical processes.

[6] This example was suggested to me by a discussion with my colleague, Professor J. C. Rees, as indeed was the realization for the necessity for this whole section.

There is a certain respect, indeed, in which Collingwood pays insufficient attention to the manner in which a way of thinking and the historical situation to which it belongs form one indivisible whole. He says that the aim of the historian is to think the very same thoughts as were once thought, just as they were thought at the historical moment in question.[7] But though extinct ways of thinking may, in a sense, be recaptured by the historian, the way in which the historian thinks them will be coloured by the fact that he has had to employ historiographical methods to recapture them. The medieval knight did not have to use those methods in order to view his lady in terms of the notions of courtly love: he just thought of her in those terms. Historical research may enable me to achieve some understanding of what was involved in this way of thinking, but that will not make it open to me to think of *my* lady in those terms. I should always be conscious that this was an anachronism, which means, of course, that I should not be thinking of her in just the same terms as did the knight of his lady. And naturally, it is even more impossible for me to think of *his* lady as he did.

Nevertheless, Collingwood's view is nearer the truth than is that most favoured in empiricist methodologies of the social sciences, which runs somewhat as follows—on the one side we have human history which is a kind of repository of data. The historian unearths these data and presents them to his more theoretically minded colleagues who then produce scientific generalizations and theories establishing connections between one kind of social situation and another. These theories can then be applied to history itself in order to enhance our understanding of the ways in which its episodes are mutually connected. I have tried to show ... how this involves minimizing the importance of ideas in human history, since ideas and theories are constantly developing and changing, and since each system of ideas, its component elements being interrelated internally, has to be understood in and for itself; the combined result of which is to make systems of ideas a very unsuitable subject for broad generalizations. I have also tried to show that social relations really exist only in and through the ideas which are current in society; or alternatively, that social relations fall into the same logical category as do relations between ideas. It follows that social relations must be an equally unsuitable subject for generalizations and theories of the scientific sort to be formulated about them. Historical explanation is not the application of generalizations and theories to particular instances: it is the tracing of internal relations. It is like applying one's knowledge of a language in order to understand a conversation rather

[7] R. G. Collingwood, *The Idea of History* (Oxford, 1946), Part V.

than like applying one's knowledge of the laws of mechanics to under-stand the workings of a watch. Non-linguistic behaviour, for example, has an 'idiom' in the same kind of way as has a language. In the same kind of way as it can be difficult to recapture the idiom of Greek thought in a translation into modern English of a Platonic dialogue, so it can be misleading to think of the behaviour of people in remote societies in terms of the demeanour to which we are accustomed in our own society. (Think of the uneasy feeling one often has about the authen-ticity of 'racy' historical evocations like those in some of Robert Graves's novels: this has nothing to do with doubts about a writer's accuracy in matters of external detail.)

The relation between sociological theories and historical narrative is less like the relation between scientific laws and the reports of experi-ments of observations than it is like that between theories of logic and arguments in particular languages. Consider for instance the explana-tion of a chemical reaction in terms of a theory about molecular struc-ture and valency: here the theory *establishes* a connection between what happened at one moment when the two chemicals were brought together and what happened at a subsequent moment. It is only *in terms of the theory* that one can speak of the events being thus 'connected' (as opposed to a simple spatio-temporal connection); the only way to grasp the connection is to learn the theory. But the application of a logical theory to a particular piece of reasoning is not like that. One does not have to know the theory in order to appreciate the connection between the steps of the argument; on the contrary, it is only in so far as one can already grasp logical connections between particular state-ments in particular languages that one is even in a position to under-stand what the logical theory is all about ... Whereas in natural science it is your theoretical knowledge which enables you to explain occurrences you have not previously met, a knowledge of logical theory on the other hand will not enable you to understand a piece of reason-ing in an unknown language; you will have to learn that language, and that in itself will suffice to enable you to grasp the connections between the various parts of arguments in that language.

Consider now an example from sociology. Georg Simmel writes:

The degeneration of a difference in convictions into hatred and fight occurs only when there were essential, original similarities between the parties. The (sociologically very significant) 'respect for the enemy' is usually absent where the hostility has arisen on the basis of previous solidarity. And where enough similarities continue to make confusions and blurred outlines pos-sible, points of difference need an emphasis not justified by the issue but only by that danger of confusion. This was involved, for instance, in the case of Catholicism in Berne ... Roman Catholicism does not have to fear any threat to its identity from external contact with a church so different as the Reformed Church, but quite from something as closely akin as Old-Catholicism.[8]

Here I want to say that it is not *through* Simmel's generalization that one understands the relationship he is pointing to between Roman and Old Catholicism: one understands that only to the extent that one understands the two religious systems themselves and their historical relations. The 'sociological law' may be helpful in calling one's attention to features of historical situations which one might otherwise have overlooked and in suggesting useful analogies. (Here for instance one may be led to compare Simmel's example with the relations between the Russian Communist Party and, on the one hand, the British Labour Party and, on the other, the British Conservatives.) But no historical situation can be understood simply by 'applying' such laws as one applies laws to particular occurrences in natural science. Indeed, it is only in so far as one has an *independent* historical grasp of situations like this one that one is able to understand what the law amounts to at all. That is not like having to know the kind of experiment on which a scientific theory is based before one can understand the theory, for there it makes no sense to speak of understanding the connections between the parts of the experiment except in terms of the scientific theory. But one could understand very well the nature of the relations between Roman Catholicism and Old Catholicism without ever having heard of Simmel's theory, or anything like it....

[8] Georg Simmel, *Conflict* (Glencoe, Ill., 1955), Ch. 1.

III

THE PROBLEM OF 'COVERING LAWS'

MAURICE MANDELBAUM

IN recent years the question of what constitutes a historical explanation has probably been more frequently discussed by English and American philosophers than has any other question concerning history. Willam Dray's interesting and influential book, *Laws and Explanation in History*, is perhaps the focal point for this discussion, and from that book I shall borrow the term 'covering-law theorists', using it (as does Dray) to refer to that group of theorists which includes Popper, Hempel, and Gardiner, among others. But since I shall need some term to denote those who have recently reacted against the views of these theorists, as have Professors Dray, Donagan, Nowell-Smith, and Berlin, I shall (if I may) use the term 'reactionists' to refer to them. I do so not in order to suggest that their works are merely reactions against the views of the covering-law theorists, but rather in order to distinguish them from another group of philosophers of history who also reject the covering law model of explanation, namely, the idealists.[1] To be sure, there are some points at which Professors Dray, Donagan, and Nowell-Smith seem to make common cause with idealists such as Croce or Collingwood or Oakeshott; and the example of W. H. Walsh shows how closely the two positions may seem to approach one another. However, what characterizes the starting-point of the reactionists is their assumption that a proper analysis of historical explanation must conform to the statements which historians actually make when they are giving what they take to be explanations of particular occurrences. The idealists assuredly made no such assumption; nor would idealist accounts of what constitutes a historical explanation actually fit this criterion of adequacy. Furthermore, the reactionists do not accept the general arguments by means of which idealists have attacked non-idealist theories,

From *History and Theory*, I, 3 (1961), 229–42, and originally published under the title 'Historical Explanation: The Problem of "Covering Laws"'. Reprinted by permission of the author and the editor of the Journal.

[1] Passmore, in his review of Dray's book, seems to identify Dray with the idealists. Cf. *Australian Journal of Politics and History*, 4 (1958), 269.

and in their frequent discussions of Collingwood they have been apt to expunge or radically reinterpret his more general metaphysical and epistemological theses.[2] I therefore find it useful to distinguish between the idealists and the reactionists. The actual lineage of the reactionists seems to be quite different: each of them appears to stem from that newer branch of analytic philosophy which may be called ordinary-usage analysis, and which is to be distinguished from the science-oriented form of analysis which the covering-law theorists represented. In this case, as in a variety of other cases, ordinary-usage analysts can be found as allies of philosophers of very different sorts, one common bond which unites them being the conviction that it is a mistake to hold that scientific explanation serves as the correct model for all forms of explanation.

I find myself in the position of wishing to defend those who regard scientific explanation as the model for all explanation, and yet I cannot do so without abandoning certain of the assumptions usually associated with that view. In other words, I share the general sort of conclusion which covering-law theorists maintain, although I do not find it possible to defend the assumptions which are used in reaching that conclusion. This is an embarrassing position since I am certain that covering-law theorists attach far more importance to the particular assumptions which I wish to abandon than they do to their interpretation of what constitutes a historical explanation. The assumptions on which I disagree with them concern the meaning of the term 'cause', the relation between the concepts of 'cause' and of 'law', and the supposed tem-

---

[2] The relevant works by Dray, in addition to his book (Oxford, 1957) are: 'Explanatory Narrative in History', *Philosophical Quarterly*, 4 (1954), 15–28; 'R. G. Collingwood and the Acquaintance Theory of Knowledge', *Revue Internationale de Philosophie*, 11 (1957), 420–32; 'Historical Understanding as Rethinking', *University of Toronto Quarterly*, 27 (1957–8), 200–15; ' "Explaining What" in History', in *Theories of History*, Patrick Gardiner, ed. (Glencoe, Ill., 1959), pp. 403–8. The relevant works by Donagan are 'The Verification of Historical Theses', *Philosophical Quarterly*, 6 (1956), 193–203; 'Social Science and Historical Antinomianism', *Revue Internationale de Philosophie*, 11 (1957), 433–49; 'Explanation in History', *Mind*, 66 (1957), 145–64. P. H. Nowell-Smith's article, 'Are Historical Events Unique?', appeared in *Proceedings of the Aristotelian Society*, 57 (1956), 107–60. Concerning the immediately relevant works of Isaiah Berlin, see below, p. 54 n. 4. One further scholar who might be grouped with the reactionsits, but who evidently does not share their common origin, is A. C. Danto. Cf. 'Mere Chronicle and History Proper', *Journal of Philosophy*, 50 (1953), 173–82; 'On Historical Questioning', *Journal of Philosophy*, 51 (1954), 89–99; 'On Explanations in History', *Philosophy of Science*, 23 (1956), 15–30. Danto's position apparently grew out of a dissatisfaction with the position of W. H. Walsh; it is also apparently related to the position adopted by Reis and Kristeller in 'Some Remarks on the Method of History', *Journal of Philosophy*, 40 (1943), 225–45.

poral priority of cause to effect.[3] Merely to mention my disagreement
on these points is to suggest the extent of my embarrassment. None
the less, what I wish to do is to support the general position reached by
covering-law theorists, and to reject the position of the reactionists regarding the differences between historical and scientific explanation. In
doing so, I shall first attack the covering-law theorists, but in a way
different from that which characterizes the reactionists.

I

Viewing the matter in historical perspective, one should recall that
covering-law theorists were in rebellion against a very widespread and
influential movement in German thought which attempted to show
that the methods of the historian were necessarily different from the
methods employed in the natural sciences. The contrasts between
'Naturwissenschaft' and 'Geisteswissenschaft', between 'erklären' and
'verstehen', between 'the repeatable' and 'the unique', between nomo-
thetic and ideographic disciplines, were the stock-in-trade of those
against whom the covering-law theorists rebelled. This the reactionists
have scarcely taken into account. Therefore, while the reactionists have
been unsparing in their criticisms of covering-law theorists, they have
not in fact noticed one point which should by now be abundantly clear:
that these earlier distinctions between historical understanding and
other forms of understanding were either falsely drawn or were badly
overdrawn. For example, no historical event could even be described,
much less could it be in any sense explained, if it were wholly unique.
To have insisted upon this and allied points, and to have done so effectively, is something which we must surely place to the credit of the
covering-law theorists.

None the less, as Dray and the other reactionists have pointed out,
there is something quite odd in viewing the task of the historian as that
of explaining the events of history by showing that they follow deductively from a general law. What is odd is not that the covering-law
theorists claim that there should be such laws, though they are of course
often criticized for this by the idealists. What is odd is that we do not

[3] It is to be noted in this connection that Hempel and Gardiner have severely
criticized my views with respect to causation, while Dray seems to have a certain
sympathy with them, though he regards them as being inadequate because they
do not conform to 'the usual sense of the term [cause] in history'. Cf. Hempel:
'The Function of General Laws in History', *Journal of Philosophy*, 39 (1942),
35–48, especially notes 1 and 7; Patrick Gardiner: *The Nature of Historical Explanation* (Oxford, 1952), pp. 83–6; Dray: *Laws and Explanation in History*,
p. 110.

really have the laws which, according to the covering-law model, would
serve to explain the particular events which we wish to explain. As
Dray has insisted, those general statements which might be claimed to
serve as the grounds for acceptable explanations are too loose and too
porous to serve as laws from which the particular events of history
might be deduced. And, as Dray has also shown, when these laws are
tightened and sealed, we find that they are not really general laws, but
statements so particularized that we would not expect them to apply to
any other instance in the world, save the one which they purportedly
explain. All of this part of Dray's argument I accept, and in fact (as
Dray would acknowledge) these difficulties were at least adumbrated
by Gardiner, and even earlier by Hempel when the latter found himself forced to distinguish between an explanation and 'an explanation
sketch'. But what, then, has gone wrong with the covering-law argument, that it should have shown that generalizations must be in some
sense, or in some ways, present in historical explanation; and yet that
it should have failed to offer an analysis which conforms to what historians actually do? On this point, it seems to me, the reactionists have
not thrown any light.[4]

Taking Hempel's article, 'The Function of General Laws in History',
as the *locus classicus* for the covering-law theory, I think it is easy to
see what has gone wrong. Hempel holds the position that historians are
mistaken if they believe that it is their essential task to describe particular events. He holds this position because he apparently believes that

[4] Isaiah Berlin's 'History and Theory: The Concept of Scientific History', *History
and Theory*, I (1960), 1–31, reached me too late to receive the attention which it
would otherwise deserve. Fortunately, I was already familiar with his general views
on the subject, both through his *Historical Inevitability* (Oxford, 1954), and
through having been privileged to attend a seminar which he gave on the subject
at Harvard University in the fall of 1954. It does not seem to me that his article
forces a revision of the position which I here wish to defend, although the
particular way in which he casts his argument at some crucial points demands
careful analysis.

A second article which came to my attention too late to be taken into account
in my paper was Ernest Nagel's 'Determinism in History', *Philosophy and
Phenomenological Research*, 20 (1960), 291–317. [See this volume, pp. 187–215, Ed.]
I derive considerable satisfaction from finding that I am apparently not in disagreement with Nagel's analysis of the current situation with respect to the theory of
historical explanation. In section III, 4 of his article (pp. 301–4), where he deals
with the same problem with which I am here concerned, he too points out that it
is doubtful whether even in the natural sciences the pattern of deductive explanation
is followed in explaining 'concrete individual occurrences'. However, in his discussion of Maitland's explanation of a concrete historical occurrence (p. 303) he
does use the sort of generalization which I shall be criticizing Hempel for employing as a basis for historical explanation; I am therefore unsure as to whether
he would accept the argument which I am propounding in this paper.

it is only by doing so that he can assimilate the methods of historical explanation to the methods of scientific explanation. The mixture of these two theses can be seen in the opening two sentences of his article. He says:

It is a rather widely held opinion that history, in contradistinction to the so-called physical sciences, is concerned with the description of particular events of the past rather than with the search for general laws which might govern those events. As a characterization of the type of problem in which some historians are mainly interested, this view probably cannot be denied; as a statement of the theoretical function of general laws in scientific research, it is certainly unacceptable.

This is a brambly pair of sentences. Surely it should be clear that historians might be interested in particular events, and yet this might not distinguish them from natural scientists; natural scientists too might be interested in particular events, such as the formation of a particular geologic deposit, or the appearance of a new biological variety in a particular environment. It might also be the case that in order to describe, to understand, or to explain particular events of the past, historians must utilize general laws; however, it need not be the case that it either has been, or should be, their primary concern to discover such laws. As the next sentence of Hempel's article makes perfectly clear, the essential point which he wished to establish was that general laws have a necessary explanatory function in historical inquiry, and that historical explanation does not therefore utilize a different type of explanation from that which it to be found in the natural sciences.[5] And with this fundamental thesis, as I have said, I agree.

What has in my opinion led to an unnecessary confusion is the fact that in making his point Hempel has spoken as if the nature of scientific explanation were restricted to the formulation of laws. Now, no one will deny that scientists do formulate laws. However, as Hempel himself rightly insists, every law is a statement which connects one *type* of event with another *type* of event: no law is a statement which directly refers to a single event, nor does it cover every aspect of those events to which it can be applied.[6] To take an example from Hempel's

[5] This sentence reads: 'The following considerations are an attempt to substantiate this point by showing in some detail that general laws have quite analogous functions in history and in the natural sciences, that they form an indispensable instrument of historical research, and that they even constitute the common basis of various procedures which are often considered as characteristic of the social in contradistinction to the natural sciences.'

[6] Cf. para. 2.2 of Hempel's article. However, it does not follow that *explanation* is always of a type of event only, and not of a particular event. As I have suggested, I do not think that Hempel wishes to confine explanation to types of event, although his emphasis at this point does not make his intentions clear. However, Hayek adopts this view of explanation, and even of prediction. In an

own article, in explaining a particular event, such as the cracking of an automobile radiator on a cold night, we must be able to state a law concerning the relation between the type of event which constitutes a drop in temperature to another type of event which is water freezing, and we must also connect water freezing with an expansion of its volume, etc. Now, clearly such statements which connect one type of event with another type of event are not intended to apply to this case only; if they only applied to this one event we should not consider them as explaining it. None the less, it is also clear that these laws are only invoked in this particular case because we wish to explain *it*. Neither the ordinary man nor the scientist would be interested in laws unless they could be used to explain, or to predict, particular cases. With this I am sure that Hempel would not disagree. But we now come to the crucial point, and one on which Hempel's article is singularly ambiguous. Is it the case that in order to explain this particular event, the cracking of this radiator on this particular night, there should be a law concerning the cracking of radiators; or is it sufficient in order to explain this particular event that there should merely be the general laws which connect temperature and freezing, freezing and expansion, and the like? This is a crucial question which demands clarification because in dealing with the question of what constitutes a causal explanation of an event, Hempel makes the following statement:

The explanation of the occurrence of an event of some specific kind E at a certain place and time consists ... in indicating the causes or determining factors of E. Now the assertion that a set of events—say, of the kinds C_1, C_2, ... Cn—have caused the event to be explained, amounts to the statement that, according to certain general laws, a set of the events of the kinds mentioned is regularly accompanied by an event of the kind E. (para. 2.1)

This surely sounds as if Hempel holds that in order to explain the cracking of *this* radiator we would have to find some set of events which regularly accompanies the cracking of radiators; but this is precisely the sort of thing which the arguments of Dray and of Donagan have shown that we *cannot* do in history. Nor, I submit, can we do it with respect to the cracking of radiators, the failure of missiles to leave their

---

article entitled 'Degrees of Explanation', Hayek says: ' "Explanation" and "prediction" of course never refer to an individual event but always to phenomena of a certain kind or class; they will state only some and never all the properties of any particular phenomenon to which they refer' (*British Journal for Philosophy of Science*, 6 (1955–6), 215). One would think that the prediction of a specific solar eclipse, or the explanation of that eclipse, would count as referring to a particular event even if it does not refer to all aspects of the event, such as the temperature of the sun, or the effect of the eclipse on the temperature of the earth, and the like. [For Hempel's comments, see below, pp. 96–7—Ed.]

launching pads, and many other events which no one (I should suppose) would deny to be wholly explicable in terms of physical laws. While we *do* explain these events through the introduction of laws, the laws which we introduce are not laws of cracking-radiators or of missile-failures: there is, I assume, no one set of conditions which is invariantly linked to a missile failure, nor to a cracking radiator, since (for example) radiators can crack when we pour water into them when they are overheated, no less than when we allow them to stand outdoors on a cold night without anti-freeze in them.

In short, what I am contending is that the laws through which we explain a particular event need not be laws which state a uniform sequence concerning complex events of the type which we wish to explain.[7] Rather, they may be laws which state uniform connections between two types of factor which are contained within those complex events which we propose to explain. This should be perfectly clear from Hempel's own analysis. What he wishes to explain is 'the cracking of an automobile radiator during a cold night', and he holds that that event is explained when 'the conclusion that the radiator cracked during the night can be deduced by logical reasoning' from a knowledge of the initial conditions plus 'empirical laws such as the following: Below 32° F., under normal atmospheric pressure water freezes. Below 39·2° F., the pressure of a mass of water increases with decreasing temperature, if the volume remains constant or decreases; when the water freezes, the pressure again increases. Finally, this group [of statements] would have to include a quantitative law concerning the change of pressure of water as a function of its temperature and volume' (para. 2.1). In short, there is not a word about radiators in the laws by means of which the cracking of the radiator is to be explained.

Bearing this in mind, we can see that Dray was quite right in objecting to what he significantly called the covering-law model of explanation in history: the law (or laws) by means of which we explain a particular case is not (or surely need not be) a law which 'covers' that case in the sense that the case is itself an instance of what has been stated by the law. Rather, the case is explained by the law because those types of factor with which the law is concerned are present in it. If this

[7] I use the expression 'need not be', rather than 'is not', for I wish to leave it an open question as to whether there are any cases in which the laws which explain a particular type of complex event are merely laws in which such an event is related to another type of complex event, or whether *in all cases* the explanation of a particular type of complex event does not demand a resolution into laws of particular component factors within it.

is true, then it should not be surprising that in history we cannot, for example, find laws which 'cover' the case of a particular migration of population in the sense that there is a law of population migration such that this case is an instance of it. Rather, the laws which we could expect to find (if we are to find explanatory laws) would be in one sense more general; in another sense, they would also be more limited than the event which they are to explain. They would be more general, since they would presumably also serve to explain other types of case, and not only population migrations; they would be more restricted because they would not concern all of the aspects of the complex event designated as a population migration, but only some one aspect of it. Thus, for example, we might expect some social psychological law to be useful in explaining a population migration, but such a law, if it were genuinely a law of social psychology, would also be relevant in explaining particular events which are not population migrations. At the same time such a law would be restricted to dealing with some one factor in the population migration, and not with the complex event as a whole. And Hempel, of course, does argue for the importance of precisely such sorts of law in our explanations of historical events.[8] Yet he has opened himself to misinterpretation, if not to error, by insisting that the universal hypotheses by means of which we explain complex events of a given type consist in finding the conditions which always accompany events *of this type*. Thus, in his discussion of population migrations he says:

Consider, for example, the statement that Dust Bowl farmers migrate to California 'because' continual drought and sandstorms render their existence increasingly precarious, and because California seems to them to offer so much better living conditions. *This explanation rests on some such universal hypothesis as that populations will tend to migrate to regions which offer better living conditions.* (para. 5.2; my italics)

Hempel then quickly admits that it would be difficult to state this hypothesis in the form of a general law which is well confirmed by all other cases of migrations. And this illustrates what sort of law he is seeking: he is seeking a covering law which states a regularity of connection between some particular complex type of event and a particular complex set of conditions. However (to revert to my earlier illustration), this is as if in the physical sciences the laws with which we are concerned were laws of radiator-crackings or missile-failures.

In my opinion, it is not difficult to see how this error—for I believe

[8] For example, in his use in para. 5.2 of the quotation from Donald W. McConnell's *Economic Behavior*.

it to be a fundamental error—cropped up in Hempel's article. As Dray has pointed out, all of the covering-law theorists accept a Humean view of causation.[9] Now, to speak of a Humean view of causation may mean a number of different things, but what I here have in mind is the fact that for Hume, and for those most directly affected by his arguments, the notion of what constitutes the cause of an event is another event which uniformly precedes it in time. To know the cause of an event is, therefore, to know that there is a law which connects this type of event, which we call the effect, with another type of event, which we call the cause. A causal relation is, then, simply an instance of some empirically established law.

Such a view has certain necessary consequences, two of which we may single out for particular attention. In the first place, if a causal relation is merely an instance of a regularly occurring sequence, a causal attribution does not consist in the analysis of this particular event, but in the formulation of what happens in cases of a particular type, or kind. It is small wonder, then, that those who accept a Humean view of causation should insist, as does Hempel, that causal analysis is really not the explanation of a particular case, but simply of what happens in a kind of case. In the second place, if a causal relation is simply an instance of a regularly recurring sequence, we shall have to distinguish between that particular event which we denominate as 'the cause' of a specific event and 'the conditions' which merely accompany the occurrence of this event. We must draw such a line of demarcation, if we accept the Humean view, since any particular event will be preceded in time by more than one particular event (or condition), and since, also, more than one event (or condition) will presumably also be spatially contiguous with it. Those aspects of the state of affairs which precede the occurrence of the effect, and which are *not* regularly present whenever an effect of this type occurs, will then be denominated as being merely 'conditions' of the effect, but not its cause. What is called 'the cause' will be confined to whatever aspect of the total state of affairs obtaining in a particular case is also present in all other cases of the same general type. But this means that the Humean view identifies the cause of an event with what we should consider a *necessary* condition of its occurrence, and does not include as part of its cause the *sufficient*, as well as the necessary, conditions of that effect.

It is small wonder, then, that Dray can charge that Hempel's analysis is really remote from the tasks which most historians have set them-

---

[9] *Laws and Explanation in History*, pp. 3, 60, and *passim*. A similar point is made by Nowell-Smith.

selves. In the first place, as Hempel found himself forced to admit, much of the historiography of the past has been concerned with the particular nature of particular events, rather than with describing what a number of events may have in common, and therefore with what constitutes a particular type of event. In the second place, it may be added, the explanations with which historians customarily have been concerned have been explanations which attempt to portray the conditions which were *sufficient* to account for the occurrence of the event; their aim has not been to discover what conditions are *necessary* for the occurrence of events of a given type.[10] In fact, they have not infrequently denied that any statements concerning necessary or invariant conditions would be true. For these two reasons the Humean view of the nature of the causal relation seems singularly inappropriate to deal with what the historian means by 'causation', and it seems to me that in point of fact the historian is concerned to explain—in some non-Humean causal sense of the word 'explain'—particular events.

However, it would be unfair to Hempel to leave the impression that he could not in any way deal with particular cases on the basis of the covering-law model. What is individual about a particular case is introduced into his account by the fact that the laws which explain events must be applied to the initial and boundary conditions obtaining at a particular time and place. However, what Hempel overlooks is that the establishment of the precise nature of these initial and boundary conditions is a complicated task, *and is itself the task of the historian.*[11] An accurate delineation of these conditions is precisely what I should suppose many historians to mean by 'the description of particular events', and Hempel nowhere shows that such an analysis of what actually constituted the initial and boundary conditions under which a given effect occurred can itself be reached by the use of the covering-law model. Later, I shall examine to what extent it is in fact necessary to presuppose a knowledge of certain regularities, or laws, in order to analyse the nature of the relevant initial and boundary conditions. Here it is only necessary to point out that it is misleading to claim that the historian

[10] W. B. Gallie in 'Explanations in History and the Genetic Sciences' (*Mind*, 64, (1955), 160–80) would seem to hold the exact opposite of this position, viz. that the historian is only interested in the necessary conditions, while natural scientists are interested in the sufficient conditions. The difference, however, is, in part, a difference in the ways in which we are using the terms 'necessary' and 'sufficient'. In the terminology which I am here using 'a necessary condition' is one which is invariantly associated with the type of event to be explained.

[11] This is why, in the review of Dray already cited, Passmore points out that much of the time the historian's task is really not one of explaining at all, but is merely one of describing, i.e. of 'telling how', not 'explaining why'.

is not interested in describing particular events, if in fact it is necessary for him to do so before he has the data to which he can apply those general laws which purportedly explain the event which he wishes to explain. To say this is merely to say that it is perfectly reasonable to demand of any person who claims to have explained a particular event that he should not only have indicated the *necessary* conditions which presumably always obtain when an event of this type occurs, but that he should also have indicated the *sufficient* conditions for the occurrence of the particular event which he seeks to explain. And in the non-Humean language which I myself used on an earlier occasion, and which Hempel has criticized, this means that the explanation of an event involves a causal analysis of that event, and not merely (or even primarily) the statement of a general law.

By way of drawing together my criticisms of Hempel's position, let me cite the fact that Hempel states that 'a set of events can be said to have caused the event to be explained only if general laws can be indicated which connect "causes" and "effects"' (para. 3.1.). Now this, I submit, is not what is usually involved when we speak about the cause of a particular event. When I ask what caused a man to fall off a ladder, or what caused a person to commit suicide, I do not expect to be given an answer which states a regular conjunction between any other type of event and the type of event which constitutes falling off a ladder or committing suicide. To be sure, in order to account for the man's fall I must know that unsupported bodies do fall. If the man's fall was connected with the fact that he fainted, I must also know that when fainting occurs one's muscles relax, since this will account for the fact that he lost his grip. However, even though Hempel is correct in insisting that my causal explanation presupposes a knowledge of such laws, it is simply not true that there is any law which explains all of the particular cases in which men fall from ladders. Yet Hempel has seemed to insist that a causal explanation would involve the discovery of such a law. Instead, I submit, the causal analysis of any particular case in which a man falls from a ladder involves analysing that complex event into a component series of sub-events, such as the man's fainting, his grip relaxing, his centre of gravity shifting, and then his falling to the ground. It is this sort of analysis of a particular complex event into its connected parts that we are called upon to make if we are asked why the man fell when he did and how he did. And to give an answer to this question is (I should suppose) to give a causal explanation of what occurred.

II

It would seem that the preceding argument has brought us around to the position of Professor Dray, in which historical explanation is conceived on the model of what he terms 'a continuous series'. And this analysis of historical explanation is in many ways similar to what W. H. Walsh has referred to as the historian's task of 'colligation'.[12]

The paradigmatic case used by Dray is not the case of a radiator cracking, although it too is drawn from automotive mechanics. It is the case of the engine seizure (pp. 66 ff.). Dray wishes to show that causal explanations are not to be given in terms of causal laws, but in terms of tracing a continuous series of sub-events which serve to explain what has occurred. His paradigmatic case runs as follows:

Suppose that the engine of my motor-car seizes up, and, after inspecting it, the garage mechanic says to me: 'It's due to a leak in the oil reservoir.' Is this an explanation of the seizure? I should like to argue that it depends upon who says it and to whom ... To me, who am ignorant of what goes on under the bonnet, it is no explanation at all ... If I am to understand the seizure, I shall need to be told something about functioning of an auto engine, and the essential role in it of the lubricating system. I shall have to be capable of a certain amount of elementary trouble tracing. I need to be told, for instance, that what makes the engine go is the movement of the piston in the cylinder; that if no oil arrives the piston will not move because the walls are dry; that the oil is normally brought to the cylinder by a certain pipe from the pump, and ultimately from the reservoir; that the leak, being on the underside of the reservoir, allowed the oil to run out, and that no oil therefore reached the cylinder in this case. I now know the explanation of the engine stoppage.

However, it should be obvious that such an explanation presupposes a knowledge of certain uniformities concerning the relations of types of events, that is, it presupposes a knowledge of general laws, and this fact is not pointed out by Professor Dray.[13] For example, the explanation of why the engine stopped presupposes a knowledge of general laws concerning friction, and concerning the relation between the absence of lubricants and the presence of friction. It also presupposes a knowledge that liquids flow through openings in the underside of reservoirs, and this too depends upon a knowledge of general laws. In short, Dray's own knowledge of general laws is presupposed in each step of the continuous-series explanation, as he has given it. Furthermore, a know-

---

[12] W. H. Walsh, *Introduction to Philosophy of History* (London, 1951), pp. 23–4 and 59–64. [See also Walsh's essay in this volume, pp. 127–44—Ed.] For Walsh's views on historical explanation, cf. also pp. 16f., 22–4, 29–47, 64–71.

[13] This point is also clearly brought out by J. Pitt, 'Generalizations in Historical Explanation', *Journal of Philosophy*, 61 (1959), 582f.

ledge of general laws is tacitly involved not only in tracing these connections but in distinguishing between what constitute relevant conditions, and what is irrelevant to engine trouble. For example, is the
fact that the engine stopped just as another car passed it, a circumstance
which must be introduced into our account of the cause of the seizure?
Our judgement will in this case surely be negative, but that is only
because we have learned that, in general, the way most man-made
machines function, and in particular the way in which automobiles
function, is that they are designed to be independent of what happens in
their environments. In short, what alone makes it possible to trace a
continuous series between concrete events such as are here in question,
is a background knowledge of laws describing uniformities among given
types of events. Such a knowledge is necessary to tracing such a series
in two respects: first, it alone provides the necessary linkage between
at least some of the components within the series; second, it is necessary
in order that we can rule out features of the environment which are
irrelevant to the series.

I am not certain that Dray would deny this, but I think it likely that
he would. What he seems to wish to defend is the proposition that a
causal analysis of a particular event depends upon what he calls 'judgement', and that judgement can function independently of a knowledge
of general uniformities or laws. This seems to me to be a mistake. I
think that what I have just said about the explanation of the engine
seizure shows it to be a mistake.

But why, one might ask, does Professor Dray apparently cast aside
all appeal to general laws in historical explanation, if, indeed, that is
what he has done? The answer seems to me to lie in the fact that he
has inadvertently accepted too much from the Humean position of his
opponents, the covering-law theorists. He has assumed with them that
in fields other than the sorts of fields with which historians deal, it is
appropriate to telescope the notions of cause and law, and he himself
does telescope these notions by speaking of 'causal laws'.[14] But then he
finds that he must also speak of 'causal explanations' in history, and
these explanations he regards as having a logic of their own, distinct
from the logic of those explanations which are supposedly given

---

[14] It is noteworthy in this connection that when Hempel shifts from a Humean
type of explanation to an explanation in terms of laws characterizing relations
among sub-events, Dray simply calls this a more complicated version of the
covering-law model (cf. pp. 52–4). However, in my opinion, the shift from what he
calls a 'holistic' to a 'piecemeal' approach represents the adoption of a totally
different model of explanation, and not merely a shift in the scale of the events
dealt with.

through a use of the causal-law model. The distinction which one might have expected him to draw between the statement of a *law* concerning a *type* of event and the statement of the cause of a *particular* event is not, to my knowledge, drawn by him. If it were to be drawn, it seems to me unlikely that Dray would have distinguished between the logic of those explanations which scientists give and the logic of the explanations given by historians. Rather, his position, like mine, would then have more nearly approached the position which I take to be essential to Hempel's article: that, in point of fact, at least an implicit appeal to a knowledge of general laws is needed in history.

III

In summary, let me say that the contrast between historians and scientists which we find in the idealists as well as in most of the reactionists is based not only on a misconception concerning the function of general laws in history, but also on a failure to appreciate the role of description in the generalizing sciences. If one asks where, in fact, the generalizations of science must take their rise, it is surely to descriptions of particular complex events and states of affairs that we must ultimately look. And even if we were to regard scientific generalizations as products of the free play of the imagination, which, while they might depend upon some observations, did not demand a painstaking investigation of the particular nature of specific events, still it would remain the case that no confirmation of such a generalization can be given without appealing to specific cases. And these specific cases must be carefully analysed. In laboratories, where conditions are controlled, the description of the particular event which did occur will not have to introduce as many variables as is the case when the scientist describes what has occurred in a state of nature. None the less, the description of a specific case even in a laboratory, is not an entirely simple matter. We must describe not merely all of the relevant conditions obtaining at that time and place, and all of the equipment used, but we must also state what happened in each successive phase of the experiment. As knowledge of general laws advances, the description of what are the relevant initial conditions, and what are the relevant phases in the experiment, becomes greatly simplified. Yet a concern with what is specific to a particular case, and the contrast between this and what happens in all cases, will presumably always remain to be drawn when we are seeking the confirmation of a general law. And it so happens that in the field of those societal events which historians and social scientists treat, the description of particular events is an extremely difficult task. If I am correct in my argument against Dray, this task can never be fulfilled without utilizing generalizations which state (or attempt to state) what uniformly happens in certain types of cases. However, if I am correct in the point which I have just been making, then the task of the traditional historian will never be rendered obsolete, as Hempel apparently thought and hoped that it would be. For no social scientist will ever be able either to discover or to confirm those generalizations in which he is interested, without making an appeal to the descriptive analyses of historians. And since in the absence of the possibility of establishing most of their generalizations under laboratory conditions, social scientists will have to rely upon a comparative method, the range of the relevant historical materials will increase, rather than contract, as the range of the generalizations spreads. For this reason what Hempel termed 'scientific historical research', a term doubtless disliked as much by the reactionists as by the idealists, will continue to be concerned with the analysis of the concrete nature of particular events, though it will surely continue to utilize, in ever growing measure, not only the common-sense generalizations of everyday life, but the best available generalizations which social scientists have been able to formulate on the basis of a knowledge of history.

IV

THE HISTORICAL EXPLANATION OF ACTIONS RECONSIDERED

WILLIAM DRAY

In the last ten years or so a good deal has been written by analytically minded philosophers about the nature of historical explanation. The discussion has centred in particular upon the question whether, and if so to what extent and in what way, such explanation involves, requires, or entails corresponding empirical laws. Less than five years ago, in a monograph entitled *Laws and Explanation in History*, I offered a contribution myself to what was then already a discussion well under way. If I now essay some further remarks on the subject, my excuse must be that, to judge from what is being read at philosophical conferences and written in the journals, the controversy has not yet lost its interest. In addition, I welcome this opportunity to try to take account of some of the criticisms that have come my way, and to contrast a position I should still want to defend with a number of interesting alternative views which have recently been advanced.

In the present paper, I hasten to add, I shall not attempt to defend all the main contentions of the monograph referred to. My concern will be limited to a single, but I think central, issue: the question of the analysis to be given of characteristic explanations of the actions of individual historical agents. This does not mean that I believe that only individual human actions are subject-matter for historical explanations properly so-called; indeed, I should agree with Professor Maurice Mandelbaum that individual actions as such are below the threshold of proper historical interest; they enter history only in so far as they have 'societal significance'.[1] 'But even those who would insist that the unit of historical study is a social rather than human individual, would seldom deny that explanations at the level of talk about nations, institutions, and movements usually involve the historian in explaining the actions of particular men and women. It is characteristic of historical inquiry to explain social occurrences piecemeal. Without wanting to raise here

From *Philosophy and History: A Symposium*, ed. Sidney Hook (New York University Press, 1963), pp. 105–35. Copyright © 1963 by New York University. Reprinted by permission of the publishers.

[1] *The Problem of Historical Knowledge* (New York, 1938), p. 9.

the question of the exact logical relation between assertions about social events and about the actions of human individuals, I shall therefore proceed on the assumption that, although no consideration of the historical explanation of such actions could claim in itself to offer a comprehensive theory of 'the nature of historical explanation', it will at any rate deal with an important aspect of that larger problem.

My procedure will be to state first, in section I, the theory of explanation which has given rise to most of the discussion of the present problem—a theory which, as previously, I shall call by the inelegant and also somewhat misleading name, 'the covering-law theory'.[2] Having stated it, I shall contrast it with what I should myself want to say about typical historical explanations of actions. In sections II and III, I shall go on to consider some objections to my claims, and to review, necessarily briefly, six alternative positions, none of which seems to me to be fully acceptable. Finally, in section IV, in the hope of clarifying the issue further, I shall call attention to certain relationships between my own analysis and some larger philosophic issues.

I

The classical statement of the covering-law theory is to be found in Professor Carl Hempel's article, 'The Function of General Laws in History'.[3] The central claim there advanced is that to explain an occurrence is to show that a statement asserting it is deducible from (1) certain statements of antecedent or simultaneous conditions, and (2) certain empirically testable universal laws or theories. Unless the *explanandum* is in this way logically entailed by what is offered as *explanans*, Hempel would say, the alleged explanation is, at best, incomplete—a mere approach to an explanation. This account of the logical structure of explanation is offered as applicable generally, regardless of subject-matter, and hence as applicable to reputable historical explanations too. What explanation *means*, it would seem, is showing the deducibility of what is to be explained from something else in accordance with universal 'covering' laws.

Those who agree with Professor Hempel about the universal applicability of such a theory of explanation, do not usually quarrel with the

[2] It may be misleading in seeming to imply that explanation should employ a *single* law linking *explanans* and *explanandum*. It also fails to distinguish (as Professor Donagan has done) between claiming that explanation must be deductive and that it must employ universal laws; either of these criteria might be satisfied independently.

[3] Reprinted in *Theories of History*, ed. P. Gardiner (Glencoe, Ill., 1959), pp. 344–56.

judgement that most of the explanations actually offered by historians in the course of their work fail to satisfy its demands. From such an admission, however, they would draw conclusions, not about the cogency of the covering-law model, but about the looseness of ordinary historical practice. Other philosophers have argued that such a discrepancy between logical theory and historical practice is a sign of an illegitimate 'a priorism' on the part of the Hempelians. Their claim would be that, in the case of a 'going concern' like history, the task of philosophers is not to *stipulate* a meaning for 'explanation', but to elicit it from practice generally agreed to be acceptable within the discipline concerned. If historical practice does not conform to covering-law theory, then so much the worse for the theory.

Now it seems to me that each of these positions has a certain kind of right-mindedness about it. I should not myself want to limit the philosopher's task to a mere *description* of what historians do. His job, as Professors Arthur Danto and J. H. Pitt insist, is to explicate, not to duplicate; we expect from the philosopher a 'rational reconstruction' which may not, in every instance, coincide exactly with what a practising historian does.[4] On the other hand, to point out that practice deviates widely and stubbornly from a logical theory at least creates a presumption against the latter; it raises with some urgency the question *why* there should be such a gap between the formula and what it supposedly explicates. I want to argue that the trouble, in the present case, is that what historians usually *mean*, in offering an explanation of a human action, simply does not coincide *conceptually* with showing an action's performance to have been deducible from other conditions in accordance with empirical laws. What is lacking in covering-law theory, it seems to me, is sensitivity to the *concept* of explanation historians normally employ. A 'rational reconstruction' may indeed properly deviate from practice. But we must be careful that such deviation is not due to its being the wrong *kind* of reconstruction.

Let me try to sketch briefly what I take to be the conceptual foundation of most explanations of human actions in history. The function of an explanation is to resolve puzzlement of some kind. When a historian sets out to explain a historical action, his problem is usually that he does not know what reason the agent had for doing it. To achieve understanding, what he seeks is information about what the agent believed to be the facts of his situation, including the likely results of taking various courses of action considered open to him, and what he

[4] A. Danto, Review, *Ethics* (July 1958), 299. J. H. Pitt, 'Generalization in Historical Explanation', *Journal of Philosophy* (1959), 579-80.

wanted to accomplish: his purposes, goals, or motives. Understanding is achieved when the historian can see the reasonableness of a man's doing what this agent did, given the beliefs and purposes referred to; his action can then be explained as having been an 'appropriate' one. The point I want to emphasize is that what is brought out by such considerations is a conceptual connection between understanding a man's action and discerning its rationale. As Professor Hook once put it, there is a difference between showing an action to be peculiar and showing it to be confused.[5] There is similarly a difference between showing an action to be routine and showing it to have point.

Explanation which tries to establish a connection between beliefs, motives, and actions of the indicated sort I shall call 'rational explanation'. The following is a particularly clear example of it. (I hope I may therefore be pardoned for using an example I have used before for the same purpose.)

In trying to account for the success of the invasion of England by William of Orange, Trevelyan asks himself why Louis XIV withdrew military pressure from Holland in the summer of 1688—this action being, he tells us, 'the greatest mistake of his life'.[6] His answer is: 'Louis calculated that, even if William landed in England there would be a civil war and long troubles, as always in that factious island. Meantime he could conquer Europe at leisure.' Furthermore, 'he was glad to have the Dutch out of the way (in England) while he dealt a blow at the Emperor Leopold (in Germany)'. He thought 'it was impossible that the conflict between James and William should not yield him an opportunity'. What makes Louis's action understandable here, according to Trevelyan, is our discovery of a 'calculation' which was 'not as absurd as it looks after the event'. Indeed, the calculation shows us just how appropriate Louis's unfortunate action really was to the circumstances regarded as providing reasons for it. In fact, of course, the king, in a sense, miscalculated; and his action was, in a sense, not appropriate to the circumstances. Yet the whole purpose of Trevelyan's explanatory account is to show us that, for a man in Louis's position, with the aims and beliefs he had, the action was appropriate at least to the circumstances as they were envisaged.

For explanations of the kind just illustrated, I should argue, the establishment of a deductive logical connection between *explanans* and *explanandum*, based on the inclusion of suitable empirical laws in the

---

[5] 'A Pragmatic Critique of the Historico-Genetic Method', in *Essays in Honor of John Dewey* (New York, 1929), pp. 163–71.
[6] *The English Revolution* (London, 1938), pp. 105–6.

former, is neither a necessary nor a sufficient condition of explaining. It is not necessary because the aim of such explanations is not to show that the agent was the sort of man who does in fact always do the sort of thing he did in the sort of circumstances he thought he was in. What it aims to show is that the sort of thing he did made perfectly good sense from his own point of view. The establishment of such a connection, if it could be done, would not be a sufficient condition of such explanation either, since it would not itself represent the relation between the agent's beliefs and purposes and what he did as making the latter a reasonable thing to have done.

I might perhaps add—to avoid possible misunderstanding—that the issue between the appropriateness of applying the covering-law and rational 'models' to such cases has nothing to do with the question whether historical explanations are to be given in terms of people's 'ideas' or in terms of 'objective' conditions of their natural and social environment. For Professor Hempel, unlike certain materialist philosophers of history, would allow that the explanation of action is peculiar, at least in the sense of usually and properly making reference to the motives and beliefs of the agents concerned. He would admit, I think, that in offering explanations of the *doing* of actions, by contrast with, say, their success or failure, it is not *actual*, but *envisaged*, states of affairs to which we need to refer. Apart from this, however, explanations of action are, for Hempel, 'not essentially different from the causal explanations of physics and chemistry'.[7] For 'the determining motives and beliefs', he says, '... have to be classified among the antecedent conditions of a motivational explanation, and there is no formal difference on this account between motivational and causal explanation'. In view of what has been said about non-deducibility of the *explanandum*, it should be clear that my quarrel with this is that it does get the form, not the content, of rational explanations wrong.

II

A number of critics have found something to disagree with in the account I have just given of rational explanation in history. The objections which have come to my attention can conveniently be treated under four heads. The first, and perhaps least important, is that few, if any, historical explanations would get very far if it were necessary to

[7] C. G. Hempel and P. Oppenheim, 'The Logic of Explanation', reprinted in H. Feigl and M. Brodbek (eds.), *Readings in the Philosophy of Science* (New York, 1953), pp. 327–8.

discover the calculation of the agent. For, as Professor Nowell-Smith has objected, if we find that our historical agent did not go through the relevant calculation, then the explanation would thereby be falsified.[8] And he seems to assume that few such agents would very often have acted in such a self-conscious, intellectualistic manner.

Now I should certainly agree that there will be many actions in history for which no such calculation can be found; and the difficulty of finding them does call attention to a limitation of the scope of such explanations. Nor should I want to rule out *a priori* the possibility of some such actions being explained in other ways. It may be, however, that the very word 'calculation' is misleading in this connection. For what makes an action understandable rationally, is not necessarily a set of propositions which the agent recited to himself. Our understanding of his action may arise out of our perception of a rational connection between an action and the motives and beliefs we ascribe to the agent without any such psychological implications. What is claimed is rather that understanding of what he did is achieved by ordering such ingredients, once made explicit, in the *form* of a practical calculation. The philosopher's point is one about the kind of logical relation which must subsist between *explanans* and *explanandum*. Interpreted in this non-intellectualistic fashion, the scope of the rational explanation of actions in history will be far from insignificant. I should expect it, indeed, to be operative in most of the explanations given by narrative historians.

A second objection amounts to the suspicion that the scope of such alleged rational understanding is in fact so broad as to be trivial, and possibly also dangerous. For understanding, as I have described it, may appear to be indistinguishable from that activity, after the event, which we refer to pejoratively as 'rationalization'. 'We all know,' observes Professor John Passmore, 'how hollow-sounding are the explanations of our conduct we give to other people.'[9] It is 'as if they were constructed to satisfy our audience rather than as explanations of our actions'. The historian will similarly be inclined 'to make of our behaviour something much more a matter of principle than it actually is'.

Now once again, I should not want to deny the danger to which the critic points. But I should regard his objection as calling into view a special hazard of any search for the reasons of actions—a way in which rational understanding can go wrong—rather than something which rules out the possibility of rational understanding as such. The

[8] Review, *Philosophy* (April 1959), 170–2.
[9] Review, *Australian Journal of Politics and History* (1958), 269 ff.

claim that the perception of appropriateness is the historian's usual criterion of understanding was, after all, a claim of conceptual logic. Its acceptance does not imply that whenever we think we know what an agent's reasons were, we *really do* know. What it implies is a conceptual connection between the claims to understand an action and to perceive its rationale; and this is a matter of correctness of *form* in explanation. Correctness of form, however, is obviously not a guarantee of correctness of content; and a similar point could, with equal propriety, be made about explanation on the covering-law model. For the latter, we need to know universal laws; but can we be so certain that we have discovered them—particularly in historical cases where (unlike the thoroughly interconnected and theoretically grounded laws of physical science) they will be simply generalizations from experience?

The third objection is more troublesome; yet I think it too can be met. In this case the objector admits that our claim to understand an action is often conditional upon our discovering the agent's reasons for acting. But this, he points out, is very different from perceiving the *rationality* of the action; for the latter involves our *endorsing* the agent's reasons as *good* reasons. Thus Mr. P. F. Strawson observes, with regard to my claim that we *do*, in some sense, have to 'certify' the agent's reasons, that although I condemn 'anything which stops short of this as spectatorism in history', he thinks 'anything which goes as far as this makes history impossible'.[10] It is true that my saying only that the reasons must be good ones 'from the agent's point of view', and that the appropriateness of his act is to be assessed only in relation to the circumstances as *he* envisaged them, goes some way towards meeting the objection. But the critics will deny that it goes far enough. For there are 'differences of intelligence, temperament, ability and character', Strawson reminds us, as well as of beliefs and purposes. And human action can fall short of an ideal of rationality because of defective *judgement*, as well as defective *information*.

Now there is certainly something correct about this line of criticism, but I do not think it destroys the position I am trying to maintain. For it is obvious that we cannot claim rational understanding of the making of a logical error, any more than we can claim such understanding of a physical failure to implement a decision. Since both of the latter sorts of things can sometimes be explained, it follows that the present criterion of understanding cannot be the only one, even in history. And it was not my intention to claim that it is. My claim is only that the criterion of rational appropriateness does function for actions not

10 Review, *Mind* (April 1959), 268.

judged to be defective in various ways; and that it sometimes *is* found to be applicable. And I add that when we do employ this criterion, we cannot help certifying the agent's reasons as good ones, from his point of view, for doing what he did. That is what is *meant* by 'following his argument' or 'seeing the relevance of the considerations he took into account'. It is out of a very proper recognition of this fact, it seems to me, that controversial theories of 'empathy' in history derive their plausibility, for there is an important sense in which the claim to understand implies a claim to be able to 'rethink' the thoughts of the historical agent. And one cannot rethink a practical argument one knows to be invalid.

The fourth objection accepts the contention that understanding of actions is achieved by knowledge of the agent's reasons, but denies that the assertion that he acted for these reasons can be made without committing the historian to the truth of a covering law. For once it becomes clear that what the historian needs to discover is the agent's *actual* reasons, and not just *good* reasons there might be for acting as he did, it will be alleged that, if the explanation is to be justified, we shall need to know some generalization to the effect that an agent who has such actual and good reasons will act as this agent in fact did. As Nowell-Smith has put it: if we argue that the agent acted as he did because he went through a certain rational calculation, our evidence will have to include general knowledge of how such men behave when they so calculate.[11] Thus even if it is true that actual reasons must also in some sense be good reasons, if they are to be explanatory, it may be claimed that there is the *additional* requirement that good, actual reasons be linked to the actions being explained by covering empirical laws.

Now it does not seem to me that when I say 'He did so-and-so because he thought so-and-so', my use of the word 'because' commits me to any such thing; and I cannot agree that my evidence for the statement must include the kind of general knowledge indicated. It should be noted, in this connection, how especially implausible it would be to claim that this is required by what I mean by such 'because' statements, when the actions which I claim to be able to explain are my own. For in my own case, too, I distinguish between finding reasons which would justify my action, and getting straight the actual reasons for which I acted; and when I do the latter, I do not need to know that all men like me, or even I myself on all similar occasions, act in the way I do on this occasion, for good, actual reasons. The claim I would make to be

[11] Ibid.

able to act *arbitrarily*—i.e. contrary to good reasons which I actually acknowledge to be so—would in itself make it impossible for me to agree with the present objection. For what I mean by such 'because' statements when they are self-applied, is also what I want to mean when I explain the actions of others on the rational model.

The exact force of Nowell-Smith's objection is in any case not entirely clear, in view of some further remarks he makes. For he seems to allow that, in 'one sense of explain', we *do* explain an action if we show that what the agent did was 'the rational thing for a person so situated to do'. But this, he continues, does not explain *why he did the rational thing*—why he acted in accordance with the good reasons he had. To answer the latter question, Nowell-Smith says, we should need to cite some such 'platitude' as that 'rational men who have worked out appropriate plans tend to act on them unless prevented'; and 'it is this sense of "explain"', he claims, 'that the covering law theory was designed to analyse.' I must confess that I cannot see that in making this distinction Nowell-Smith really disagrees with me. For to characterize in this way a difference between explaining why the agent did an *act as specified* and explaining why he did *the rational thing*, it is surely implied that rational explanation, short of appeal to the platitude, can be *complete of its kind, or at its level*. And nothing I have said about it need be taken as ruling out the possibility of giving explanation (at the second level) of a man's acting rationally at all. We might, for example, explain the present rationality of a person's actions by referring to the casual efficacy of a certain sort of shock treatment he has undergone since last we saw him. One might still have doubts as to whether such explanations, if they could be given, would consist of showing anything more than the satisfaction of a certain necessary, rather than sufficient, condition of acting rationally. But that issue would be beside the present point. And the kind of explanation involved would in any case be rarely required in history.

I might add that another critic, Professor J. Cohen, scores a good point in this connection, by quoting against me the remark that in history there operates as a 'standing presumption' the 'general belief that people act for sufficient reasons'.[12] The fact that such a presumption might be regarded as trivial is, as he says, irrelevant; the question is whether it is *logically required* by what was above called the first level of explanation of actions in terms of actual, but good, reasons. My reply must be that my declaration of the presumption of rationality was incautiously strong. It is true that it was only stated as a 'presump-

---

[12] Review, *Philosophical Quarterly* (April 1960).

tion', and was really intended only to reinforce the claim that historians give priority to the search for rational explanations over non-rational ones. The important point is that any such 'presumption' does not rule out the possibility of there being an indefinite and variable number of cases to the contrary. Nor does it imply that cases to the contrary will be explicable failures to act rationally. There is no assumption in history (as there may be in physical science) that everything is, in principle, explicable. Any 'presumption of rationality' is thus logically quite different from what methodologists and logicians would mean by a covering empirical law.

III

There are a number of philosophers who would not accept the analysis I have given and tried to defend in the preceding sections, who would never the less agree that there is something wrong with the covering-law model as originally formulated, if it is to be an elucidation of the logical structure of explanation in history. What generally drives them to this conclusion, I think, is a problem which Sir Isaiah Berlin has expressed thus.[13] If we challenge a historical explanation by asking for the law which renders it deductive, we can usually, in fact, think of some fairly plausible universal generalization which would bring the proffered explanation into line with the requirements of the model. By any ordinary standards, however, the inductive warrant we could claim for the laws we could, with a certain amount of ingenuity, in this way often provide, is not very strong. More significantly, it is generally much less strong than our confidence in the explanation given. We are thus left with the paradox that, on covering-law theory, good explanations have to be represented as deriving logically from questionable laws.

In the face of this paradox, and despite the supposed obviousness, *a priori*, of its original claims, a number of proposals have been made for the modification of the covering-law model, while retaining its central idea. In particular, it has been suggested that something less than a law, in the sense of 'a statement of universal conditional form', may give force to a historical explanation. In this section, I want to take note of six different ways in which it has been suggested that laws may be weakened or defective and still perform their explanatory role. For it may be argued that it is with reference to the resulting, modified versions of the covering-law theory, rather than the austere original, that

[13] 'History and Theory: The Concept of Scientific History', *History and Theory*, I, 1 (1960), 19.

the need for recognizing a 'rational' model of explanation, in the case of actions, should be judged. No thorough examination of any of the six alternatives can be attempted here, although I shall make some remarks about each of them. I hope at any rate to say enough to make it profitable for us to carry the discussion of them further.

The first is a view which I shall associate with the names of Mr. Patrick Gardiner and Sir Isaiah Berlin (although it is not the only view held by either of them on the subject). Both of these authors link the difficulty of representing historical explanation as deductive, in the full Hempelian sense, with the fact that the language of historical description is not that of a technical discipline like physics or psychology, but is the language of the plain, if educated, layman. Nor do they regard this as a defect of history, for it is, they would say, a *requirement* of the study if consumers of history are to grasp what is produced. The concepts of ordinary language, however, are notoriously loose and vague, and these features are consequently features also of any general laws formulated in terms of them. Words like 'revolution' or 'conquest', Gardiner points out, do not have precisely defined rules of application; indeed, their meaning may even change through time.[14] Similarly, although Berlin accepts the claim that all historical judgements 'embody' generalizations, he adds that 'few are sufficiently clear, sharp, precisely defined to be capable of being organized in a formal structure which allows of systematic mutual entailments or exclusions....'[15]

Berlin sometimes offers an additional reason for resisting the covering-law model in any strict or literal version. This is the claim that ordinary language is not only vague, but also ineradicably *evaluative*. The whole language of human action is bound up with its user's appraisal of what is done, and uncertainty as to whether a concept applies, therefore, may be due to differences of evaluation, not only to genuine indeterminacy of meaning. Some philosophers of history, like F. A. Hayek, Leo Strauss, and Peter Winch, would go further and say that the very notion of a historical or social fact is, in its ordinary sense, a quasi-evaluative notion.[16] Any laws into which such notions are to enter would consequently be evaluative too.

Now it does not seem to me that what Berlin and Gardiner bring out in this way, even if true, represents any insuperable obstacle for the claims of covering-law theory as a 'rational reconstruction'. For it

[14] *The Nature of Historical Explanation* (Oxford, 1952), pp. 53, 60–1.
[15] *Historical Inevitability* (London and New York, 1953), p. 54.
[16] See *The Counter-Revolution of Science* (Glencoe, Ill., 1952); *Natural Right and History* (Chicago, 1953); *The Idea of a Social Science* (London, 1958), respectively.

surely follows that, since the historian's explanations employ the same language as the laws, any looseness introduced by the language will affect the explanations too. The really puzzling argument, however, is one which represents a good explanation as resting on poor laws. To argue that only vague or evaluative laws function in a vague or evaluative inquiry, is surely to *accept* the covering-law model as the statement of a functioning logical ideal. And this presumably is all that a Hempelian would want to claim—although he might regret that historians should care more about speaking to the general public in its own language than giving completely adequate explanations.

A second and more radical way of trying to meet the original difficulty concentrates, not upon the language, but upon the subject-matter of history. It agrees that either the subject-matter itself, or the state of inquiry into it, is such that plausible universal laws can seldom, if ever, be discovered, so that if explanations are to be given at all, we must make a virtue of necessity, and abandon the strict *deductive* criterion. A straightforward version of this position is to say that *statistical* as well as universal laws may explain what falls under them. From a statistical law we cannot, of course, deduce the occurrence of a particular event or action to be explained; but we can at least show it to have been probable. We might therefore claim to be able to explain it *inductively*. Such a modified analysis, it might be claimed, would apply to all those cases of explanation in history for which we could formulate a plausible general statement incorporating some such qualification as 'usually' or 'for the most part'. For the notion of a statistical law here is simply the notion of a generalization which asserts a connection, not between *all* cases of what is specified by *explanans* and *explanandum*, but between a certain *proportion* of them. And such a law could, of course, be vague or precise, stating either that most, or a certain definite percentage, of cases were concerned. A modification of the covering-law model along these lines was suggested by Hempel himself, even in its earliest formulations; and it has also recently been advocated by Professor Nicholas Rescher.[17]

Now the modification of the original claim involved in the abandonment of the deductive criterion and the acceptance of statistical laws seems to me quite a major one from the standpoint of conceptual analysis of explanation. For the new claim is not, presumably, simply that a *partial* explanation, or a mere *approach* to explanation, can be given by this means (a doctrine which would not go beyond Hempel's

---

[17] 'The Function of General Laws in History', op. cit., p. 350; 'The Logic of Explanation', op. cit., p. 350.

theory of the explanation 'sketch'). The claim appears rather to be that an event can be *completely* explained (although perhaps in a different sense) without subsuming it under a universal law licensing its deduction, and consequently without showing that it had to happen. One may perhaps wonder whether the withdrawal of what was at first received as obvious is anything more than a convenient stipulation of a new meaning for 'explain'. One may wonder, too, how acceptable the concession really is to those who were at first attracted to the covering-law model because of its logical elegance. Professor Michael Scriven, I suspect, speaks for many of them when he objects to the way particular occurrences 'rattle around' in statistical explanations.[18] It was a strength of the deductive theory, he observes, that it focused attention on precisely what was to be explained. Statistical laws, however, are compatible with both the occurrence and non-occurrence of what they are supposed to explain; they 'abandon the hold on the individual case'.

It may be of interest, in this connection, to note that in spite of its not being deductive in Hempel's sense, a *rational* explanation actually has a better claim than a statistical one to meet Scriven's objections against explanation which appears to lose its grip on the case. For although a rational explanation does not show that a particular action had to *occur*, it may show (in a rational sense of 'had to') that a particular action *had to be done*. I say only 'may' because I do not think that the puzzlement which leads a person to ask why someone did something is, even in the rational sense, always expressible as 'Why did he *have* to do that?' Sometimes all we really want to know, when we ask for an action to be explained, is how it could have seemed rationally possible or 'all right' to do it; and here an issue like that between deductive and inductive approaches to the covering-law model arises *within* the class of rational explanations. When we do ask why an action had to be done, however, an answer bearing directly on the case is often possible—an answer involving the rational ruling out of all possible alternatives. There is no counterpart of this in the assertion of a purely statistical connection.

A third sort of modification of the covering-law model has been suggested by Professor Scriven himself.[19] Scriven's proposal takes its rise from the difficulties already sketched: first, that universal laws elicited from most historical explanations are doubtful; second, that a mere statistical law, since it fails to rule out the non-occurrence of what is

[18] 'Truisms as the Grounds for Historical Explanations', reprinted in *Theories of History*, p. 467.
[19] Ibid., pp. 464 ff.

being explained, fails to explain why *it* happened rather than something else. Scriven's solution is to attribute the implicit generality of a historical explanation to a type of general statement which is neither of these sorts, but a kind of logical hybrid, with (he would claim) the important advantages of each.[20]

Thus, to use a simplified version of one of his examples, if we ask why William the Conqueror did not invade Scotland, and answer that it was because he had no desire for additional lands, we may say the explanation is grounded in some such truism as 'Rulers don't normally invade neighbouring territories if they are satisfied with what they have.' Such a generalization, Scriven insists, would clearly not be *intended* to be taken as unequivocally ruling out all cases to the contrary; yet it says more than that rulers *seldom* do this sort of thing, as a truly statistical generalization would do. It makes a stronger assertion than this because it represents what is specified by the law as the normal or standard case, to which any counterexamples stand as strange exceptions. Scriven calls such a generalization 'normic'. It allows us to *deduce* the occurrence of what is to be explained, provided we have no reason for thinking the circumstances extraordinary. Such generalizations often betray their special sense, he says, by containing one or other of a number of normic 'modifiers': words like 'ordinarily', 'typically', 'properly', 'naturally', 'under standard conditions'—the logic of which, Scriven argues, is quite different from 'all', 'most', or 'some'. He cautions us, however, that not every generalization employing such modifiers is asserted with true normic force, and that some generalizations omitting them may yet be asserted with such force. Correct diagnosis thus often requires close attention to the context.

The problem, of course, is to get clear just how we are to operate with the notion of 'exceptional conditions', and how we are to represent, not only as justifiable, but even as fully intelligible, the distinction between apparent counterexamples which do, and which do not, falsify a normic generalization. For Scriven does not deny that such generalizations are empirical assertions, and they must therefore be falsifiable in principle. It seems to me that, when pressed, such generalizations are in danger of sliding in one of two directions. They will tend either towards an ordinary universal or statistical law, or towards what might be called the agent's principle of action, as it would function in a rational explanation.

It is Scriven's contention that a knowledgeable and skilful practitioner of a discipline (whether it be history or medicine) knows how

[20] Ibid., p. 464.

to handle normic statements because, although he cannot spell out in advance all the sorts of things that would count as exceptional circumstances, he at least grasps the principle at work: the network of exceptions, he says, is 'complex but understandable'.[21] In this connection Scriven makes a good deal of the learned capacity or trained judgement of the historian, about which little more can be said; and perhaps he is right in thinking that no adequate account of the nature of historical explanation can be given without some reference to such a notion. But even if we accept the claim that the network can be known without being articulable, it is difficult to see that any logical novelty is introduced which would give normic generalization, so conceived, a different force from universal or statistical laws. The problem would appear to be only that of saying in full what the 'understood' generalization is.

There are hints, however, in what Scriven says about the 'norm-defining' function of such generalizations, and about their dependence upon the historian's judgement, that they may be logically peculiar after all, in not being straightforwardly empirical generalizations. It is notable, for example, that in offering a very miscellaneous list of the kinds of statements that may have to be interpreted normically, Scriven includes 'rules, definitions and certain normative statements in ethics' (although he rather mysteriously refers to the latter as normic statements operating in 'other fields').[22] It seems to me that in its explanatory role, a statement like 'Rulers do not normally invade neighbouring territories if they are satisfied with what they have' may quite intelligibly be interpreted as stating a 'norm' in the sense of reminding us of what it is reasonable to do—and thus, of course, of what people in fact do, *except* when they act foolishly, ignorantly, arbitrarily, and so on. So interpreted, the explanatory function of the normic statement would be to display the rationale of William's non-invasion of Scotland. And this would assimilate explanation in terms of normic generalizations to what I have called the 'rational' kind.

A fourth and equally interesting attempt to provide a more plausible type of explanatory law for historical cases has been elaborated by Professors N. Rescher, C. B. Joynt and O. Helmer.[23] According to these authors, although historians do often use universal laws brought in

[21] Ibid., p. 466.
[22] Ibid., p. 464.
[23] N. Rescher and O. Helmer, 'On the Epistemology of the Inexact Sciences', *Management Science* (October 1959), 25–40; C. B. Joynt and N. Rescher, 'On Explanation in History', *Mind* (1959), 383–7; N. Rescher and C. B. Joynt, 'The Problem of Uniqueness in History', *History and Theory*, I, 2 (1961), 150–62.

from the various sciences, both natural and social (chiefly to establish the 'boundary conditions' for action), they also themselves *discover* generalizations of a logically different sort. As part of their own proper inquiry, historians are said to formulate, not general laws, but restrictive generalizations, limited by spatio-temporal considerations, but fully valid and lawlike within them. Examples would be: 'Officers of the pre-Revolutionary French Navy were selected from those of noble birth', or 'Heretics were persecuted in seventeenth century Spain.'[24] What makes such generalizations of special interest in the present context is their relation to a certain characteristic objection of historians, when presented with the original claims of covering-law theory. This is the objection that universal laws would commit them to making unsupported claims regarding what happens in unexamined regions of historical space and time. Explanations given in terms of *limited* generalizations would employ only general knowledge of the kind historians would claim to have—namely, knowledge of 'the period'.

It might be added that Rescher also points out that most limited generalizations actually in use in history are loose in the more familiar sense of admitting counterexamples, although not too many—*within* their proper sphere of application. This admission raises no special problem for him since he allows that statistical laws and probability hypotheses, when known, can also function in an explanatory role. The point of importance here is that such generalizations could in principle be perfectly general, in the sense of not allowing any counterexamples within the limited scope of their application; and they would thus, although themselves not strictly universal, afford *deductive* explanations in favourable cases. In considering the Rescher–Joynt–Helmer thesis as making a novel point, by contrast with others noted in this paper, we may therefore concentrate upon the claim they make regarding restricted generalizations which are non-statistical.

Now the most natural interpretation to place upon the examples noted is that they are really *summative* generalizations. The form of any explanation given in terms of them might therefore be thought to be like that given in terms of drawing a red ball from a bag when it is pointed out that only red ones were put into the bag in the first place. One could hardly deny that this would be to give an explanation, although it might be doubted that such explanations would be of any importance in historical studies. It might be claimed, at any rate, that the explanation has greater force than, say, a derivation from a mere statistical, although otherwise unrestricted, generalization. And there

[24] 'On the Epistemology of the Inexact Sciences', op. cit., pp. 27 and 29.

doubtless are true summative generalizations in history: for example, 'All the Reformation Parliaments were packed', a statement which would presumably be asserted on the basis of independent knowledge of all of them. But the present authors explicitly repudiate such an interpretation of the restricted generalizations in view. For these are said to apply to unexamined cases as well as examined ones; and they also have counterfactual force. They apply not only to known French naval officers and Spanish heretics, but also to unknown ones, and to ones who might have existed but didn't.

When we ask, however, on what basis we can assert them, limited generalizations, like normics, seem gradually to dissolve into something more familiar (although it is not entirely clear why they have to). This comes out especially in the discussion of a favoured example (which unfortunately is not itself the explanation of an action): the explanation of the defeat of Villeneuve at Trafalgar, in part by reference to the generalization, 'In seafights, 1653–1805, large formations were too cumbersome for effectual control.'[25] We can have confidence in this, we are told, because of our general knowledge of the state of eighteenth-century naval ordnance; our knowledge of the latter reinforces the mere generalization by showing *why* the regularity holds in the period and area indicated. What we have, in fact, is a 'transitory regularity', which is itself explicable in terms of universal regularities, in conjunction with local conditions. The crucial point for the interpretation of the Rescher–Joynt–Helmer doctrine is whether the limited generalization would be explanatory even if no such link with universal laws were known. Do we at any rate need to have this further information to know what the spatio-temporal limits of the limited generalization are? To make either admission would surely be to concede all that an exponent of the original covering-law theory would require. And as far as I can see, these authors concede it. The only caveat, as in the case of Scriven's normics, concerns the inarticulateness of the knowledge of supporting generalizations. There is only 'a vague knowledge of underlying regularities'.[26]

A fifth sort of modification of the covering-law doctrine which has been proposed tries to take account of the resistance of historians to admitting universal empirical laws by narrowing the extent of their alleged commitment in still a further way. This is the suggestion that, in the case of the explanation of an individual human action, at least, the general statement providing the link between what is explained and

[25] Ibid., p. 28.
[26] Ibid., p. 38.

the motives and beliefs which explain it, need only be a 'lawlike' statement, formulated to apply to a range of actions of a specified *individual*. The doctrine in question entered current discussion in philosophy of history as an application of Professor Gilbert Ryle's account of dispositional explanation in *The Concept of Mind*. Ryle pointed out that dispositional statements we make about individuals—for example, character statements like 'Disraeli was ambitious'—are 'lawlike' in licensing singular hypothetical statements of the form, 'If Disraeli sees an opportunity to obtain a position of leadership, he will take it.' Unlike true laws, however, they make no assertion connecting *kinds* of beliefs or motives (or people) with *kinds* of actions. If they are explanatory, statements which are defectively general in the dispositional sense, like Rescher's limited generalizations, would appear to be especially useful in historical studies. For it is a commonplace that it is dangerous to generalize about individuals in history. The historian must, as Strawson puts it, get to *know his man*, which is, he says, quite different from knowing 'platitudes about men in general'.[27] To know one's man is, in this view, to discover the dispositional complex we call his character. We can then, it is claimed, explain what he does as *characteristic* of him.

It is clear that a dispositional statement about an individual is not itself a law. The question arises, however, whether we can assert such statements without committing ourselves to, or deriving them from, laws. Ryle has declared that we can; he has even claimed that we learn dispositional truths about particular things, even in the study of nature, *before* we know corresponding laws. It is unfortunate that his best-known example is poorly selected for illustrating this claim. For if I try to explain the shattering of *this* pane of glass when hit by a stone, by saying it was brittle, it is hard to see how I could have known this apart from general knowledge of the properties of glass. I certainly could not have experimented relevantly in the past with this particular pane. In other cases, however, where prior manifestations of a disposition would not entail destruction of the object, it does not seem out of the way to say we could have such knowledge. And we could similarly discover that a particular person was disposed to act in a certain way by noticing the way he has acted already in relevant circumstances.

It has been argued, however, that there is no logical peculiarity of *human* dispositions which brings any such claim into question. In introducing the dispositional model into the discussion of explanation in history, Gardiner made a great deal of Ryle's own admission of the looseness of the prediction of action which is licensed by dispositional

[27] Review, *Mind* (April 1959), p. 268.

statements about people. Ryle puts the point by saying that human dispositions are highly determinable rather than determinate; there are usually a number of alternative ways of actualizing them, so that knowing a man's dispositions is not necessarily being able to predict in any detail what he will do. Professor Jonathan Cohen has argued that this complexity of human dispositions may well manoeuvre the historian giving dispositional explanation into assuming universal laws.[28] Cohen's point is that if the statement, 'Disraeli was ambitious', licenses us to expect, not a specific expression of ambition previously noted in his behaviour, but only one or other of quite a number of alternatives, then if we are going to base our explanation of Disraeli's attack on Peel in 1847 on our knowledge that he was ambitious, we need something more to warrant our inference than our having found Disraeli acting ambitiously in *other* ways in the past. We need to know that he is disposed to act ambitiously in this particular way as well. Cohen suspects, therefore, that the historian, in giving the explanation, really assumes some such universal law as that a person who is disposed to act ambitiously in some ways is disposed to act so in others as well. Such an argument, it should be noted, does not show that what is *asserted* by the dispositional statement about Disraeli is a universal law, or even that it could not be *established* by observing Disraeli's past behaviour alone (provided that he had already acted ambitiously in the requisite number of ways). It does suggest, however, that in typical cases in history, what is asserted may *in fact* rest on assumed universal connections.

Still a sixth type of modification has been suggested by some other philosophers. Professor Charles Frankel, for example, having accepted from Hempel the conclusion that the failure of historical explanations to display a tight covering-law pattern may often be due to their offering incomplete explanations, goes on to distinguish between this kind of deviation and another not attributable to the historian's not finishing what he begins. Historical explanations, Frankel claims, may fail to be deductive (and hence lack predictive force) because they state only certain *necessary* or *essential*, not sufficient, conditions of what occurred. This also happens in other domains, he reminds us, but when it does, the stating of sufficient conditions still remains the ideal of explanation. In history, on the contrary, stating certain necessary conditions often 'seems fully to satisfy our demand for an explanation'.[29] To

[28] Review, *Philosophical Quarterly* (1960), 192.
[29] 'Explanation and Interpretation in History', reprinted in *Theories of History*, p. 412.

give such an account, especially as part of tracing the necessary stages in a process, according to Frankel, 'is one of the stable and accepted meanings of "explain" '; and it would therefore be incorrect to regard it as in any proper sense incomplete—a mere 'explanation sketch'. We must realize 'that not all satisfactory explanations supply us with exactly the same type of information, and that not all requests to have something explained are unequivocal requests for a single kind of answer'.

An explanation in terms of necessary or essential conditions does not aim to represent the *explanandum* as deducible from the *explanans*. It nevertheless, Frankel goes on to say,

rests as much as does a fully predictive explanation on tacit or expressed generalizations. Otherwise we could not distinguish between a mere succession of events and a series of connected events. For it is only in terms of generalizations to the effect that events of a given type do not take place unless they are conjoined with other events of a given type that we are able to say what we mean by an 'historical process'. . . .

In his general account of *genetic* explanation, Professor W. B. Gallie says much the same thing. If a historian explains the rapid rise of Christianity by referring to its possession of the proselytizing platform of the Jewish synagogue, he points out, this does not commit him to arguing that the development was either necessary or probable. The force of the explanation is rather to show how Christianity got its opportunity. An everyday example of the same pattern would be the explanation of an angry retort by reference to the taunt which evoked it. Once again, there is no claim to show the retort to be deducible or predictable. It is rather that *but for* the taunt, 'the statement would remain unintelligible in the sense of lacking an appropriate historical context'.[30]

Professor Gallie has been criticized for assuming that we could have knowledge of a necessary condition of an occurrence which is logically independent of knowledge of its sufficient conditions, and hence for implying that we could ever offer a properly warranted explanation of the so-called genetic type without filling out antecedent conditions and laws to the point where we have the materials for a covering-law, deductive explanation.[31] I cannot see why we should deny that we can discover, empirically, laws of the form, 'Only if so-and-so then so-and-so', which could warrant the assertion of mere necessary condition in a

---

[30] 'Explanations in History and the Genetic Sciences', reprinted ibid., p. 387.
[31] A. Montefiore, 'Professor Gallie on "Necessary and Sufficient Conditions" ', *Mind* (October 1956), 534 ff.

particular case. Nor does it appear questionable that knowledge of such conditions alone may in some contexts be explanatory. They are especially likely to be explanatory, it might be added, when the puzzlement giving rise to the demand for explanation is of the kind most naturally expressed in such questions as 'How could that have happened?' where it seems at first that a certain essential condition was not fulfilled.

All I should want to point out is that, in explaining *actions* non-deductively in the rational way, it is no more required that we establish certain antecedent conditions, such as the agent's motives or beliefs, as necessary by virtue of corresponding 'only if' laws, than it is that we establish them as sufficient conditions. It is enough that what provides the agent with a reason for acting be a *rationally* necessary condition—that is, that it be shown that without it, he had no reason to do what he did. It is not required that we show that he *could not* have acted in the same way without having that reason. It has already been argued that, when we show that an agent *had* to do what he did because there was no reasonable alternative open to him, we do not commit ourselves to representing his action as predictable from the fact that he had sufficient reason for performing it. Similarly, in the present case, when we show that but for the taunt, the agent would have had no reason for his response, we do not commit ourselves to representing the taunt as *retrodictable* from the fact of his angry remark. The proposed weakening of the covering-law model to include explanations in terms of 'laws of necessary condition' is thus still not sufficiently radical to encompass the relevant forms of the rational explanation of actions. It does, however, so far as it goes, indicate a genuine way in which the claims of the original model can go wrong.

IV

This completes our brief review of some of the more important proposals which have been made for modifying the covering-law theory. In every case, what we are offered seems to be a concession by logical theory to the realities of historical knowledge. These concessions, as we have seen, are of logically different sorts; and there may be better reasons for accepting some of them than others. It might be noted, however, that although the various deviations from the original conception of what would count as a covering law were presented as *alternatives*, they are not (with the possible exception of statistical and normic generalizations) *exclusive* alternatives. It has, in fact, already been pointed out that some of the authors treated represent explanatory laws in history as being 'defective' in two or more ways at once. It might be added that anyone who accepted the legitimacy of each type of modification separately, could also accept them as functioning together: one might conceive of an explanatory law which fell short of the ideal in all six ways at once. It might assert *vaguely* that the beliefs, purposes, and actions of a certain *individual* are *normally* connected, in a certain *proportion* of cases, in a restricted *geographical area*, and during a limited *period*, in such a way that *but for* his having those beliefs and purposes, the actions would not be performed.

A philosopher who was prepared to recognize such a maximally modified 'law' as satisfying the demand for generality in a historical explanation, could certainly not be accused of failing to keep theory in touch with practice. And it might very well be that a sufficient accumulation of such modifications would break down completely the usual resistance of historians to admitting that the particular explanations they give either explicitly contain, or implicitly commit them to, a law or laws. The commitment, after all, can come to look pretty innocuous. Yet, for reasons which I sketched in the first section of this paper, it seems to me that it is misleading to say that even the most innocuous law is what gives typical explanations of action in history their force. To point out that an action which puzzles us falls under a law of any kind—even if this is true—is to make a claim in the wrong 'universe of discourse' for the answering of typical 'why' questions in history.

It may perhaps be useful, in concluding this paper, to try to link this position with some considerations arising out of broader philosophical questions. There are two points I should especially like to touch on. The first is the relation between the acceptance of the rational model of explanation and the holding of a libertarian metaphysical position. The second is the relation between the giving of rational explanations and a certain view of the nature and purpose of historical inquiry.

Let me confess that I do in fact hold a libertarian position, and that I think the rational model of explanation to be of special interest to anyone who does. It is of interest because it shows a way in which explanation can be given in history which is logically *compatible* with indeterminism regarding human actions. The incompatibility of representing actions as both free and explicable has often been asserted. But if the contentions of this paper are correct, this doctrine holds only for explanation on the covering-law model, with an assertion of a deductive connection between an action and its explanatory conditions.

In saying this, it should be clear that I am not *arguing* for the acceptibility of the rational model of explanation from liberation meta-physics as premiss. I am arguing on conceptual grounds that there is a meaning of 'explain' which is already current in history, as well as everyday affairs, which does not entail determinism. I should like to point out also that I am not arguing from the possibility of giving rational explanations to the truth of libertarianism. For I cannot see—as some like Professor Winch apparently believe[32]—that the giving of a rational explanation excludes the giving of a covering-law explanation; that rational explanation entails *indeterminism*. I cannot see that we need agree even with what appears to be Professor Donagan's view on this: that rational explanations would at any rate have *point* only so long as we cannot give law-covered explanations of the same things.[33] The two sorts of explanations are better regarded as belonging to different logical and conceptual networks, within which different kinds of puzzlement are expressed and resolved.

I have suggested that the compatibility of rational explanation and libertarianism may provide some philosophers of history with a justi-fiable motive for emphasizing the conceptual differences between such explanation and the covering-law model in all its forms. There is also, however, a reason for accepting the rational model, and believing that it *should* function in historical inquiry, which ought to appeal to deter-minists as well. This claim will put me at odds with any philosopher who, having accepted the compatibility thesis, argues that since ex-planations which are logically 'tight' are obviously superior to 'loose' ones, whatever the reason for the looseness, covering-law explanations are clearly to be preferred wherever they can be given; so that it would be legitimate to hope that a 'defective' rational model in history would gradually be replaced by something better. I want to argue that even if covering-law explanations were always available, it would still be valu-able and proper to explain the actions of historical agents in the rational way.

My reason for saying this arises out of an answer I think we should give to the question: What is the study of history for? Certainly one reason people study history is the hope of gaining knowledge of past human activities which may help them in coping with present prob-lems. And, as in the study of nature, it would often be very helpful in-deed to be able to explain and predict on the covering-law pattern. As Professor Donagan has on more than one occasion eloquently urged, the possibility of pursuing such a study with very significant success

---

[32] Op. cit., pp. 72, 93–4.
[33] 'Explanation in History', *Mind* (1957), 153.

still remains to be shown; and he is surely right to say that it would be foolish to abandon 'antinomian' social inquiry, which has been going on for centuries, on the mere *promise* of something 'better'.[34] I should like, however, to push this point a little further. For it seems to me that, even if a 'science' of history employing covering-law explanations were well advanced, there would *still* be no good reason for abandoning an inquiry giving non-deductive, rational explanations, and very good reason for continuing it—if necessary, alongside the other.

For what drives us to the study of history, as much as anything else, is a humane curiosity: an interest in discovering and imaginatively reconstructing the life of people at other times and places. To discover and understand their life, we need to be able to do more than regularize, predict, and retrodict their actions; we need to apply to those actions the categories and concepts of *practice*; we need to take a view of them, as R. G. Collingwood might have put it, *from the inside*. Even if we are not libertarians, we are ourselves, and believe others to be, agents; and even if we accept the possibility and usefulness of covering-law explanation for some purposes, we may still surely share the desire to extend such understanding and evaluation of human life *from the standpoint of agency*. The slogan, 'Historical study is vicarious experience', like all such slogans, fastens on only one facet of the truth. But it *is* a facet of the truth, and one which covering-law theorists are likely to ignore. What we should be careful to remember is that history is not only (possibly) a branch of the science of society, but is also (actually) a branch of the humanities. My chief complaint against acceptance of the covering-law doctrine in history is not the difficulty of operating it, in either fully deductive or mutilated form. It is rather that it sets up a kind of *conceptual barrier* to a humanistically oriented historiography.

---

[34] 'Social Science and Historical Antinomianism', *Revue Internationale de Philosophie* (1957), 448–9.

V

REASONS AND COVERING LAWS IN HISTORICAL EXPLANATION

CARL G. HEMPEL

I. DEDUCTIVE AND PROBABILISTIC EXPLANATION BY COVERING LAWS

As a background for the following discussion of historical explanation, which is prompted mainly by Professor Dray's substantial and stimulating paper [IV in this volume], I propose to present first a brief sketch of, and some amplificatory comments on, the covering-law analysis of explanation.

The suggestive term 'covering-law model of explanation' was introduced by Professor Dray in his monograph, *Laws and Explanation in History*, in which, after a very fair-minded presentation of this conception of explanation, he develops a number of interesting arguments against its general adequacy, particularly in the field of historical inquiry.

In his book, Mr. Dray used the term 'covering-law model' to refer to the construal of an explanation as a deductive subsumption under covering laws. In an explanation of this kind, a given empirical phenomenon—in this paper, I will normally take it to be a particular event—is accounted for by deducing the *explanandum* statement, which describes the event in question, from a set of other statements, called the *explanans*. This set consists of some general laws and of statements describing certain particular facts or conditions, which usually are antecedent to or simultaneous with the event to be explained. In a causal explanation, for example—to mention one important variety of deductive explanation by covering laws—an individual event (e.g. an increase in the volume of a particular body of gas at a particular place and time) is presented as the 'effect' of certain other particular events and conditions (e.g. heating of that body of gas under conditions of constant pressure), from which it resulted (from whose realization its occurrence can be inferred) in accordance with certain general laws (e.g. gas laws).

From *Philosophy and History: A Symposium*, ed. Sidney Hook (New York University Press, 1963), pp. 143–63. Copyright © 1963 by New York University. Reprinted by permission of the publishers.

In explanations of the deductive, or 'deductive-nomological', kind the covering laws are all of strictly universal form; i.e. schematically speaking, they are statements to the effect that in *all* cases where a certain complex F of conditions is satisfied, an event or state of kind G will come about; in symbolic notation: $(x)\,(Fx \supset Gx)$.

But there is a second, logically quite different, kind of explanation, which plays an important role in various branches of empirical science, and which I will call 'covering-law explanation' as well. The distinctive feature of this second type, to which Mr. Dray briefly alludes in his paper, is that some of the covering laws are of probabilistic-statistical form. In the simplest case, a law of this form is a statement to the effect that under conditions of a more or less complex kind F, an event or 'result' of kind G will occur with statistical probability—i.e. roughly: with long-run relative frequency—q; in symbolic notation: $ps\,(G,F) = q$. If the probability q is close to 1, a law of this type may be invoked to explain the occurrence of G in a given particular case in which conditions F are realized. By way of a simple illustration, suppose that after one particular rolling of a given set of four dice, the total number of dots facing up is greater than 4. This might be explained by the following information (whose factual correctness is, of course, an empirical matter and subject to empirical test; it would not be true, for example, if one of the dice were loaded): (i) For every one of the dice, the statistical probability for any particular face to show up as a result of a rolling is the same as for any other face, and (ii) the results yielded by the individual dice, when rolled jointly, are statistically independent of each other; so that the statistical probability for a joint rolling (R) of all four dice to yield a total of more than four dots (M) is: $ps\,(M,R)$ $= 1295/1296 = 0.9992\ldots$ This general-probability statement, combined with the information that the particular occurrence under consideration, say i, was a case of joint rolling of the four dice (or briefly that Ri), does not logically imply that in the particular case i the total number of eyes facing up will be more than four (or that Mi, for short): but the two statements provide strong inductive grounds, or strong inductive support, or, as it is sometimes put, high inductive probability, for the assumption or expectation that Mi. The logical character of this explanatory argument may be represented by the following schema:

(*Explanans*)	$\begin{cases} ps\,(M,R) = 1295/1296 \\ Ri \end{cases}$	confers high inductive proba-bility on
(*Explanandum*)	Mi	

The probability which the *explanans* is here said to confer upon the *explanandum* is clearly not of the statistical kind; it does not represent an empirically determined quantitative relation between two kinds of event, such as *R* and *M*; rather, it is a logical relation between two statements—in our case, between the conjunction of the *explanans* statement on one hand and the *explanandum* statement on the other. This relation of inductive-logical support or probability is the central concept of the logical theories of probability developed by Keynes and by Carnap, to mention two outstanding examples. Carnap's theory, which is applicable to formalized languages of certain kinds, in fact provides ways of giving an explicit definition of logical probability in quantitative terms. To what extent these systems of inductive logic are applicable to actual scientific contexts is still a subject of study and debate; but that does not affect the basic thesis that in an explanation by means of probabilistic-statistical laws, the 'subsumption' of the *explanandum* statement under the 'covering laws' rests, not on a deductive implication, but on a relation of inductive support between the *explanans* and the *explanandum* statement. I will therefore refer to this kind of explanation as *probabilistic or inductive explanation*. Explanations of this kind play an important role in several areas of scientific inquiry; for example, the irreversibility of certain macrophenomena, such as the mixing of coffee and cream, is probabilistically explained by the assumption of certain purely statistical uniformities at the level of the underlying microevents.

II. A NECESSARY CONDITION OF ADEQUACY FOR EXPLANATIONS

The two kinds of explanation by covering laws have this feature in common: they explain an event by showing that, in view of certain particular circumstances and general laws, its occurrence was to be expected (in a purely logical sense), either with deductive certainty or with inductive probability.[1] In virtue of this feature, the two modes of

[1] For a fuller account of the deductive-nomological model see, for example, C. G. Hempel, 'The Function of General Laws in History', *The Journal of Philosophy*, 39 (1942), 35–48. Reprinted in *Theories of History*, ed. P. Gardiner (Glencoe, Ill., 1959), pp. 344–56. See also C. G. Hempel and P. Oppenheim, 'Studies in the Logic of Explanation', *Philosophy of Science*, 15 (1948), 135–75. Secs. 1–7 of this article are reprinted in *Readings in the Philosophy of Science*, eds. H. Feigl and M. Brodbeck (New York, 1953), pp. 319–52. The former of these articles also deals with the relevance of covering-law explanation to historical inquiry. A more detailed logical analysis of inductive-probabilistic explanation has been attempted in C. G. Hempel, 'Deductive-Nomological vs. Statistical Explanation', in *Minnesota Studies in the Philosophy of Science,* ed. H. Feigl and G. Maxwell, III (Minneapolis, 1962), 98–169.

explanation clearly satisfy what is, I submit, a general *condition of adequacy* for any account that is to qualify as a rationally acceptable explanation of a given event. The condition is that any such explanation, i.e. any rationally acceptable answer to a question of the type 'Why did X occur?', must provide information which constitutes good grounds for the belief that X did in fact occur.[2] To state the point a little more fully: if the question 'Why did X occur?' is answered by 'Because Z is, or was, the case', then the answer does not afford a rationally adequate explanation of X's occurrence unless the information that Z is, or was, the case constitutes good grounds for expecting or believing the X did occur; otherwise, the explanatory information would provide no adequate grounds for saying, as it were: 'That explains it—that does show why X occurred!'

Two amplificatory remarks may be indicated. First: the condition of adequacy just stated is to be understood as a necessary condition for an adequate explanation, not as a sufficient one; certain kinds of information—such as the results of a scientific test—may provide excellent grounds for believing that X occurred without in the least explaining why.

Secondly, the covering-law concepts of explanation, as schematically represented by the models, refer to the logic, not to the psychology, of explanation, just as metamathematical concepts of proof refer to the logic, not to the psychology, of proving mathematical theorems. Proofs and explanations that are adequate in the psychologic-pragmatic sense (which is of interest and importance in its own right) of making someone 'understand' whatever is being proved or explained may well be achieved—and are in fact often achieved—by procedures that do not meet the formal standards for the concepts of proof or explanation construed in a non-pragmatic, metatheoretical sense. For example, it may be sufficient to call to a person's attention just one particular fact or just some general principle he had overlooked or forgotten or not known at all: taken in combination with other items in his background knowledge, this may make the puzzling item, X, fall into place for him: he will 'understand why' X is the case. And since the proofs and explanations offered by mathematicians and empirical scientists in their writings, lectures, and informal conversations are normally formulated

---

[2] The condition can readily be formulated so as to cover also explanations that are intended to account, not for an individual event or state of affairs, but for some general uniformity, such as that expressed by Kepler's second law, for example. But explanations of this latter kind—which are discussed, for example, in the second and third of the articles mentioned on p. 92 n. 1—need not be considered in this paper.

with some particular kind of audience in mind, they are accordingly elliptic in varying degrees. But this surely does not show that attempts to construct non-pragmatic metatheoretical concepts of proof and explanation are either mistaken in principle or at any rate bound to be unilluminating and theoretically unprofitable. In the case of proof-theory, the contrary is well known to be the case. And while the logical theory of explanation cannot claim achievements comparable in depth and importance to those of recent proof-theory, it has led to some significant insights. For example, certain results by Ramsey and by Craig illuminate the role of 'theoretical entities' in scientific theories and shed light on the possibility of avoiding reference to such entities in scientific theories without loss of explanatory import; and problems such as these clearly concern the logic, not the psychology, of explanation.

As I mentioned a moment ago, the explanatory accounts actually offered by investigators in various fields of empirical inquiry, ranging from physics to historical research, will often fail to meet the condition of adequacy set forth above, and yet those accounts might intuitively be quite satisfactory. Clearly, in appraising the logical adequacy of a proposed explanation we must in fairness take into account not only what it explicitly tells us in the *explanans*, but also what it omits as not requiring mention, as tacitly taken for granted and presumed to be understood. Of course, it is not the task of a logical theory of explanation to tell us how to carry out an appraisal of this kind—any more that it is the task of a logical theory of inference to tell us how to judge whether a proposed argument that falls short of the formal standards of deductive validity is to be qualified as invalid or as deductively valid but elliptically formulated. The parallel to the case of mathematical proof is clear.

The condition of adequacy here proposed conflicts with a claim that has been made particularly, but not exclusively, with respect to historical explanation, namely, that sometimes an event can be quite adequately explained by pointing out that such-and-such antecedent conditions which are necessary but not sufficient for its occurrence, were realized. As Mr. Dray mentions in his survey of various modifications that have been suggested for the covering-law construal of explanation, this idea has been put forward by Frankel and by Gallie; it has also been strongly endorsed by Scriven, who offers this illustration in support of his view:[3] paresis occurs only in persons who have previously

[3] M. Scriven, 'Explanation and Prediction in Evolutionary Theory', *Science*, 130 (1959), 480.

suffered from syphilis; and the occurrence of paresis in a given patient can therefore be properly explained by antecedent syphilitic infection —and thus by reference to an antecedent which constitutes a necessary but far from sufficient condition; for in fact, only quite a small percentage of syphilitics develop paresis. This 'explanation' clearly violates the condition of adequacy proposed above. Indeed, as Scriven is the first to point out, on the information that a person has had syphilis, 'we must . . . predict that [paresis] will *not* occur'.[4] But precisely because the statistical probability for syphilis to lead to paresis is so small, and because therefore on the given information we must rationally expect the given person *not* to have developed paresis, the information that the patient has had syphilis (and that only syphilitics can develop paresis) clearly no more explains the actual occurrence of paresis in this case than a man's winning the first prize in the Irish Sweepstakes is explained by the information that he had bought a ticket (and that only a person who has bought a ticket can win the first prize).

III. INDIVIDUAL EVENTS AND 'COMPLETE' EXPLANATION

In his paper, Mr. Dray touches briefly upon a question that has received a good deal of attention in the recent literature, namely, whether any individual event admits of a *complete* explanation, and in particular, whether such an explanation could possibly be achieved by means of covering laws. I would like to comment briefly on this issue.

In any covering-law explanation of an individual event, the event in question is always characterized by a *statement*, the *explanandum* statement. Thus, when we ask why a given body of gas, g, increased in volume between 5·00 and 5·01 P.M. or why the particular rolling i of our four dice yielded a total of more than four dots facing up, the *explanandum* events are described by the statements 'the body of gas, g, increased in volume between 5·00 and 5·01 P.M.' and 'the particular rolling i of the four dice yielded a total of more than four dots facing up'. Clearly then, only individual events in this sense, as described by statements, can possibly be explained by means of covering laws. (This is not to say, of course, that every such event can actually be so explained: the covering-law analysis of explanation presents a thesis about the logical structure of scientific explanation, but not about the extent to which individual occurrences in the world can be explained; that depends on what laws hold in the world and clearly cannot be determined just by logical analysis. In particular, therefore, the cover-

---

[4] Ibid. (Italics the author's.)

ing-law analysis of explanation does not presuppose or imply universal determinism.)

Quite frequently, however, the notion of an individual event is understood in a very different way. An event in this second sense is typically characterized, not by a statement describing it, but by an individual name or by a definite description, such as 'the Children's Crusade', 'the October Revolution', 'the eruption of Mt. Vesuvius in A.D. 79', 'the assassination of Julius Caesar', 'the first solar eclipse of the 1960s', and the like. Individual occurrences thus understood cannot be explained by covering laws or in any other way; indeed, it is unclear what could be meant by explaining such an event. For any event thus understood has infinitely many aspects and thus cannot be even fully described, let alone explained. For example, the various aspects of Julius Caesar's assassination include the fact that it was plotted by Brutus and Cassius: that Brutus and his fellow conspirators were in such-and-such political positions and had such-and-such expectations and aspirations; that Caesar received such-and-such wounds; and—if I may trust an estimate I read some time ago, which may be quite well supported by physical theory—that with every breath we draw today, we inhale some of the molecules of oxygen and nitrogen that Caesar exhaled in his dying breath. Evidently, a complete characterization, let alone explanation, of an individual event in this sense is impossible.

For lack of a better expression, I will use the phrase *'concrete event'* to refer to individual events understood in this latter sense. Individual events of the only kind admitting in principle of explanation by covering laws, i.e. events describable by statement, might then be said to constitute particular *aspects of, or facts about, concrete events.*[5]

I need hardly add that concrete events are not limited to the domain of the historian. An event such as the first total solar eclipse of the 1960s also exhibits infinitely many physical, chemical, biological, sociological, and yet other aspects and thus resists complete and, *a fortiori*, complete explanation. But certain particular aspects of it—e.g. that it is visible from such-and-such a region on the earth, that the duration of its totality is so many seconds, etc.—may well permit of explanation by covering laws.[6]

But it would be incorrect to say that an explanation by covering laws

[5] At the end of the present section, a derivative sense will be suggested in which one might speak of more or less complete covering-law explanations of concrete events.

[6] The gist of what I have so far said here about individual events and their explanation was briefly, but quite explicitly, stated already in Hempel, 'The Function of General Laws in History', section 2.2.

can explain only some *kind* of event rather than an individual event. For, first of all, a *kind* of event would be represented by a predicate-expression, such as 'total solar eclipse visible from Alaska'; and since such expressions, not being statements, cannot be the conclusions of any deductive or inductive argument, a kind of event cannot be explained in accordance with the covering-law models. Secondly, what might be also explained is the *occurrence of an event of a certain kind in a particular space-time region*; for example, a lengthening of the mercury column in a particular thermometer at a particular place during a specified period of time, or a particular individual developing yellow fever after being exposed to mosquitoes of a certain type. But what is thus explained is very definitely an individual event, of the sort that can be described by a statement. On this point, therefore, I agree with Mandelbaum, who rejects Hayek's thesis that explanation and prediction never refer to an individual event but always to phenomena of a certain kind, with the comment: 'One would think that the prediction of a specific solar eclipse, or the explanation of that eclipse, would count as referring to a particular event even if it does not refer to all aspects of the event, such as the temperature of the sun, or the effect of the eclipse on the temperature of the earth, and the like.'[7]

I said earlier that a concrete event, having infinitely many aspects, cannot be completely described, let alone explained. But there is at least one other sense in which the possibility of a complete explanation has recently been discussed and questioned, even in regard to individual events described by statements. Mr. Dray raised the issue in his paper when he asks whether an event can be *completely* explained by subsuming it under statistical rather than strictly universal laws, and thus without showing that it 'had to happen'. And indeed, as was noted earlier, the *explanans* of a statistical explanation confers upon the *explanandum* only a more or less high inductive probability, but does not imply it with deductive necessity, as is the case in deductive-nomological explanations. The latter might be said, in this sense, to be complete; probabilistic explanations, incomplete.[8] If the terms are thus understood, however, it is important to bear in mind that a more complete explanation of an event is not one that explains more aspects of it; in fact, the idea of completeness here under consideration applies only to

[7] M. Mandelbaum, 'Historical Explanation: The Problem of "Covering Laws"', *History and Theory*, 1 (1961), 223, n. 6. [p. 56 of this volume. Ed.]

[8] Completeness and incompleteness of explanation are obviously understood in this sense by J. Pitt, 'Generalizations in Historical Explanation', *The Journal of Philosophy*, 56 (1959), 580–1.

the explanation of events described by statements, whereas the notion of aspects of an event was introduced in specific reference to concrete events.

Finally, it is now possible to specify a sense in which one might speak of partial explanations of concrete events and in which some of those explanations might be called more complete—in a third sense of the term—than others. First, any set of deductive-nomological explanations, each of which explains some aspect of a concrete event, might be called a partial deductive-nomological explanation of that event; and if the aspects explained in one of the sets form a proper subset of those in the other, the former set might be said to provide a less complete explanation of the concrete event than the latter. These notions can be generalized so as to apply also to sets containing probabilistic explanations, but this is not the place to enter into further details.

IV. EXPLAINING ACTIONS BY REASONS

4.1 *Dray's construal.* I now turn to some comments on the central topic of Mr. Dray's paper, the concept of rational explanation. Dray holds that the method, widely used by historians among others, of explaining human actions in terms of underlying reasons cannot be construed as conforming to the covering-law pattern: to do so, he says, would be to give the wrong kind of reconstruction, it would get the form of such explanations wrong. In my opinion, Dray's arguments in support of this verdict, and his own alternative construal of such explanations, form a substantial contribution towards the formulation and clarification of the perplexing issues here at stake.

According to Dray, the object of explaining an action by reference to the reasons for which it was done is 'to show that what was done was the thing to have done for the reasons given, rather than merely the thing that is done on such occasions, perhaps in accordance with certain laws'.[9] The explanatory reasons will include the objectives the agent sought to attain and his beliefs concerning relevant empirical matters, such as the alternative courses of action open to him and their likely consequences. The explanation, according to Dray, then provides 'a reconstruction of the agent's *calculation* of means to be adopted towards his chosen end in the light of the circumstances in which he found himself',[10] and it shows that the agent's choice was appropriate, that it was the thing to do under the circumstances. The appraisal thus

    [9] W. Dray, *Laws and Explanation in History* (Oxford, 1957), p. 124.
    [10] Ibid., p. 122 (Italics the author's.)

made of the appropriateness of what was done presupposes, not general laws, but instead what Dray calls a 'principle of action', i.e. a normative or evaluative principle of the form 'When in a situation of type C, the thing to do is X.'[11]

4.2 *The problem of criteria of rationality.* Before considering the central question whether, or in what sense, principles of this kind can explain an action, I want to call attention to what seems to me a problematic assumption underlying Dray's concept of a principle of action. As is suggested by the phrase 'the thing to do', Dray seems to assume (i) that, given a specification of the circumstances in which an agent finds himself (including, I take it, in particular his objectives and beliefs), there is a clear and unequivocal sense in which an action can be said to be appropriate, or reasonable, or rational under the circumstances; and (ii) that, at least in many cases, there is exactly one course of action that is appropriate in this sense. Indeed, Dray argues that on this score rational explanation is superior to statistical explanation because the question why an action had to be done often permits an answer that involves the rational ruling out of all possible alternatives—a result that cannot be achieved in a probabilistic explanation.

But the two assumptions just listed seem to be unwarranted or at least highly questionable. First of all, it is by no means clear by what criteria of rationality 'the thing to do' in a given situation is to be characterized. While several recent writers assume that there is one clear notion of rationality in the sense here required,[12] they have proposed no explicit definitions; and doubts about the possibility of formulating adequate general criteria of rationality are enhanced by the mathematical theory of decisions, which shows that even for some rather simple types of decision-situation several different criteria of rational choice can be formulated, each of which is quite plausible and yet incompatible with its alternatives.[13] And if this is so in simple cases, then the notion of *the* thing to do under given circumstances must be regarded as even more problematic when applied to the kinds of de-

---

[11] Ibid., p. 132.

[12] For example, Q. Gibson, in his stimulating study, *The Logic of Social Enquiry* (London and New York, 1960), asserts: 'there may be various alternative ways of achieving an end. To act rationally ... is to select what on the evidence is *the best* way of achieving it' (p. 160; italics the author's); and he refers to 'an elementary logical point—namely, that given certain evidence, there can only be one correct solution to the problem as to the best way of achieving a given end' (p. 162).

[13] For a clear account and comparative analysis of such criteria, see, for example, R. D. Luce and H. Raiffa, *Games and Decisions* (New York, 1957), Ch. 13.

cision and action the historian seeks to explain. I think, therefore, that the presuppositions underlying the idea of a principle of action require further elaboration and scrutiny.

However, in order not to complicate the remainder of my discussion, I will disregard this difficulty from here on and will assume, for the sake of the argument, that the intended meaning of the expression '*X* is the appropriate, or rational, thing to do under circumstances of kind *C*' has been agreed upon and adequately specified by objective criteria.

4.3 *The explanatory import of citing reasons for an action.* The question we have to consider then is this: How can a principle of action serve in an explanatory capacity? Dray's account, both in his paper and in his book, would seem to suggest that a rational explanation of why agent *A* did *X* would take the following form:

Agent *A* was in a situation of kind *C*.
When in a situation of kind *C*, the thing to do is *X*.

Therefore, agent *A* did *X*.

The first statement in the *explanans* specifies certain antecedent conditions; the second is a principle of action taking the place which, in a covering-law explanation, is held by a set of general laws.

Thus conceived, the logic of rational explanation does indeed differ decisively from that of covering-law explanation. But precisely because of the feature that makes the difference it cannot, I submit, explain why *A* did *X*. For by the general condition of adequacy considered earlier, an adequate *explanans* for *A*'s having done *X* must afford good reasons for the belief or the assertion that *A* did in fact do *X*. But while the *explanans* just formulated affords good grounds for asserting that the appropriate thing for *A* to do under the circumstances was *X*, it does not provide good reasons for asserting or believing that *A* did in fact do *X*. To justify this latter assertion, the *explanans* would have to include a further assumption, to the effect that at the time in question *A* was a rational agent, and was thus disposed to do what was appropriate in the given situation. When modified accordingly, our *explanans* takes on a form which may be schematized as follows:

Agent *A* was in a situation of kind *C*.
A was a rational agent at the time.
Any rational agent, when in a situation of kind *C*,
   will invariably (or: with high probability) do *X*,

and it will then logically imply (or confer a high inductive probability on) the *explanandum*:

A did *X*.

Thus modified, the account will indeed provide an explanation of why *A* did in fact do *X*. But its adequacy for this purpose has been achieved by replacing Dray's evaluative principle of action by a descriptive principle stating what rational agents will do in situations of kind *C*. The result is a covering-law explanation, which will be deductive or inductive according as the general statement about the behaviour of rational agents is of strictly universal or of probabilistic-statistical form. This construal of an explanation by reasons is evidently akin to Ryle's conception of an explanation by reference to dispositions;[14] for it presents *A*'s action, as it were, as a manifestation of his general disposition to act in characteristic ways—in ways that qualify as appropriate or rational—when in certain situations.

It might be objected[15] to the broadly dispositional annalysis here proposed that the 'covering law' allegedly expressed by the third statement in the *explanans* is not really an empirical law about how rational agents do in fact behave, but an analytic statement of a definitional character, which expresses part of what is *meant* by a rational agent— so that the given action is not actually explained by subsumption under a general law. However, this objection does not, I think, do justice to the logical character of concepts such as that of a rational agent. The reason, stated very briefly, is that such concepts are governed by large clusters of general statements—they might be called symptom statements—which assign to the dispositional characteristic in question various typical manifestations or symptoms; each symptom being a particular manner in which a person who has the dispositional characteristic will 'respond to', or 'act under' certain specific ('stimulus-') conditions. The third statement in our *explanans* is then just one of many symptom statements for the concept of rational agent. But the totality of the symptom statements for a given broadly dispositional concept will normally have empirical implications, so that they cannot all be qualified as definitional or analytic; and it would be arbitrary to attribute to some of them—e.g. the one invoked in our *explanans*—the analytic

14 G. Ryle, *The Concept of Mind* (London, 1949). The construal here intended, which has been outlined only sketchily, differs, however, in certain respects from what I take to be Ryle's conception. To indicate this, I refer to the analysis here envisaged as 'broadly dispositional'. For a fuller account, see Hempel, 'Rational Action', in *Proceedings and Addresses of the American Philosophical Association*, vol. 35 (Yellow Springs, Ohio, 1962); section 3.2 of that article, in particular, states and discusses the differences in question.

15 An objection to this effect was in fact raised in the discussion by Professor R. Brandt.

character of partial definitions and to construe only the remaining ones as having empirical import.[16]

In sum, then, I think that Dray's very suggestively presented construal of explanations by reasons has a basic logical defect, which springs from the view that such explanations must be based on principles of action rather than on general laws. Dray explicitly makes a distinction between the two on the ground that the phrase 'the thing to do', which characteristically occurs in a principle of action, 'functions as a value-term', and that therefore there is a certain 'element of *appraisal*' in a rational explanation, for it must tell us in what way an action 'was *appropriate*'.[17] But—and this seems to me the crux of the matter—to show that an action was the appropriate or rational thing to have done under the circumstances is not to explain why in fact it was done. Indeed, no normative or evaluative principle specifying what kind of action is appropriate in given circumstances can possibly serve to explain why a person acted in a particular way; and this is so no matter whether the action does or does not conform to the normative principle in question.

The basic point of the objection here raised has also been made by J. Passmore, who states it succinctly as follows: '... explanation by reference to a "principle of action" or "a good reason" is not, by itself, explanation at all.... For a reason may be a "good reason"—in the sense of being a principle to which one *could* appeal in justification of one's action—without having in fact the slightest influence on us.'[18]

It might perhaps be suspected that in arguing for a broadly dispositional analysis which presents explanations by reasons as having basically the logical structure of one or other of the covering-law models, we are violating a maxim of which Mr. Dray rightly reminds us in his paper, namely, that a sound logical analysis must refrain from forcing historical explanation on to the Procrustean bed of some preconceived general schema, and that instead it must take careful account of the practice generally agreed to be acceptable within the discipline con-

[16] This idea is presented somewhat more fully in Hempel, 'Explanation in Science and in History', in *Frontiers of Science and Philosophy*, ed. R. G. Colodny (Pittsburgh, Pa., 1962), section 6; also section 3.2 of Hempel, 'Rational Action', has a direct bearing on this issue.

[17] Dray, op. cit., p. 124. (Italics the author's.)

[18] J. Passmore, 'Review Article: Law and Explanation in History', *Australian Journal of Politics and History*, 4 (1958), 275. (Italics the author's.) Passmore then goes on to argue very briefly also that an explanation by reasons amounts to an explanation 'by reference to a general statement', for to 'take a "reason" to be the actual explanation of anyone's conduct ... is to assert, at least ... the general statement: "People of type X, in situation Y, act in such a way as to conserve the principle Z." ' (Ibid.)

cerned; that it must show sensitivity to the concept of explanation historians normally employ. No doubt a historian who adduces an agent's presumptive reasons in order to explain his actions, may well conceive it to be his main task to show that in the light of those reasons, the action was the appropriate thing to have done. But in giving his account, the historian undoubtedly also intends to show why in fact the agent acted as he did—e.g. to take Dray's example, why Louis XIV in fact withdrew military pressure from Holland. And this question cannot be answered by showing that the action was a (or even 'the') reasonable thing to do, given Louis's objectives and beliefs; for after all, many agents on many occasions do not actually do the rational thing. This observation seems akin to an objection raised by Strawson, to which Dray refers in his paper. Dray agrees there that human action can fall short of the ideal of rationality and he stresses that his claim is only that the criterion of rational appropriateness does function for actions that are not judged to be defective in various ways. But this seems to me the crucial point: if an explanation by reasons invokes standards of rationality then, to have the desired explanatory force, it must in addition make the empirical assumption that the action was not defective in relevant ways, i.e. that the agent was at the time disposed to act in accordance with the standards invoked, and that the external circumstances did not prevent him from doing so.

And it seems clear to me that a historian would simply see no point in displaying the appropriateness or rationality of an action if he did not assume that the agent, at the time in question, was disposed to act rationally (as he might not be under conditions of extreme fatigue, under severe emotional strain, under the influence of drugs, and the like). And since, in an explanation by reasons, this essential presupposition will normally be taken for granted, it will not, as a rule, be explicitly mentioned; it is rather when departures from rationality are considered that the need is felt explicitly to specify disturbing circumstances. But while an elliptic formulation that forgoes explicit mention of the assumption of rationality may be quite satisfactory for practical purposes, i.e. in the pragmatic-psychological context of explanation, it obscures the logic of the explanatory argument; and surely, an analysis that makes explicit this essential assumption underlying the historian's account does not thereby force the method of explanation by reasons upon a Procrustean bed.

I think the broadly dispositional analysis I have outlined applies also to the intriguing case, invoked by Mr. Dray, of explaining one's own actions by reference to the reasons for which they were done. To be sure, in an account of the form 'I did X for reasons R', explanation and justification are almost inextricably fused, and yet, we do distinguish between a genuine explanation and a mere rationalization in such contexts; and an account of the form 'I did X for reasons R' would be suspected of being a rationalization if there were grounds to believe that I had not actually done X for the reasons given: e.g. that I had not in fact had the reasons and beliefs adduced in my account, or that I had been in a state in which I might well have tended not to take an action appropriate to my objectives and relevant empirical beliefs. Thus again, a statement given by me of the reasons for my action can have explanatory force only on the assumption of a disposition to act rationally in the given situation.

4.4 *The 'rationality' of non-deliberate actions.* A dispositional construal of rational explanation can also resolve a difficulty inherent in a view that Mr. Dray expresses in his book, and to which he briefly adverts again in his paper. According to Dray, there are certain actions that qualify as rational although they are decided upon without the benefit of actual deliberation or calculation. Indeed, in his book he argues that in so far as an action is purposive at all—no matter at what level of conscious deliberation—it is capable of rational explanation because 'there is a calculation which could be constructed for it', a calculation the agent might have performed had he had the time, and which he might produce if questioned later.[19] But since, by hypothesis, no such deliberation or calculation did take place, since considerations of rationality actually played no role in the agent's action, an explanation of the latter by reference to such calculations seems to me to be simply fictitious.

Responding to an objection by Nowell-Smith which appears to be aimed at this point, Mr. Dray states again in his paper that the reasons adduced in a rational explanation need not actually have been considered by the agent in adopting his course of action, and he adds that our understanding of that action may arise out of our perception of a rational connection between the action and the motives and beliefs the rational explanation ascribes to the agent. But again, our awareness of such a logical connection surely cannot show why the action was taken by the agent, who, by hypothesis, took no account of that connection at all.

But I think Mr. Dray has a point in regarding some of those actions that are decided upon 'in a flash', without reflection, as being akin to those which are prompted by careful deliberation. And it is possible to

---

[19] Dray, op. cit., p. 123.

do justice to this idea by giving it a different—and again broadly dispositional—construal. Under this construal, a 'rational explanation' of such an action is effected by ascribing to the agent certain behavioural dispositions acquired through a learning process whose initial phases did involve conscious reflection and deliberation. Consider, for example, the various intricate manoeuvres required in using a typewriter, in driving a car through heavy traffic, in drilling and filling a patient's teeth: all these are learned in training processes that involve more or less elaborate deliberation in the beginning; but eventually they become 'second nature' and are performed routinely, with little or no conscious reflection.

A particular act of this kind might then be explained, not by a reconstructed calculation or deliberation which the agent in fact did not perform, nor by pointing out that his action was appropriate to his putative objectives, but by presenting it as a manifestation of a general behaviour pattern that the agent had learned in the manner just alluded to.[20] And clearly, this derivative kind of rational explanation would again be broadly dispositional, and hence of the covering-law variety.

To adopt the general conception I have presented here of explanation by reasons is by no means to deny that, as Mr. Dray rightly stresses, the historian adducing motivating reasons in explanation of an action normally does seek to show that the action 'makes sense' when considered in the light of the purposes and the beliefs that presumably prompted it; nor is it to deny that perceiving an action as thus making sense can be a source of great intellectual satisfaction. What I have tried to argue is rather that—apart from the problematic status of the requisite concept of appropriateness—the presentation of an action as being appropriate to the given situation, as making sense, cannot, for purely logical reasons, serve to explain why in fact the action was taken.

---

[20] In a similar vein, I. Scheffler, in 'Thoughts on Teleology', *British Journal for the Philosophy of Science*, 9 (1959), 269–75, has suggested that an interpretation in terms of learning may shed light on some types of non-purposive teleological behaviour.

VI

'SOCIAL MEANING' AND THE EXPLANATION OF SOCIAL ACTION[1]

QUENTIN SKINNER

I

A SOCIAL action may be said to have a meaning for the agent performing it. The acceptance of this rather vague claim represents the one major point of agreement in the continuing debate between those philosophers who wish to assert and those who wish to deny the naturalist thesis[2] to the effect that social actions can sufficiently be accounted for by the ordinary processes of causal explanation. The significance of the fact that social actions have a 'meaning' has of course been emphasized in each of the three main traditions of anti-naturalist opposition to the idea of a social science. The followers of Dilthey, and of the whole tradition which has insisted on the importance of *verstehen*, stress that the special feature of 'the human studies' is their concern 'with a world which has meaning for the actors involved'.[3] Similarly, the phenomenologists stress that the aim of the social sciences must be to gain 'insight into the meaning which social acts have for those who act'.[4] And the followers of Wittgenstein stress that the 'forms of activity' studied in the social sciences will characteristically be those 'of which we can sensibly say that they have a *meaning*'.[5]

This emphasis on the meaning of social actions has been no less marked, however, in the various strands of thought which have converged in accepting the theoretical possibility of establishing a causal and predictive science of human action. Those who have wished to vindicate a generally 'scientific' approach to the study of social action

From *Philosophy, Politics and Society* (Fourth Series), ed. Peter Laslett, W. G. Runciman, and Quentin Skinner (Oxford: Basil Blackwell, 1972), pp. 136–57. Slightly revised by the author and reprinted with his permission.

[1] I am particularly indebted to Dr. John Burrow, Mr. John Dunn, and Mr. Geoffrey Hawthorn for comments on earlier drafts of this paper.

[2] Here and throughout I adopt the terminology suggested by Sidney Morgenbesser, 'Is it a Science?', *Social Research*, 33 (1966), 255.

[3] H. P. Rickman, *Understanding and the Human Studies* (London, 1967), p. 23.

[4] Alfred Schutz, 'The Social World and the Theory of Social Action', *Social Research*, 27 (1960), 203.

[5] Peter Winch, *The Idea of a Social Science* (London, 1958), p. 45.

still concede the need to take account of 'the meaning of people's move-ments'.[6] Similarly, those who have wished to claim that even an agent's reasons may be the causes of his actions still allow for the fact that such agents will characteristically see 'a point or meaning' in their actions.[7] And even those who have wished to maintain the strictest thesis of positivism, to the effect that an individual action must always be explained by deducing it from some known general law covering such movements, continue to concede that 'what distinguishes a mere bodily movement from an action' is 'the *meaning* of that movement'.[8]

It is in fact possible, as I shall next seek to show, to see the entire debate between the social science naturalists and their opponents in terms of the different conclusions which the two sides of the debate have drawn from their common stress on the fact that 'the acting individual' (as Weber puts it) 'attaches a subjective meaning to his social behaviour'.

The anti-naturalists have traced a logical connection between the meaning of a social action and the agent's motives for performing it. And they have seen the recovery of the agent's motives for acting as a matter of placing the agent's action within a context of social rules. This view of social meaning has led them to the following two conclusions about the explanation of social actions. First, they have claimed that to decode the meaning of a social action is equivalent to giving a motive-explanation for the agent's performance of that action (Thesis A). Secondly, they have claimed that since the recovery of an agent's motives for acting is a matter of placing the agent's action in a context of rules rather than causes, so to cite the social meaning and the motives of an action is to provide a form of explanation which stands in contrast with, and is in fact incompatible with, a causal explanation of the same action (Thesis B).

These anti-naturalist conclusions about the idea of a social science have in part derived, and have gained great strength, from the powerful impact of Wittgenstein's later philosophy upon recent philosophical psychology. This is most clearly evident in a work such as A. I. Melden's *Free Action*—with its stress on 'making sense' of the meaning of actions (p. 102), its insistence that this is essentially a matter of recovering the agent's motives (pp. 87–8), by way of grasping the 'background against which both the man and his action can be understood'

---

[6] Quentin Gibson, *The Logic of Social Enquiry* (London, 1960), p. 52.
[7] A. J. Ayer, 'Man as a Subject for Science' in P. Laslett and W. G. Runciman, eds., *Philosophy, Politics and Society*, Series III (Oxford, 1967), p. 23.
[8] May Brodbeck, 'Meaning and Action', *Philosophy of Science*, 30 (1963), 309.

(p. 104), and its conclusion that this process makes causal explanation 'wholly irrelevant to the understanding' of social actions (p. 184).

There is also a much longer tradition of analysis, however, lying behind this type of anti-naturalist commitment. In the philosophy of history it is best represented by Collingwood's insistence, in *The Idea of History*, that to explain an action is always 'to discern the thoughts' of its agent, and that this study of individual motivation means that the historian who seeks to 'emulate the scientist in searching for the causes or laws of events' is simply 'ceasing to be an historian' (pp. 214–15). This contrast, moreover, between understanding actions in terms of motives and explaining events in terms of causes looks back to Croce and Dilthey, and forward to the development of this argument by Dray, Donagan, and others. And in the philosophy of social science a similar commitment has always informed the Weberian tradition of analysis. Weber himself never wished to suggest that the concepts of *verstehen* and causal explanation are incompatible. But he did begin the *Wirtschaft und Gesellschaft* by discussing motive-explanations, and he did at that point specifically equate the 'understanding of motivation' with the business of 'placing the act in an intelligible and more inclusive context of meaning' (tr. Henderson and Parsons, p. 95). Since then, moreover, a much more strongly anti-naturalist case has been developed by at least two schools of thought which have acknowledged Weber's influence. On the one hand the phenomenologists (such as Schutz, at least in certain moods) have gone on to insist both that an understanding of 'the meaning which social phenomena have for us' is a matter of recovering 'typical motives of typical actors', and that this is a form of understanding 'peculiar to social things' (op. cit., pp. 206, 211, 214). And on the other hand the Wittgensteinians (such as Winch) have insisted both that 'the notion of meaningful behaviour is closely connected with notions like *motive* and *reason*', and that the explanation of such behaviour, by way of relating the agent's motives to a context of social rules, requires 'a scheme of concepts which is logically incompatible with the kinds of explanation offered in the natural sciences' (op. cit., pp. 45, 72).

The naturalists, by contrast, have given an account of social meaning from which they have drawn two conclusions opposed to those I have just set out. First, they have claimed that the decoding of the meaning of a social action merely provides a method of redescribing it. And they have insisted that since mere redescription cannot in itself be explanatory, so it must be a mistake to suppose that the placing of a social action in its context, or the decoding of its social meaning, can ever serve in itself as an explanation of the given action (Thesis C). Secondly, they have claimed that if the idea of decoding the meaning of an action is so much extended that it becomes equivalent to recovering the agent's motives for performing it, then there is no incompatibility between the ideas of social meaning and of causal explanation, since the provision of an explanation by way of citing an agent's motives, or even his intentions, is itself a form of causal explanation. They have thus concluded that there is nothing in the fact that a social action may have a meaning or consist of the following of a rule from which it follows that such episodes may not be entirely explicable simply by the ordinary processes of causal explanation (Thesis D).

These naturalist conclusions, like those of their opponents, have been in part derived from, and have been greatly influenced by, a recent movement in philosophical psychology. This is the current and increasing movement of reaction against the Wittgensteinian assumption that motives and intentions cannot function as causes of actions. This has already generated some powerful arguments (best stated by Davidson),[9] and has caused several philosophers (notably Hamlyn and MacIntyre) to recant their previously published anti-naturalist views about the explanation of action. The implications of the reaction can be seen at their clearest in an essay such as Ayer's on 'Man as a subject for science'—with its insistence both that to redescribe a phenomenon cannot be 'in any way to account for it', and that to cite either a motive or an intention to explain an action, as we do 'in the normal way', must always be ultimately to point to 'lawlike connections' which are causal in form. The conclusion is that even if we can 'estimate an action in terms of its conforming to a rule', and even if we need to understand such actions 'in terms of their social contexts', these factors affect the agent only as 'part of his motivation', and give us no grounds for doubting that the action can be sufficiently explained 'by means of a causal law'. There is thus said to be 'nothing about human conduct that would entitle us to conclude a priori that it was in any way less lawlike than any other sort of natural process' (op. cit., pp. 16, 17, 21, 22–3).

As with the anti-naturalist commitment, there is a considerable tradition of analysis lying behind this type of claim. In the philosophy of history the idealist tradition represented by Dilthey and Collingwood has always been confronted by a positivist tradition stemming from the philosophy of science. This is perhaps best represented by Hempel's classic essay on 'The Function of General Laws in History', originally

[9] Donald Davidson, 'Actions, Reasons and Causes', *Journal of Philosophy*, 60 (1963), 685–700.

published in the *Journal of Philosophy* for 1942. The attempt, it is there
claimed, to explain the actions of historical individuals in an *ad hoc*
manner, in terms of 'the circumstances under which they acted, and the
motives which influence their actions' 'does not in itself constitute an
explanation'. And the fact, it is claimed, that the historian may concern
himself with 'the "*meanings*" of given historical events', as well as with
motives and actions, does nothing to vitiate the claim that any genuine
explanation of any historical phenomenon will have to consist of 'subsuming it under general empirical laws' (pp. 44–5). And similarly, in
the philosophy of social science, the school of Weber has always been
confronted by the school of Durkheim, with his dismissal of the need to
study individual intentions and motives, and his insistence (in *The Rules
of Sociological Method*) on the 'principle' that 'the determining cause of
a social fact', in which he included social actions, 'should be sought
among the social facts preceding it, and not among the states of individual consciousness' (tr. Solovay and Mueller, p. 110).

The two opposed theoretical traditions I have now sketched have
both been represented in the two most recent volumes of *Philosophy,
Politics and Society*. In Series II MacIntyre's essay made use of the
anti-naturalist approach, and he committed himself to theses A and B.
(See especially pp. 56–7.) In Series III Ayer's essay put the case for the
naturalist approach, and argued for theses C and D. (See especially
pp. 21–3.) My aim in what follows is to reconsider the two opposed
theoretical traditions I have now sketched out by attempting to do three
things. I shall first try very briefly to make a new start (Section II) on the
analysis of the required sense of 'meaning', and to give some examples
of this analysis in action. I shall then try to show (Section III) that if this
analysis is sound, then there seem to be some grounds for doubting each
of the four theses I have now set out. (Here I shall in part attempt to
adapt and apply an account of explaining social actions which I have
already published.)[10] Finally, I shall try (Section IV) to suggest certain
methodological implications of these conclusions for historians and
social scientists, at least in so far as they are concerned with explaining
the social actions of individual agents.

[10] See my article 'On Performing and Explaining Linguistic Actions', *Philosophical Quarterly*, 21 (1971), 1–21. I make use of this material here by permission of
the Editor.

II

There is a tendency, particularly among the anti-naturalists, to apply the concept of social meaning in a rather over-extended way. (This is perhaps evident from several of the quotations I have already given.) I shall begin therefore by restricting myself to considering the way in which the concept is used in the discussion of a single class of social actions. Later I shall try tentatively to extend the application of this analysis. But at first I shall concentrate on the class of social actions in which the concept of somebody meaning something (in or by saying or doing something) has its clearest and most obvious application, namely in the class of *linguistic* actions.

The classic analysis of the concept of a linguistic action has been provided by J. L. Austin in his William James Lectures, edited and published by J. O. Urmson as *How to Do Things with Words*. Austin's central contention is that any agent, in issuing any serious utterance, will be doing something as well as merely saying something, and will be doing something *in* saying what he says, and not merely as a consequence of what is said. Austin reached this conclusion by way of claiming that to issue any serious utterance is always to speak not only with a certain meaning but also with a certain intended force, corresponding to what Austin dubbed the 'illocutionary' act being performed by the agent in issuing his given utterance. Austin's claim is thus that to gain 'uptake', as he put it, of this element of illocutionary force co-ordinate with the ordinary meaning of the locution will be equivalent to understanding what the agent was *doing in* issuing that given utterance.

A single example will make clear the sense in which the issuing of any serious utterance constitutes, according to Austin, the performance of a type of social action. Consider the case of a policeman who sees a skater on a dangerous pond and issues to the skater the following serious utterance: 'The ice over there is very thin.'[11] Here the policeman is obviously issuing a meaningful utterance: he is saying something and the words mean something. But Austin's further point is that the utterance also has an illocutionary force, corresponding to the fact that the policeman will be doing something in issuing this meaningful utterance:

---

[11] Here I adopt an example from P. F. Strawson, 'Intention and Convention in Speech Acts', *Philosophical Review*, 73 (1964), 439–60. I also follow the argument of this article (i) in extending (and in this sense rejecting) Austin's concept of a convention and (ii) in relating Grice's theory of meaning to Austin's theory of illocutionary force. I have tried to defend both these commitments in my article 'Conventions and the Understanding of Speech Acts', *Philosophical Quarterly*, 20 (1970), 118–38.

he may for example be performing the illocutionary act of *warning the skater.*

I now wish to suggest that this account of linguistic action may be used to establish two crucial claims about the sense of 'meaning' with which I am concerned in discussing the meaning of social actions. The first is that the idea of decoding the meaning of an action seems, at least in the case of linguistic actions, to be equivalent to gaining uptake of the nature of the illocutionary act performed by the agent in issuing that particular utterance. To understand, that is, that the policeman, in issuing his utterance 'The ice over there is very thin' was performing the illocutionary art of warning seems equivalent to understanding the meaning of issuing the utterance itself. It is to understand what the policeman (non-naturally)[12] meant by performing his given (linguistic) action.

The second point is that to ask about this non-natural sense of meaning, at least in the case of linguistic actions, seems to be equivalent to asking about the agent's intention in performing his given social action. It is perhaps necessary to be more precise, and to stress that to ask this question is to ask about the agent's *primary* intention. It is arguable that Austin's way of stating his theory encourages the belief that there must be a correspondence between single intentions and single actions. But an agent may well have several different intentions in performing a single social action, some of which may be less important than others from the point of view of characterizing what the agent is doing, all of which may nevertheless form part of a complex set of intentions which are realized in the given action. It remains true, however, that to understand (in the example I am considering) that what the policeman meant to do in issuing his utterance 'The ice over there is very thin' was to warn the skater is equivalent to understanding what the policeman's primary intention was in performing that particular (linguistic) action.

It might be doubted, of course, whether this analysis of 'social meaning' in terms of understanding the intended illocutionary force of an agent's (linguistic) action can possibly be applied in the case of ordinary non-linguistic social actions. If we accept Austin's own claim, however, that certain illocutionary acts are invariably performed non-verbally (p. 118), there seems some reason to suppose that the analysis can be used at least to decode the meaning of the 'ritual and ceremonial'

[12] See H. P. Grice, 'Meaning', *Philosophical Review*, 66 (1957), 377–88 and his revisions in 'Utterer's Meaning and Intentions', *Philosophical Review*, 78 (1969), 147–77.

acts in which Austin was chiefly interested, even if many of these turn
out to be non-linguistically performed. If we accept Strawson's argument, moreover, to the effect that the account which Austin gave of the
conventions of illocutionary force may have been excessively narrow in
scope, then there seems some reason to assume that the analysis can
also be used to decode the meaning of a whole range of ordinary non-
ritual as well as non-linguistic actions. Finally, it is relevant to recall that
the main aim of Grice's original discussion of non-natural meaning was
'to show that the criteria for judging linguistic intentions are very like
the criteria for judging non-linguistic intentions', and thus to show
'that linguistic intentions are very like non-linguistic intentions' (op. cit.,
p. 388).

These suggestions may be corroborated by considering some examples of such non-linguistic as well as linguistic actions. Consider first
a case of a ritual but non-linguistic social action. (Hollis has popularized
the following example.)[13] Certain Yoruba tribesmen 'carry about with
them boxes covered with cowrie shells, which they treat with special
regard'. Hollis's interest in this example (concerned with the need for
the Yoruba to have rational thought-processes) is not relevant to my
argument at this point. My interest is in the meaning of this social action
and in the nature of the questions we need to ask and answer in order to
decode it. In the first place, the crucial question to ask certainly seems to
be about what the agent may be *doing in* performing just this action.
The answer (Hollis tells us) is that the tribesmen believe 'that the boxes
are their heads or souls' and that what they are doing in treating the
boxes in a reverent way is protecting their souls against witchcraft. This
in turn suggests that to ask and answer this question about the illocutionary force of the action is, as I have suggested, equivalent to asking
about the intentions of the agent in acting in this way. Notice that we do
not learn the nature of the motive which prompts (and perhaps causes)
the Yoruba to treat his box with special regard—although we may now
infer that the motive is likely to be respect or fear for the power of
unknown forces. What we learn is the Yoruba's primary intention in
acting in this way—that it is to protect his soul.

Consider next a case of a non-ritual, non-linguistic social action. (I
derive the following example from one of the case-histories reported by
R. D. Laing and A. Esterson in *Sanity, Madness and the Family*
[2nd. edn., London, 1970].) An adolescent girl becomes an apparently
compulsive reader, 'burying herself in her books' and refusing to stop
or allow herself to be interrupted (p. 46). Laing and Esterson's interest

[13] Martin Hollis, 'Reason and Ritual', *Philosophy*, 43 (1968), 231.

in the case lies primarily in their suggestion that the behaviour can be seen as a strategy, a deliberate social action, and not just as the symptom of an illness. My interest is again in the meaning of the behaviour, and in the appropriate questions to ask in order to determine whether it has any meaning, and if so how it should be decoded. Again it seems that the crucial question to ask is what the girl may be doing in performing just this action. The answer (Laing and Esterson suggest, p. 35) is that she is 'taking refuge' and preventing what she takes to be 'intrusions' by an overdemanding family. And again it seems that to ask and answer this question about the illocutionary force of the action is equivalent to asking about the girl's intentions in acting in this way. Notice again that this does not tell us the motives which prompted (and perhaps caused) the girl's behaviour. Laing and Esterson suggest (p. 34) that the motive may have been a desire for what they call 'autonomy' but one might infer other motives as well—such as a kind of pride, a degree of hatred, and so on. The point is that what we do learn is the girl's intentions in acting in this way—that they are to register a protest against, and to protect herself from, an excessively demanding social situation.

It may still seem, however, that to extend the discussion of non-natural meaning and illocutionary force to deal with such non-linguistic social actions is to give an illegitimate application to Austin's and Grice's theories. Consider finally, therefore, a further case of an ordinary (non-ritual) linguistic action—and not a dummy example this time, but a genuine (and historically important) utterance. Machiavelli, in Chapter 15 of *The Prince*, offers the following piece of advice: 'Princes must learn when not to be virtuous.' Several of his interpreters have asked what he may have meant by offering such advice. Here it cannot I think be doubted that the crucial question to ask, in order to answer this question, is what Machiavelli may have been doing in making this claim. One widely accepted answer (suggested by Felix Gilbert)[14] has been that Machiavelli was 'consciously refuting his predecessors' within the highly conventionalized genre of advice-books to princes (p. 477). Again it seems unquestionable that to ask and answer this question about the illocutionary force of Machiavelli's utterance is equivalent to asking about Machiavelli's intentions in writing this section of *The Prince*. Notice once more that this does not tell us the motives which prompted (and perhaps caused) Machiavelli to offer this advice. Gilbert suggests that the most likely motives might have been a mixture of frustration at the prevailing 'idealist interpretation of politics' combined with a simple

---

[14] Felix Gilbert, 'The Humanist Concept of the Prince and *The Prince* of Machiavelli', *Journal of Modern History*, 11 (1939), 449–83.

desire to shock and a belief in the importance of giving genuinely practical political advice (p. 480). The point once more is that what we do
learn is Machiavelli's intention in writing just what he did write. I do
not wish to imply here, of course, that what we learn is the intention
lying behind the writing of the particular sentence I have quoted, nor
do I wish to imply that Machievelli need have had any isolable intention in writing just that one sentence. But I do wish to claim that we
learn the intention lying behind Machiavelli's argument at this point of
his work—the primary intention (and the illocutionary force of his given
utterance) being to challenge and repudiate an accepted moral commonplace.

III

I now turn to try to bring out the philosophical interest of these
claims. This lies, as I have already indicated, in the suggestion that the
argument I have now set out seems to give some grounds for saying that
both the theses of the naturalists (C and D) as well as those of the anti-
naturalists (A and B) may be mistaken. Consider first the two naturalist
theses. Thesis C states that to redescribe an action is in no way to explain
it. I have now sought to show, however, that for at least certain classes
of social actions there can be a unique form of (illocutionary) redescription which, by way of recovering the agent's intended illocutionary act,
may be capable of explaining at least certain features of the agent's behaviour. This conclusion can perhaps be most readily corroborated by
reverting to the dummy example of the policeman issuing to the skater
the utterance 'The ice over there is very thin.' This episode might be
witnessed by a puzzled bystander who for some reason fails to grasp the
policeman's primary intention in issuing this utterance. One request for
an explanation might then take the form of asking 'Why did he say
that?' (Or more exactly, 'Why did the policeman issue that given
utterance?') And one reply, providing an explanation of the policeman's
action, might be 'He said it to warn the skater.' (Or more exactly, 'The
policeman's reason for issuing that given utterance was to give notice
to the skater of the potential danger of skating where the ice is very
thin.') The illocutionary redescription serves as an explanation of the
(linguistic) action.

There seems no doubt, moreover, about the way in which such illocutionary redescriptions may serve as genuine explanations of at least
some puzzles about a fairly wide range of social actions. For it is one
thing if the bystander understands what the policeman's utterance to

the skater means, so that he may be able to give an account of what the policeman said. But it is another and further thing if the bystander understands what the policeman's issuing of an utterance with that meaning was itself intended to mean on the given occasion, so that he may be able to give an account of why the policeman said what he said. Colloquially, we may say that what an illocutionary redescription will characteristically explain about a social action will be its *point*.

Consider next thesis D, that there is nothing in the fact that a social action may have a meaning from which it follows that the action may not be entirely explicable by means of the ordinary processes of causal explanation. I have now suggested, however, that while it may be essential in a wide range of cases to recover the meaning of a social action in order to be able to explain it, to supply this redescriptive form of explanation is certainly to supply something other than a causal explanation. Again this can most readily be corroborated by reverting to the dummy example of the policeman warning the skater. The explanation for the policeman's issuing of his given utterance is supplied by way of recovering what the policeman meant, in the non-natural sense of understanding not just what his utterance itself meant (for as Ziff has stressed it is not even necessary that the utterance should in that sense have a meaning at all) but of understanding what the act of issuing an utterance with that meaning might itself have meant in the given circumstances. This is supplied in turn by way of decoding the conventions governing the illocutionary force attaching to the policeman's utterance itself. But this can scarcely be to provide a causal form of explanation. For this is to focus on a *feature* of the policeman's action, and not on an independently specific condition of it, in the way that any causal form of explanation requires. Yet this is still to provide an explanation of the given action. For to know in the required sense what the agent meant is to know how he intended his utterance (or other action) to be taken. But this in turn is to know the agent's intention in performing that action. And this in turn is to know why he performed that particular action. We thus have a genuine form of explanation of the given action, even though it is clear that we cannot construe these sorts of intentions (intentions *in* acting) as causes of which the agent's corresponding actions can then be seen as effects.

Next consider the two anti-naturalist theses. Thesis A states that the reason the concept of social meaning can be explanatory is because it tells us the agent's motives for performing his given action. I have now sought to show, however, first that a sharp line needs to be drawn between an agent's motives and his intentions in acting, and secondly that it is these intentions, and not the agent's motives, which we need to recover in order to decode the meaning of a social action.

The possible need for this sharp division between motives and intentions does not seem to have been admitted by any of the anti-naturalist or the naturalist theorists I have cited. The anti-naturalists (such as Melden, Rickman, and Winch)[15] as well as the naturalists (such as Ayer, Davidson, and MacIntyre in his recent work)[16] write about motives and intentions in this connection—and often about reasons and purposes as well—as if they believe these concepts to be virtually interchangeable. This seems to be a mistake in itself, but it also seems to be a mistake of some consequence when we come to try to explain social actions, since it encourages the elision of what I take to be a necessary stage in the explanation of a certain range of actions. It is this extra stage, and the need to begin by considering it, which I have chiefly been concerned to emphasize—the stage, that is, at which it may be appropriate, before asking either about the agent's motives or about any deeper causes of his behaviour, to ask whether the performance of his given action itself bears any conventional element of (non-natural) meaning or (illocutionary) force.

The possible significance of isolating this extra stage can be conveniently illustrated by reconsidering the main example of a social action which Ayer chooses in his essay on Man as a subject for science. He takes the case (pp. 9–10) of a man drinking a glass of wine, and claims that this action might be explained, according to its context, either as '(1) an act of self-indulgence, (2) an expression of politeness, (3) a proof of alcoholism, (4) a manifestation of loyalty, (5) a gesture of despair, (6) an attempt at suicide, (7) the performance of a social rite, (8) a religious communication, (9) an attempt to summon up one's courage, (10) an attempt to seduce or corrupt another person, (11) the sealing of a bargain, (12) a display of professional expertise, (13) a piece of inadvertence, (14) an act of expiation, (15) the response to a challenge'.

It is true that my argument is not altogether easy to make good in terms of Ayer's particularly elaborate and eccentric list. In cases (3) and (13) it is not clear that the *explicans* yields the explanation of anything that could be called a voluntary action. In cases (6), (10), and (12) it is not clear how the *explicans* is to be understood. (It is hard to see, that

---

[15] Melden, op. cit., pp. 83–9; Rickman, op. cit., p. 69; Winch, op. cit., pp. 45–51.

[16] Ayer, op. cit., p. 9; Davidson, op. cit., p. 699; Alasdair MacIntyre, *Against the Self-Images of the Age* (London, 1971), p. 226.

is, how any of these answers could be offered as possible explanations for the action *simply* of drinking a glass of wine.) Furthermore, in cases (1), (7), (9), and (14) it does seem necessary to concede that the question of distinguishing the motives of the agent from his intentions in acting scarcely seems to arise. There scarcely seems, that is, to be any question to ask in these cases about the meaning of the given action, and it seems that, if we were to ask in these cases about the intentions of the agent in performing his given action, this would scarcely explain anything about the given behaviour. This still leaves us, however, with cases (2), (4), (5), (8), (11), and perhaps (15). The explanation in these cases, *pace* Ayer's assimilation of intentions to motives, seems to take the form of a redescription which directs us not primarily to the agent's motives, but rather to his intentions *in* performing the given action of drinking the glass of wine. Thus it does seem possible, at least in these cases, to insist on the need to begin by considering a stage of explanation which is prior to any attempt to elucidate the agent's motives, and which consists of an attempt to recover the unique illocutionary redescription of the action itself, in terms of which the agent's performance of it can be shown non-naturally to mean something. It seems therefore that the anti-naturalists must be mistaken when they equate the recovery of social meaning with the elucidation of the agent's motives for action.

Consider finally thesis B—that to explain an action by citing its meaning and the agent's motives is to provide a form of explanation incompatible with causality. This thesis is contradicted rather than sustained by the way in which I have sought to vindicate the possibility of giving non-causal explanations of social actions. I have sought only to argue that to explain a social action in terms of the agent's intentions in performing it constitutes one stage in the explanation of a certain range of social actions. I have at no point suggested that to provide such non-causal explanations is in any way incompatible with the subsequent provision of further and arguably causal explanations of the same action. One such further stage might be to provide an explanation in terms of the agent's motives. A yet further stage might be to provide an explanation in terms of the grounds for the agent's possession of just those motives. It will normally be indispensable to go on to both these further stages in order to be able to provide anything like a complete explanation of any social action. And I should wish to claim that it is strongly arguable in the case of the first of these further stages, and unquestionable in the case of the second, that to provide these further explanations will be to provide causal explanations for the performance of the given social action.

I V

I turn finally to consider the practical implications of the thesis I have argued. There is a special interest in trying to make this point, first because of the tendency among some recent philosophers of social science to deny that their views about the logic of explanation entail any methodological recommendations,[17] and secondly because of the more obvious tendency among practising historians as well as social scientists to deny that the acceptance of any particular philosophical viewpoint could possibly have any practical bearing on the study of their subjects. I now wish to suggest that if the conceptual scheme I have set out is sound, it entails at least three methodological recommendations, all of which tend, moreover, to be ignored or even explicitly denied in a good deal of current writing in history and social science. I concede, of course, the difficulty of deriving anything except negative methodological injunctions from my *a priori* arguments. Perhaps any such injunctions, if they are to stand any chance of being sensible as well as sufficiently general to be of practical value, are bound in effect to consist of injunctions not to heed methodological injunctions based on mistaken *a priori* arguments. I hope nevertheless that it may be possible to see in this section the beginnings, if only the negative beginnings, of an answer to those who have refused to accept that the dispute over causal and rational explanations of actions could possibly have anything to do with the methodology of the social sciences.

Consider first the classes (the non-linguistic as well as linguistic classes) of what Austin called 'ritual and ceremonial' actions. There are two methodological recommendations which seem, at least in these cases, to follow from the argument I have advanced. The first is the need to raise questions about the agent's ritual *beliefs* in order to be able to explain such actions. This claim appears to have been explicitly denied in some recent social anthropology,[18] and is certainly bypassed by those who have written as if they believe that ritual actions can sufficiently be explained in terms of their place in a given social structure and by reference to their social effects.[19] It is clear, however, that since there is obviously a crucial logical link between the nature and

[17] See for example Peter Winch, 'Mr Louch's Idea of a Social Science', *Inquiry*, 7 (1964), 203.

[18] For example, I. C. Jarvie and Joseph Agassi speak of 'a general criticism' in current social anthropology of 'the entire assumption that people's actions can be explained by their beliefs' in Bryan R. Wilson, ed., *Rationality* (London, 1970), p. 179. (But this is denied by J. H. M. Beattie, ibid., p. 246.)

[19] Hollis, op. cit., pp. 235–6 criticizes this type of explanation.

range of the intentions it makes sense to ascribe to an agent in acting, and the nature and range of that agent's beliefs, it must follow that in order to explain a ritual action by way of recovering the agent's intentions in performing it, we must necessarily be prepared to examine and allude to the ritual beliefs informing the intentions with which the agent performed his given ritual action.

The second recommendation is that as soon as we concede the need to enter the realm of the agent's beliefs in order to explain his social actions, it also becomes essential to raise questions about the *rationality* of these beliefs. This has of course been recently stressed, as I have mentioned, by Hollis and others. They have primarily been concerned, however, with the linguistic and logical elements in the concept of rationality. It seems clear, as they have argued, that we must be prepared to make some *a priori* assumptions about the universality of the laws of thought if we are going to be able correctly to identify (and so to translate) the nature of the speech-acts, as well as to explain the nature of the ritual actions, which may be performed in an alien culture. It also seems clear, however, that the analysis of the concept of rationality requires us to consider a further question, concerned with the nature of the procedures which will have to be followed, and the nature of the criteria met, before we can say of a given empirical belief that it is rationally held.

It might be doubted whether my basic theme—that of intentionality in relation to the explanation of action—necessarily requires an examination of this further point. To be concerned, however, with explaining actions, and thus with the examination of intentions as the means both of identifying those actions and of establishing whether they may be said to have a meaning, is to commit oneself not only (as I have just stressed) to examining the beliefs of which such intentional actions form the expression. It is also to commit oneself to asking about the rationality of the agent's beliefs, since the answer to this question must in turn affect our assessment of his intentions and actions.

It is true that the strong influence, until recently, of a positivist theory of knowledge upon the philosophy of social science has made it rather easy to oversimplify, and perhaps to overstress, the significance of this point. It has been usual to define the concept of a rational belief in terms of the agent's capacity and willingness to recognize 'that there is sufficient evidence in its favour' (Gibson, op. cit., p. 156), 'that it is based on good evidence' (Wilson, ed., op. cit., p. 173), and so on. It is clear however, that this fails to acknowledge something problematic in the very notion of holding a belief in the light of rather than in the face of 'the available evidence', since it fails to acknowledge that the question of what is to count as good or sufficient evidence in favour of holding a belief can never be free from cultural reference. This anti-positivist objection can be developed as follows. We can imagine an alien system of beliefs in which the paradigms used to connect the system together are such that none of the evidence which we should regard as evidence in favour of abandoning those beliefs is taken to count as decisive evidence either for or against them. We can then imagine an agent, operating within this belief-system, who accepts on trust these prevailing paradigms (and these prevailing canons of evidence), recognizing and following only the moves accepted as rational within the given system, but never challenging the rationality of any part of the system itself. It might now be argued, of the beliefs held by someone in this type of situation, that provided they are coherently connected together, and provided the agent recognizes their implications, they may be said to be held in an entirely rational way. There seems to be no space left for this possibility, however, if we insist on defining rational belief in terms of each individual believer's continual willingness to examine 'the available evidence' for and against each belief he holds.

A positivist might still wish to insist, however, that such an agent's beliefs cannot be rationally held, since it cannot be rational for anyone to accept on trust what are to count as the canons of evidence in favour of holding any given belief. Such an answer seems to be given, in effect, even by some of the most recent and avowedly anti-positivist writers on the topic of rationality. MacIntyre, for example, in his most recent essay on the topic, continues to rest his definition of rational belief on the (unanalysed) claim that to hold a belief rationally must be to hold the belief in the light of having engaged in a 'relevant process of appropriate deliberation', conducted according to 'the appropriate intellectual norms and procedures'.[20]

This type of reply, however, scarcely meets the original objection to the positivist way of connecting rational belief with evidence. It is clear that we all accept and act upon a large number of beliefs (particularly of a technical or theoretical character) without ever trying—or even being in a position seriously to try—either to decide in an independent spirit on the 'appropriate procedures' for falsifying them, or to reassess 'the available evidence' in favour of holding them. We accept such beliefs on trust, on the grounds that we know no better, that they look inherently plausible, and that most other people feel the same. There does not necessarily seem, however, to be anything irrational about ac-

[20] MacIntyre, op. cit., p. 247.

cepting many of our empirical beliefs on trust in this way, both with respect to the alleged evidence in favour of holding them, and with respect to what should count as evidence. It would indeed be extremely irrational in many cases if we refused to accept a number of such conventional beliefs, and always insisted on the need to try to reconsider for ourselves the status of the alleged evidence for believing them, in order to arrive at our own far more untutored conclusions.

It is true that these sorts of objections to the analysis of rational belief simply in terms of evidence and refutability have gained considerable ground in recent discussions. They have perhaps drawn some of their strength from their apparent connection with Quine's attack on the alleged distinction between analytic and synthetic statements, a distinction which underlies the positivist way of connecting rational belief with the idea of examining the facts of the case. More recently, the attack has been popularized in such methodological studies as those of Kuhn and Winch, which have converged in rejecting the assumption that we ever construct or examine our theories in the light of anything like unvarnished evidence. As the idea that our theories really act as paradigms rather than as straightforward conjectures has gained ground, however, a contrasting danger seems to have developed, which the positivists—with their simple application of a correspondence theory of truth to elucidate the concept of rational belief—at least managed to avoid.

This new danger arises with the tendency to suppose that in order to vindicate the rationality of an alien belief-system, *all* the investigator need do is to examine what counts as evidence within the given system, to assure himself that the alleged reasons which the agents may give for acting are genuinely reasons within the system, and in general to assure himself that each particular belief is connected with other beliefs in such a way as to make up a coherent and integrated cultural system. The danger with this type of emphasis lies in the tendency to assume that it must follow from this that there cannot be any trans-cultural or trans-historical criteria for applying the concept of rationality at all. Thus it has been explicitly insisted, for example by Winch, that the attempt to apply any such criteria must be altogether improper methodologically, and in any case 'not open to us', since the result will only be to contaminate our explanations with our own parochial standards of rationality.[21]

This argument between the positivists and these newly fashionable relativists has left the topic of rationality in more or less complete dis-

---

[21] This is the position taken up in Peter Winch, 'Understanding a Primitive Society', *American Philosophical Quarterly*, 1 (1964), 316.

array. Perhaps it is by now appropriate, however, to think in terms of trying to make at least a partial defence of a more positivist point of view. It may be proper, that is, first to try to stress the value of attaching *some* weight to the idea of examining and rejecting empirical beliefs in the light of the available evidence, and secondly to try to show the way in which this approach (however question-begging it may seem) may still yield a methodological injunction to the historian or the social scientist concerned with the explanation of individual social actions.

Suppose it were possible to combine the elements of a correspondence with a coherence theory of truth in the way that such an approach would seem to require. Why would this be worthwhile, from the point of view of trying to explain individual social actions? Because a belief which an agent holds rationally in this sense—in the sense of holding it in the light of considering the evidence available to him for refuting it—will generate a quite different range of social actions from the range generated out of a belief which he holds irrationally, in the sense of holding it in the face of rather than in the light of the available evidence. The reason is that the agent will have a quite different perception in each case of the appropriate action to perform. In the first type of situation, the investigator will need to find the means to assure himself that the agent's beliefs are in fact rationally held. This may require an extremely sensitive analysis of 'the available evidence', since the state of the evidence may be such that the agent's beliefs can be seen by the investigator to be false, and may nevertheless have been rationally held. (Some recent discussions have arguably failed to keep the ideas of rational and of true belief sufficiently separate.)[22] In the second type of situation, a further and different type of investigation becomes necessary if the agent's social action is to be explained. The investigator needs to be able to discover why the agent continues irrationally to hold a given belief if the evidence to refute it is in some clear sense available to him. It follows in each case that if the investigator fails to raise the question of the rationality of an agent's beliefs, in relation to the facts, he will not have established exactly what there is to be explained about the given action. He will thus be unable to avoid the danger of giving a wholly inappropriate type of explanation.

I turn finally to consider the wider class of social actions which I have suggested can in part be explained by decoding the agent's intentions in performing them. I wish to suggest that a further methodological injunction follows in these cases from my general argument. This

[22] They seem, for example, to be conflated in Steven Lukes, 'Some Problems about Rationality', *European Journal of Sociology*, 8 (1967), 262.

would be to begin by focusing not on the individual action to be explained, but rather on the *conventions* surrounding the performance of the given type of social action in the given social situation. The sense of grasping what is conventional which is relevant here is not limited to the strict sense in which we speak of understanding that a given action is being performed according to a convention of which the agent is aware, and which he deliberately follows. The relevant sense includes the wider idea of understanding what the established, conventional standards are which we may expect to see followed in the case of various types of social action within a given culture. The methodological injunction then becomes: begin not by trying to recover the agent's motives by studying the context of social rules, but rather by trying to decode the agent's intentions by aligning his given social action with a more general awareness of the conventional standards which are generally found to apply to such types of social action within a given situation.

This injunction appears to hold good even in the case of the type of abnormal social behaviour I have mentioned—such as the example out of Laing and Esterson's work on schizophrenia. It seems, that is, that the appropriate injunction to follow, in the attempt to discover whether the apparent autism of an allegedly schizophrenic adolescent may not be a case of deliberate and meaningful behaviour, must be to begin not by making an intensive study of the particular case and its possible aetiology. It must be to begin instead by trying to relate the particular case to other instances of adolescent withdrawal, in order to try to assess the extent to which the given degree of autism may not after all represent a fairly conventional form and degree of adolescent protest, rather than a straightforward set of pathological symptoms awaiting a straightforward causal explanation.

The same injunction applies even more clearly in the case of the types of linguistic action I have mentioned—such as the example out of Machiavelli's *Prince*, where there is not only a highly conventionalized genre of writing against which to measure Machiavelli's contribution to it, but also the clear presumption that Machiavelli was aware both of the genre and of the conventions usually applying in it. Here it seems unquestionable that the appropriate injunction to follow, in the attempt to disclose the meaning of such a work, must be to begin not by making an intensive study of the text in itself, but rather by trying to see what relations it bears to these existing conventions.

It is true that this injunction has been explicitly attacked by a prevailing school of historians of social and political thought, who have wished to insist that it must be possible, simply by reading such works 'over and over', to arrive at a sufficient understanding of them.[23] It will be clear by now, however, that to adopt such an approach must usually be to follow an inadequate methodology. It is surely clear (to keep to the Machiavelli example) that the fact that *The Prince* was in part intended as a deliberate attack on the moral convictions of advice-books to princes cannot be discovered simply by attending to the text, since this is not a fact contained in the text. It is also clear, however, that no one can be said fully to understand Machiavelli's text who does not understand this fact about it. To fail to grasp this fact is to fail to grasp the *point* of Machiavelli's argument in the later chapters of his book. It seems then, that some other form of study besides that of reading the text itself 'over and over' must be indispensable to an understanding of it. And it seems that this will at least need to take the form of adding a study of the general conventions and assumptions of the genre, from which the intentions of any particular contributor to it may then—by a combination of inference and scholarship—be decoded.

V

It will be clear by now that my thesis occupies a middle ground which has I believe been somewhat overlooked in the course of the current philosophical debate about the explanation of action in history and in social science. I have not been particularly concerned with exegesis, but I believe my position to be similar, at least in certain important respects, to that taken up—though by a very different route —in Weber's *Wirtschaft und Gesellschaft*. Those who have emphasized (correctly, I believe) the importance of intentions and conventions in the explanation of social action have usually written as though it follows that the attempt to explain such actions causally must represent a confusion, even a 'pernicious confusion'; that it must in any case be 'wholly irrelevant'; and that the whole vocabulary of causality ought accordingly to be 'expunged' from discussions about the explanation of social action.[24] Conversely, those philosophers who have insisted (again correctly, I believe) on the absurdity of this commitment have usually written (as I have shown in the case of all the naturalists I have examined) as though it follows that intentions and conventions must

[23] This is the commitment of the methodological introduction to J. P. Plamenatz, *Man and Society*, 2 vols. (London, 1964), 1, p. x.

[24] For these claims see respectively A. R. Louch, *Explanation and Human Action* (Oxford, 1966), p. 238; Melden, op. cit., p. 184; Raziel Abelson, 'Because I Want To', *Mind*, 74 (1965), 541.

themselves be treated simply as causal conditions of social actions. What I have essentially sought to argue is that neither of these alleged implications follows, and that both these claims seem to be mistaken.

It might finally be asked what relation these conclusions may bear to the issue of determinism with respect to voluntary human actions. This would be a vertiginous question even to broach, were it not that several proponents of the two naturalist theses I have examined seem to suggest that they lend an immediate strength to the thesis of determinism. This belief emerges, for example, at the end of Ayer's essay on Man as a subject for science. It is first pointed out there that we ordinarily explain human action by citing the agent's motives and intentions and the social context of his behaviour. It is then argued that all these conditions must be construed as causes of which the agent's actions are effects. It is then said to follow that there is 'no reason why the reign of law should break down' when we come to explain such actions. This is 'the strength of the determinists' (op. cit., p. 24).

I have sought to argue, however, that while there can undoubtedly be successful causal explanations of voluntary human actions, there can also be successful explanations of voluntary human actions which operate simply by recovering the illocutionary redescription of the given action, which are neither causal nor reducible to a causal form. If this argument is sound, then it seems possible to suggest two conclusions about the relations between the naturalist theses I have examined and the idea of the social determinism of actions, without having to commit oneself on the vexed question of the meaning of the thesis of determinism itself. The first, which must obviously be put very tentatively, is that if it is in fact essential for the defence of the thesis of the social determinism of actions that it should be possible to construe all the mental states of agents as causes of their actions, then there may be something inherently doubtful about the thesis. But the main conclusion, which can I think be expressed more confidently, is that in so far as the current arguments in favour of the thesis of social determinism have to depend upon the truth of theses C and D—including the assumption contained in thesis D that an agent's intentions must always be construed as causes of which his actions are effects—the thesis of social determinism has not yet been strengthened at all.

VII

COLLIGATORY CONCEPTS IN HISTORY

W. H. WALSH

THE activities with which I shall be concerned in this essay are familiar enough to writers and readers of history, though relatively little attention has been paid to them by those who have worked on the theory of the subject. To introduce them I shall mention only that, when we are confronted with a set of historical facts, one of our first tasks as students of history is to discover what they add up to, a result we achieve by identifying the continuing processes to which they belong or bear witness. I want to ask what assumptions are involved in thinking of this sort, and whether it requires any special type of concept. I admit that my initial description of the situation to be examined is vague; my hope is that it will be replaced by something more precise as the discussion proceeds. At the outset I can say little more than that I have questions to raise about the common historical activity of *saying what was going on* at a particular time in the past.

It will be useful to consider first in this connection a problem which is, ostensibly, not historical at all: that of a social commentator who has to write an account of contemporary Britain. We must notice immediately that, if he is to get results of any sort, he will need to understand the word 'contemporary' with a certain latitude: 'contemporary Britain' must mean, say, 'Britain since World War II' or 'Britain since 1960'. The reason for this becomes evident if we consider the kind of things a commentator of this sort could be expected to write. What I myself should look for in a work of this type would be, above everything else, a description of a series of movements or processes or trends which continued through a significant part of the period under study, though they need not have originated during it and could very well go on after it was completed. I should expect a commentator on contemporary Britain to remark on things like: the steady *growth* in the power of organized labour; the *decline* in religious belief and practice; the remarkable way in which Oxford and Cambridge *keep their hold* over

From *Studies in the Nature and Teaching of History*, ed. W. H. Burston and D. Thompson (London: Routledge and Kegan Paul, 1967), pp. 65–84. Reprinted with minor revisions by permission of the author and publishers.

the Establishment despite far-reaching changes in the educational and social systems. To make judgements of this sort he would need to see individual happenings in a special way, as going together to constitute recognizable trends or developments. It seems to me not accidental that, in speaking of what is going on in the contemporary world, we often use the term 'present developments'. It also seems obvious that, when we take different events to belong together in a single development, we do not think of them as being loose and separate in the Humean manner, but rather as having an altogether more intimate relation.

What that relation is I shall not attempt to specify at this juncture. My aim in these opening remarks is only to point out the importance of the notion of process in thinking about the contemporary world, 'process' here being a term in social theory rather than one in biology. If someone aspires to analyse the contemporary scene for us, we expect him to identify continuing processes in the welter of confusing and seemingly discordant facts, and to make clear the ways in which they are working out. Reducing the facts to order, in a case of this kind, means at least putting your finger on the main developments which are taking place, though it need not mean only this. A commentator may wish also to explore the setting in which the developments are occurring, and to trace the ways in which this is affecting what is coming about. But before he can turn to these questions he must make clear what it is that is happening, and for this must have recourse to concepts of the type I have stressed.

I now want to claim that we can find a precise parallel in the thought of the historian to this use by the contemporary social commentator of notions like process and development: the historian too has the identification of continuing processes (including of course processes of decline) as one of his primary tasks, and makes events intelligible to his readers to the extent to which he succeeds. But we should notice that there is one important respect in which a historian is better situated than any commentator on the contemporary scene when it comes to saying what is going on. The contemporary commentator is able to pronounce on present trends because, among other things, he can refer back to events before those with which he is primarily concerned and can thus see the movements in question come into being. Where he is handicapped, and where the historian is correspondingly strong, is that he does not know the outcome of the processes with which he deals. He can trace their origin and development so far; what he cannot do is say how they will eventually work out. And this means, of course, that his pronouncements are always open to question: it may well be that, for lack of information which just cannot be his, he fails to spot the real connections and so produces an account which is one-sided, if not positively false. By contrast the historian is, often at least, in a position to say what was happening with full awareness of the situation, for the processes with which he is concerned are, in typical cases, completed processes, and he can trace the stages of their history with a sure consciousness of where they were leading. In this respect he is better placed than anyone could have been at the time of which he writes: he has the gift of hindsight and knows how things went as well as how they were developing.

It is a commonplace in the theory of history to say that the historian should tell us 'precisely what happened' in the past; he must make the past come alive, as the point sometimes put, so that we see it as those concerned saw it themselves. But if what I have been arguing is correct, this cannot be the truth, or at least not the whole truth. To resurrect the past as it was is to reproduce it with all its uncertainties, to reproduce it as open to the future. But though there are historians who speak as if it were regrettable that they know the outcome and aftermath of the events of which they write, the fact is that they do know it. The historian who confines himself, in Collingwood's term, to 'rethinking' the thoughts of the agents whose deeds concern him is rendering himself incapable of performing his proper duties as a historian, for if he *only* rethinks the thoughts of the agents he must turn a blind eye to the effects of their acts. To command a clear view of the whole historical scene, and so to put his readers in the picture, he needs to see the acts of his character in relation both to what went before and to what came after. Of course it is perfectly proper for him to concern himself with Collingwood's question what they were thinking of when they acted as they did; my point is only that he cannot restrict himself to that inquiry. For he knows not only what the personages he writes of attempted, but also what they achieved. And as readers of history we are interested in results at least as much as intentions.

A number of questions can readily be posed about the activity of discerning and describing movements or processes or developments in history. We can ask first what sort of a thing history must be if the concepts mentioned are to be useful in characterizing it. An important part of the answer to this question is that it must be, to a significant degree, the product of human action: for notions such as process to apply, it must be true, at some level at any rate, that men make their own history. The processes in which historians are interested are not natural processes, which come about without any regard to the efforts of human beings, but movements which can, at least, be accelerated or retarded by men's voluntary decisions. Or if this is too strong (for historians might, after all, be interested in, say, a process of desiccation resulting in the spread of desert conditions to an area which had been fertile), their concern with the purely natural is limited to its bearing on what men do and suffer. If processes of this kind happen quite independently of choice, they gain attention because of the way they limit or circumscribe choice, or again for the efforts men make to counter their effects.

These considerations enable us to reply to the criticism that the supposition that men make their own history in any significant sense is absurd. To say that they make their own history is not to say that they make it *in vacuo*; it is not to deny the effects on their actions of natural forces, physical necessities, or physical factors beyond their control. Such elements operate to restrict their area of choice; they bring it about that, quite often, they cannot do what they would like. But there is nothing damaging in this admission so long as it is recognized that what human beings do has *some* influence on events, i.e. that, whatever the pressure of natural circumstances, there is a field for the exercise of free choice. Historians and social theorists may differ about the extent and significance of that field, for what men can choose is circumscribed not only by natural but also by social factors (e.g. existing institutions), but few of them deny its existence altogether. Nor again is it necessary, if we are to believe that men make their own history, to argue that they must always make it precisely according to their plans. Certainly we can point to some historical developments which seemingly worked out largely as planned: the Benthamite movement for legal reform in nineteenth-century England, the institution of the state of Israel, the transformation of Germany from a weak to a strong power between 1933 and 1939. But these are very much the exception rather than the rule. A historical process is, in general, an altogether more untidy affair, in which men's aspirations and attempts are constantly thwarted both by circumstances and by their fellows, and in which there is a continual struggle to make the best of unfavourable situations and achieve what one can in frustrating conditions. But these facts do not preclude us from properly taking diverse events to constitute historical movements and developments, provided always that men at the time can be shown to have had certain general aims which they were actively seeking to realize. That things worked out less easily than they initially hoped, and less in accordance with their ideas, is of smaller importance than that they were interested in long-term goals and were able to do something towards their eventual attainment.

This argument has a corollary which it may be of interest to notice in passing. Among the writers who have made a particularly prominent use of the idea that history should be seen in terms of movements or processes are the speculative philosophers of history of the late eighteenth and early nineteenth century. Kant, for example, in his celebrated essay 'Idea for a Universal History', spoke of 'Nature' or 'Providence' as pursuing a hidden plan in history, and argued that the main object of a philosophical treatment of the subject was to uncover such a plan, thus making the writing of universal history possible. But if the proviso just noted is correct, it must be agreed that no such plan could conceivably be of interest to *historians*. The movements with which the latter are concerned have, as has just been explained, a direct relation to what men set themselves to obtain or avoid; even if the end-result achieved was not explicitly aimed at by any single person or body of persons, as in the case of the Industrial Revolution, it must all the same be true that it connected directly with, and was a natural outcome of, the things at which they did aim. No one, perhaps, sought to bring about the total transformation of social, economic, and political arrangements, with all the upheaval and unhappiness it involved, which was the upshot of the industrialization of Britain between 1750 and 1850, but it remains true that from the first there were men who wanted radical changes in many spheres, and were ready to seize the opportunities created by the technical discoveries to forward their own aims. For this reason a movement of this kind can genuinely interest the historian, for though much happened that was unintended, the idea that men make their own history can clearly not be dismissed altogether in this type of case. But things seem quite otherwise when we find Kant arguing that the final aim of Nature in history is to bring about a state of affairs in which the nations of the world are united in a single federal organization, enjoying a state of perpetual peace. For, at least as Kant expounds the idea, it appears that this result is to come about naturally, i.e. without any reference to what men want to have or avoid. In these circumstances human beings are really no better than puppets in the hands of fate, and what eventuates cannot be ascribed in any way to their individual efforts. But if this is so, equally it cannot have the peculiar interest we associate with the study of history.

Kant certainly takes for granted some propositions about human behaviour, but these are drawn from psychology rather than history. In general, his approach to the past is that of the sociologist (it is instructive to observe that he was considerably influenced by Adam Ferguson's *Essay on Civil Society*). A central category of historical thought, that of a process which bears witness to human achievement or lack of achievement, appears to pass him by. In this respect he compares unfavourably with a still more famous speculative philosopher, Hegel. We all know how Hegel made play in his lectures on the philosophy of history with the suspicious-sounding concept of 'the cunning of Reason', and how he declared that 'world-historical men', figures like Julius Caesar and Napoleon, achieve altogether more than they aim at. These facts suggest that Hegel too was a historical naturalist; that his aim was to establish a pattern in history which it would have regardless of men's particular wishes. But it is by no means certain that this conclusion is correct. We cannot be sure, in the first place, that Hegel intended his language about 'Reason' and the 'World Spirit' to be taken quite literally: the 'World Spirit' seems sometimes to be almost a synonym for 'humanity'. Nor need there be anything sinister in the famous claim about 'world-historical men', for we find parallels to this in the thought of quite unphilosophical historians. It might, for instance, be argued that the union of Germany was a direct, if unintended, result of the French Revolution. But a historian who spoke in this way need not see the hand of destiny behind the developments of which he wrote: he could allow that none of the original revolutionaries wanted, or even foresaw, German unity, but could still maintain that the whole affair remained a matter of genuine historical interest because there were Germans who took advantage of the opportunities created by the Revolution and its aftermath to promote their own ends. Similarly one could, I suppose, argue that when he made the achievement of liberty the end of the whole historical process Hegel was not speaking of something which could come about without human cooperation: if social science or (worse still) logic determined what history must be in its main lines, the details were all the same filled in by individual men. No doubt Hegel's own position over the point is unclear. But in so far as it is, there is equal unclarity about whether or not his philosophy of history can have any real relevance for historians. If we interpret him, as Professor Dray suggests we should,[1] as standing in the humanist tradition and connect his talk about 'Reason' with men's rational decisions, he will certainly be relevant despite the strangeness of his language. But if he is the panlogicist monster many critics have made him out to be, he will be concerned with processes which are not historical at all.

[1] See Ch. 6 of his *Philosophy of History* (Englewood Cliffs, N.J., 1964).

I am assuming in all this that history is properly seen as a humane discipline and not as a branch of natural science, and I of course agree that this assumption might well be disputed, e.g. by Marxists. To meet such criticism I wish to make two points. First, I want to repeat that seeing history as a succession of movements or developments does not preclude further investigation of it as conditioned by the operation of natural or social forces. Nobody in his senses pretends that historical agents are exempt from natural necessities, and everyone who reflects sees that their activities are circumscribed by countless social factors— institutions, conventions, ways of proceding, moral beliefs—which in practice it is out of their power to flout or change. The investigation of the effect of such background factors is in my view entirely legitimate, and if the historian who undertakes it can summon the results of social science to his aid, so much the better. So far as I can see, one way in which modern professional historians have improved on their pre- decessors and produced a *deeper* analysis of the facts is precisely in giving more attention to such conditioning factors. But this does not mean that they have deserted the traditional historical attitude, for their chief interest remains in men's achievements and failures in the period of which they write. Their position is thus radically different from that which claims that *everything* which happens in history does so as a result of forces over which men exercise no control whatsoever. And this brings me to my second point, which is simply that no practising historian acts as if he thought history was made, wholly and solely, by factors outside human control. Even Marxists do not subscribe to the belief without reservations, despite their view that in the stages of 'pre- history', i.e. those before the institution of the communist society, men are prisoners of an economic system which is not of their own making. For they hold, notoriously, that there are circumstances in which the processes of history can be accelerated by the efforts of the prescient, and they look forward to a time when economic conditions will no longer determine what men do, but they will be free to make their own history. Despite their commitment to theory, their outlook in history is identical in essentials with that of the bourgeois historians they so much despise.

In previous discussions of this subject, especially in my *Introduction to Philosophy of History*, I employed the term 'colligation' to cover the activity by which the historian groups different events together 'under appropriate conceptions', to employ Whewell's phrase (the word 'colligation' was introduced into philosophy by Whewell). My emphasis in these discussions was different from what it is now, in a way I shall specify in a moment, but I should like for all that to retain the general term and its derivative 'colligatory concept'. I want now to ask what general role such concepts play in historical thought; what relation they have or should have to what was explicitly before the minds of the persons whose acts they serve to colligate; finally whether there are any limitations on the kind of concept which can be used for colligatory purposes. Successful answers to these questions would, I believe, throw considerable light on a notion which is as elusive as it is important, the notion of historical understanding.

When writing about colligation earlier I tended to treat it primarily as an explanatory process. My interest in it at that time arose out of an attempt to find a plausible version of the Idealist theory of history. I observed that there are cases where historical happenings are not externally connected as, according to empiricist philosophers, all events necessarily are, namely those in which an agent or group of agents pursues a long-term policy over a period of time. The earlier and later stages in the carrying out of such a policy have an intimate relationship to one another, for it is not only the case that what came subsequently was affected by what came before; it is also true that the former in a sense affected the latter, in so far as the agents concerned envisaged, or at least had some idea of, what they were going to do later when they first began to act. One point I thought important to stress about this situation was that the internal relationships here exemplified were possible only because the concern was with actions: Collingwood's emphasis on the concept of action as central in historical thinking, and the close link he saw between action and thought, seemed here to be entirely vindicated. Another was that a regular way in which historians answer the question 'Why did that happen?' is to show the place the event in question had in a continuous development, by specifying what led up to it and what it led on to, and by colligating the various happenings concerned under a single appropriate conception.

It seems to me now that this argument, though not perhaps seriously wrong, was defective in various ways. First, in making the standard case to which colligation applies that in which a planned policy is carried out without major obstruction. I mentioned at the time that there are many instances of historical development which do not answer this description, but was inclined to treat them as degenerate cases of purposive action proper. As will be obvious from the foregoing pages, I now want to argue that the ideas of process, movement, and development rather than that of realized policy should be taken as primary in this sector of historical thought, thus allowing for the disparity between men's aspirations and their actual achievements. A historical process, like a man's career, is the product of chance and opposition as well as of purpose and intention; the various stages of which it consists have accordingly only a relatively loose unity. But this is not to say that it cannot be properly treated as a single development. Nor is it to admit that such unity as it possesses is like that possessed by, say, a spell of bad weather, the later part of which grows mechanically out of the earlier. For the fact remains that the processes I have in mind, of which my earlier example the Industrial Revolution may be taken as typical, have an intimate connection with the purposive activities of human agents: our interest in them, as has already been explained, springs from our interest in what men can and cannot do. Though not solely the product of human effort, except perhaps in very rare cases, they are nevertheless continuously affected by what men set themselves to do, and their unity is often derived from the fact that, in the face of natural obstacles and opposition from their fellows, human beings tend to try again and again to realize the same long-standing aims.

A second respect in which my previous argument was defective was in not sufficiently pointing out the social or collective aspect of historical processes. Like many others who have written about this subject, I worked with the false assumption that a man's mind and actions are private to himself, when the truth is that ideas and ways of thinking and proceeding are widely shared (they would generally be unintelligible apart from their social setting), and that the causes to which men devote themselves are in nearly all instances common causes. I regard it as important to stress this feature of the situation now for two reasons. First, because historical processes typically involve many individuals; they bear witness to common rather than to merely personal achievements. There can be no question of reducing historical movements to complicated sets of individual human actions for the very good reason that individual human actions do not have the independence which is so often claimed for them: men's minds reflect their upbringing and human environment, and we should find it hard to say what was in them if we had to abstract from these. Secondly, I believe that the fact that different people can and do literally have ideas in common has a close bearing on the relationship of their actions. If persons A and B possess the same idea and are interested in the same ultimate object there is a sense in which we can properly forget that B is a different person from A when he takes up the work after A has given it up. It will then be possible to give our attention only to the development they were jointly forwarding, and this will make it legitimate to treat a process like the rise of the Independent Labour Party without constantly asking the question who were the agents ultimately concerned. It is interesting to notice that historians regularly do just this: they move at what individualist philosophers must regard as an alarming level of abstraction with no discomfort whatsoever. And this bears witness not to their logical *naïveté*, but rather to their capacity to handle ideas in practice.

A third respect in which my previous account is open to criticism concerns the main part which colligation plays in historical thought. As mentioned already, I introduced it previously in connection with the general subject of historical explanation, and my example here has been followed by Professor Dray, who argues that historians not only explain why or how things happen, but also, as in the cases I had in mind, explain what was going on.[2] I agree, however, with Mr. Marvin Levich[3] in thinking there is something suspect about Dray's phrase 'explaining what', and am now inclined to follow him in connecting the activities Dray and I are concerned with more with *interpretation* than with explanation. Many historical procedures, as Mr. Levich has stressed, fall under this general head, since it is a major task for the historian to make clear to his readers what was going on in the period under study. The basic situation here is, in fact, that depicted above: the historian and his reader initially confront what looks like a largely unconnected mass of material, and the historian then goes on to show that sense can be made of it by revealing certain pervasive themes or developments. In specifying what was going on at the time he both sums the individual events and tells us how to take them. Or again, he picks out what was significant in the events he relates, what is significant here being what points beyond itself and connects with other happenings as phases in a continuous process. I am not saying now that the procedures I have described exhaust what is meant by 'giving a historical interpretation': no doubt there can be much more to the latter than mere colligation. But I am saying that colligation is regularly invoked as a stage in historical interpretation, and that it is to this broad area of thought that it mostly belongs. We can, as I argued earlier, have recourse to colligatory concepts in the interest of explaining something: we can show why an event happened as it did by displaying how it fitted into a continuing process. But we use them for other purposes too, to characterize and analyse, and in so doing commonly aim at producing under-

---

[2] ' "Explaining What" in History' in P. L. Gardiner (ed.), *Theories of History*, (Glencoe, Ill., 1959), pp. 403–8.

[3] In a review in *History and Theory*, 4 (1965), 341.

standing and enlightenment rather than answers to the question 'Why?'

Once, however, it is agreed that to colligate in history is (typically) to interpret, we are confronted by a further problem: what is the relationship between the concepts we use to colligate events and the events themselves? To colligate is, broadly, to organize, and it would be generally agreed that any acceptable scheme of organization must have a firm foundation in fact. Yet it is apparent that the summary descriptions we offer of past periods of history, as when we speak of Rome as suffering a severe financial crisis in the time of Sulla, or of the period of the Sophists as the Greek Age of Enlightenment, are often framed in terms which are intelligible to us but would have little or no meaning for the persons whose activities and experiences they purport to sum up. Can anything be said about the conditions in which it is and those in which it is not appropriate to import the concepts of a later period in summing the events of a previous era?

We may notice first that many professional historians would be inclined to say that there are no circumstances in which any such move could be legitimate. The aim of history being to arrive at truth about the past for its own sake, historians must in their view confine themselves to describing what happened in terms which would have made sense to those alive at the time. Otherwise they fall victim to the vice of anachronism and, like journalists, distort the facts for the sake of producing something interesting. Historians who take this line are inclined to be suspicious of generalization of any kind, even summative generalization, and in consequence prefer to avoid the explicit identification and labelling of trends and movements wherever they can, substituting juxtaposition of facts for the open use of an interpretative concept. On the face of things their history consists in nothing but the recital of fairly low-level facts. This attitude goes along with the belief, already mentioned, that the historian's job is to make the past come alive as it was at the time, and with the suspicion I referred to of seeing what happened in the light of its outcome. To pay attention to the outcome is, on this way of thinking, to read history backwards, a procedure followed by the discredited Whig historians who thought that history made sense because it led up to the glories of the present. According to Professor Oakeshott, who has set out the theory of this form of 'scientific' history more boldly and with a greater show of logic than any other writer, what these men lacked was a grasp of the elementary distinction, fundamental to history proper, between the historical and practical past. The past as it figures in practical thought of any kind is a past which exists in essential relation to the present;

it is *my* past, rather than *the* past. But the past as it appears in the thought of the historian proper has no relation to anyone's present loves, hates, or aspirations; it is, strictly speaking, 'dead and irreproachable'. It is a past about which there is nothing to be done except to investigate it for its own sake. Few historians manage to live up to these austere requirements in every aspect of their historical work, but they must even so be taken as expressing the historical ideal.[4]

I cannot comment on this theory generally in the present context, but must confine myself to one or two points which bear on the immediate issue.[5] First I want to repeat what was said above, that whether historians like it or not they do, unless dealing with very recent history, know the outcome of events they investigate. If to take account of the outcome is to read history backwards, they are inevitably committed to reading history backwards. But this does not necessarily involve them in the errors of 'Whig historians', nor mean that they cannot distinguish the practical from the historical past. It is one thing to see past happenings in the light of the present, another to see them in the light of their aftermath: the first may well stir our passions, the second need not do so at all. What harm is done if we see the careers of Marius and Sulla as prefiguring the Roman Empire, provided we do not insist on viewing them as an awful warning or an admirable example? But if it is agreed that historians may, and indeed must, see events in the light of their outcome I do not see how they can refuse to identify the trends or processes to which they bear witness. Admittedly they can, if sufficiently gifted, avoid using labels in this connection: by skilful selection and juxtaposition they can show the form of the facts without explicitly naming it. But though this protects them from a number of mistaken inferences, it seems to me that they deceive themselves if they think that, in following this procedure, they are keeping closer to reality than their bolder colleagues who are not afraid to generalize, for their procedure amounts to offering an interpretation even if it does not make the organizing concept explicit. And their reticence may well involve them in the consequence of not being intelligible to their readers, a situation which is apt not to trouble the true professional, but in my opinion definitely should.

I suggest that two conditions should govern our choice of colligating

---

[4] For these views see *Experience and its Modes* (Cambridge, 1933), pp. 102 ff., and especially Oakeshott's later essay 'The Activity of being an Historian', reprinted in *Rationalism in Politics* (London, 1962), pp. 137–67.

[5] For a fuller treatment of the points discussed here see my essay 'The Practical and the Historical Past' in *Politics and Experience*, ed. Preston King and B. C. Parekh (Cambridge, 1968), pp. 5–18.

concepts in history. They must, in the first place, clearly be well founded as opposed to arbitrary, tailored to fit the facts rather than a strait-jacket into which the facts must be forced whatever their particular nature. The general test of whether this condition is satisfied lies in the evidence with which statements embodying such concepts are supported. For every authentic statement containing a colligatory concept it must be possible to produce a series of relevant and connected lower-level statements which count in its favour, are framed, by comparison, in untheoretical terms, and about whose acceptability historians are generally agreed; at the same time there must be no generally accepted statements at this level which positively count against the colligating statement. Less technically, we can say that the authenticity of a colliga-tory concept will be shown in the success which those who appeal to it have in covering detail. If there are details which will not fit, or will only fit awkwardly, into an interpretative scheme, it is obvious that the scheme is defective. For after all the pretence here is to offer a general picture of the facts; such a picture must clearly be useless if it does not cover the agreed data.

There are, however, certain caveats which need to be entered here. It should be noticed first that the question whether or not the detailed facts support a particular historical interpretation is one which can be decided only in a rough sort of way. The high-level statements here purport to summarize the low-level statements, but the latter certainly do not entail the former. A historian who refused to accept a descrip-tion of the first half of the nineteenth century in Britain as an age of improvement, to use Asa Briggs's title, would be entirely within his rights, though he might well find that, if he persisted in pressing his disagreement no matter how much evidence was produced in the des-cription's support, he was forfeiting the sympathy of his colleagues. It is important to observe in this connection that historians have working criteria of when to accept such descriptions; they know in practice how to handle colligatory concepts, even if they would find it difficult to make explicit the criteria they use. But there is another consideration which should not be neglected here. The description of an age which is given by a generalizing historian is always more or less schematic; it is achieved, if you like, always at the risk of a certain distortion of the facts. The reason for this is the same as that which makes it impossible for a map to cover more than the salient features of a piece of country-side: if it included everything, it would be no guide to the general shape of the terrain. What we want from the generalizing historian is informa-tion about what was essentially going on, and this means that he has to be prepared to stand back from the detailed events and even, in extreme cases, to turn a blind eye to contrary evidence. Again, of course, this is a matter of degree: there is a point beyond which no self-respecting historian could persist with his interpretation in the face of unassimilated data. But it is something which, all the same, needs to be insisted on and is indeed subscribed to by historians in practice. You cannot discredit the use of terms like 'the Renaissance' or 'the Enlightenment' by pointing to the existence of a few persons in the first period who retained the full medieval outlook or a few individuals in the second who had no use for the claims of reason. To this extent the formal requirements laid down in the previous paragraph need to be relaxed: the use of a colligatory concept is not invalidated if we can point to *some* facts it does not cover. They must be prominent or salient or significant facts.

I pass now to the second criterion which is employed in the choice of colligatory concepts. As well as asking if they fit the facts we can also ask if they illuminate the facts. And here what we have primarily in mind is the extent to which their use makes the past real and intelligible *to us*. The object of the whole colligatory exercise is to increase understanding, and it is obvious that the understanding in question is that of the modern student of history who looks back on a given set of events from the standpoint of the present. It is not just a regrettable fact that such a student tends to read past happenings in the terms of present-day experience; the truth is that he has to do so. For in what other terms than those of the sophisticated thought of the present can the historian frame these high-level descriptions? If the reply is made that he must confine himself to ideas which were present in the minds of the individual with whom he is concerned, we must insist that this requirement is both impossibly restrictive in practice and quite indefensible in theory. It is impossibly restrictive in practice because there are periods in which men had no explicit grasp of such simple ideas as 'government', 'sea power', 'economic structure': is the historian to be precluded from using terms of this sort when he offers a picture of such an age? And if it is said that he must show that men had thoughts which corresponded at least in a rudimentary way to the description given, the difficulty is to know how to apply this very unspecific prescription. It is, as I have already pointed out, entirely legitimate to demand that a high-level characterization of a historical period or movement be supported by lower-level statements framed in less theoretical terms. But such statements need only depict a state of affairs which *we* can properly describe in a certain way; whether or not anyone at the time would or could have employed the description is another matter. I am not, of course, denying that some large-scale historical descriptions do reflect the explicit thoughts of past persons, only saying that it is not necessary that they should. But I hold that the attempt to make out that they must in every case can be clearly seen to be faulty, if only because of the fact that contemporaries are often not in a position to say what is going on. The processes with which they are confronted are largely uncompleted, and for that reason it is hard to command a clear view of them. But this is just what the historian can do, as I argued before: he has the advantage of knowing not only what was happening but also what ensued, and this means that he can offer an altogether better-founded description. To insist that any such description must be such that men alive at the time could have understood it is to insist on an absurdity.

Needless to say, this is not intended as a defence of deliberate anachronism in history. To claim that we must describe the past in terms intelligible to the present is not to claim that *any* such terms can be made to apply. A Namier would, on my view, be entirely justified in refusing to allow the propriety of a description of eighteenth-century politics in terms of party rivalries, provided he could show that there was nothing in the eighteenth-century scene which *we* should describe as a political party. But nothing general follows from this and similar cases. The fact that a type of concept is sometimes, or even often, misused is not enough to show that it must always be misused. No doubt it is true that popular historians are prone to sum their facts dubiously or at best superficially, but the remedy for this is not to refuse to sum them altogether. The historian who thinks he can escape the hazards of large-scale generalizing history by confining himself to the investigation of particular facts and detailed problems about them deceives himself. You cannot, in the first place, give a small-scale description or analysis of a set of events without placing it in a wider setting, the general shape of which is taken as clear. Nor is it true, as this suggestion assumes, that there is an ideal distance from which the historian can record events without compromising their innocence. In one sense, historical facts can never speak for themselves: no statement of fact, however simple, is entirely independent of the outlook of the historian and his readers. But if it is claimed that there is another sense in which, in sophisticated modern history, the facts are left to speak for themselves, the comment must be that they are made to do so, by skilful selection and juxtaposition on the part of the historian.

The points I have been trying to urge are simple and, I believe, really quite uncontroversial. I hold that the historian has a double task: he must do justice to his evidence and at the same time must do his duty by his readers. The latter want from him not just a bare recital of what happened, but also guidance on what it amounted to, and this guidance must be given in terms they can understand. Because of the difficulty in performing both parts of the task there is a constant temptation for the historian to skimp one part or the other: he may make his history bright at the expense of being accurate, or he may stay so close to the evidence that he fails altogether to make it intelligible. In the latter case he is likely to console himself with the thought that making the shape of events clear is really a job for the vulgarizer: it is not something which need trouble the true scholar when he writes an article for a learned periodical or composes a monograph. I hope I have at least shown the falsity of this view. If there were no general history, there could be no monograph history. And if historians refuse to say what was going on generally, they make it impossible to ask any questions about history whatsoever.

The final problem I wish to raise is whether there is any limitation on the range of concepts which can serve to colligate events in history; an alternative way of putting it would be to ask if the concepts which actually fulfil this role have any marked logical pecularities. Let me begin the discussion of this point by listing a few concepts which are used for the purposes of which I am speaking: a new renaissance, the emergence of a fresh social hierarchy, a widespread shift of allegiance, a continuing crisis of confidence, a prolonged struggle for political independence, a revolution made by intellectuals will perhaps suffice in this connection. The historian employs these concepts in a concrete way: he is apt to speak of 'the Greek Age of Enlightenment' or 'the rise of the bourgeoisie' instead of using the abstract form, but that is not surprising in view of his concern with the characterization of individual happenings. The logical status of such phrases is that of definite descriptions: they pick out what is taken to be a single subject of discourse and predicate something of it. I incline to think that, in the case of the descriptions I have in mind, there are peculiarities both in what is picked out and in what is said about it.

It seems clear in the first place that the subjects of discourse which are designated by colligating phrases are one and all complex particulars: each of them has a temporal and also a spatial spread ('the rise of the bourgeoisie in western Europe'). But there are many kinds of complex particular which are of no interest for purposes of historical interpretation: a weather system would supply one example, the fourteenth hole on a golf course another. The peculiarity of the complex particulars in which historians are above all interested is that they themselves have a history. Broadly, they can be characterized as complex states of affairs which are systematically changing as a result of human effort or lack of effort. The ultimate subjects concerned are doubtless individual men and women, but the historian's primary attention is not so much on these as on the patterns and relationships into which they enter as a result of their social environment and mutual interaction, such patterns as constitute the class structure of a society, its economic organization, and cultural life. It is characteristic of these complex particulars that they are not static, but are rather in process of continuous development or decay. Nor is the change here involved the exclusive product of natural forces, though it can, of course, be influenced by such factors; it also comes about because of what men do or fail to do, particularly men acting in a social capacity. And this feature, as I indicated earlier, has a close bearing on our belief that in cases like this we are dealing with unitary processes rather than aggregates of externally connected events. The presence here of a continuing theme in diverse material is to be explained, at bottom, by the fact that men have ideas in common and pursue long-term aims, the realization of which demands different actions in different circumstances. In ideal cases we can see that the different parts of such a development must be internally related, since they are steps in the realization of a single purpose or goal. And though the processes with which historians are concerned are only exceptionally as close-knit as this, we find in all of them features which answer in some degree to this pattern. We find a set of events which can be intelligibly treated as the vicissitudes of a single subject, even though it is patently clear that such a subject cannot act in isolation from the rest of the historical world.

If this argument is correct, it seems to me that the right kind of concept to use for colligatory purposes in history is the Hegelian concrete universal. Hegel contrasted the 'concrete' with the 'abstract' universal by saying that, whereas the latter served to distinguish merely general features of things, the former had the advantage of enabling us to 'think the individual'. His claim was obscure and dubious, both because of the implied suggestion that there is something unsatisfactory about thinking in general terms (the term 'abstract' here was clearly pejorative), and because not enough attention was given to specify *what* individuals could be thought by means of the concrete universal. It is surely obvious that the concrete universal, which is the thought of something as a unity in diversity, is of no relevance to many things which can be described as individual because they are singular subjects of predicates, for example this piece of paper. It is obvious again that its value is, to say the least, questionable when we are dealing with individuals which are complex but mechanically constituted, like a chemical reaction. But things begin to look entirely different when we turn to the individuals with which historians are most typically concerned: persons, nations, institutions, movements, processes. Here the formula 'unity in diversity' is immediately applicable; when we examine a revolution or the growth or decline of an institution it is clear that we are concerned with a central subject possessing something like a life of its own, a life expressed in phenomena which are diverse but recognizably related, and in which the same themes keep recurring though never in a simply repeated form. That there are individuals of this kind in the universe, and that the human mind has the means to pick them out and grasp them each as a unity in diversity, do not seem to me matters for dispute. Hegel was certainly not wrong to insist on them; his mistake, if he made one, was only in pushing them too hard. He wanted to proceed from the obvious, though unappreciated, point that there is a sphere for the proper application of the concrete universal to the far bolder thesis that the whole universe must be seen in this way, and he thought it necessary to denigrate all other conceptual mechanisms in order to establish this point of view. I do not see myself that he could possibly have been right in the second of these steps, for ability to operate with ordinary ('abstract') universals appears to be a necessary condition of ability to operate with concrete universals: I must be able to pick out and characterize particulars as such if I am to pick out and characterize the special sort of complex particular to which the concrete universal is appropriate. But fortunately we have no need to prove conclusions on these difficult logical and metaphysical issues in order to show the importance of the concrete universal for historians. It would be absurd to suggest that they think in these terms alone. But it would be equally absurd to deny that they do think in these terms, above all when they are engaged in the colligatory activities which have been the subject of this paper.

VIII

THE OBJECTIVITY OF HISTORY

JOHN PASSMORE

'THERE'S one thing certain,' said a historian of my acquaintance when he heard the title of this paper, 'that's a problem which would never perturb a working-historian.' He was wrong: a working-historian first drew it to my attention; and in one form or another it raises its head whenever historians discuss the nature of their own inquiries. Yet in a way he was right. His mind had turned to the controversies of epistemologists, controversies about 'the possibility of knowledge'; historians, he rightly felt, do not trouble their heads about such matters.

When, indeed, the historian asks whether history can be objective, he is not suffering from a generalized, or epistemological, scepticism. That some forms of inquiry—he would instance physics—can be objectively conducted, he does not doubt; the only question, for him, is whether this is true of history. One cannot allay his qualms, therefore, as Mr. Christopher Blake has recently suggested in *Mind* ('Can History be Objective?', January 1955), by an appeal to 'the principle of non-vacuous contrast'. This principle would forbid us to deny that history is objective unless some forms of inquiry are objective, but the distinction between objective and non-objective need not be exhibited within history itself.

A striking feature of philosophical words, however, is that it is very easy to fall into the trap of so defining them as to make them vacuous in either of two directions: they may become vacuous through applying to nothing at all, or through applying to everything, thereby losing their usefulness as modes of distinguishing. Thus, for example, some philosophers have defined 'present' so rigidly that it would never be proper to say of anything that it is 'present', others so loosely that the present swallows up both the past and the future. Similar considerations apply to 'objectivity'.

Consider the following arguments, the first constructed but by no means, I think, implausible, the second a quotation from an article by A. J. P. Taylor (*The Times Literary Supplement*, 6 January 1956), intended to disprove the objectivity of history. *Argument One:* 'Of course

From *Philosophy*, 33, 125 (1958), 97–111. Reprinted by permission of the author and The Royal Institute of Philosophy.

history is objective: no one really doubts such facts as that Magna Charta was signed in 1215.' *Argument Two:* 'Historians seek to be detached, impassionate, impartial. In fact, however, no historian starts out with his mind a blank, to be gradually filled by the evidence.'

Now if an inquiry is objectively conducted provided only that the inquirer sometimes asserts true propositions, then every inquiry is objective; the most arbitrary of partisans will tell the truth sometimes, if only by accident. On the other side, if only those inquiries are objective in which the inquirer begins with a blank mind, then no inquiry whatsoever is objective. By the time we begin to inquire we already, and inevitably, have beliefs, expectations, interests. What Hegel says of the historian—'Even the average and mediocre historian who perhaps believes and pretends that he is merely receptive, merely surrendering to the data, is not passive in his thinking'—applies to all scientists. Not even the worst of them, the dreariest laboratory drudge, is objective—in Taylor's sense of the word. Thus on *Argument One* objectivity no longer discriminates; on *Argument Two* it no longer applies. Yet so treacherous is the ground on which we are now standing that neither of these arguments is wholly outrageous. Each has a certain contact with quite ordinary ways of using the word 'objective'.

Since it is my object to compare and contrast history with other forms of inquiry, I shall dismiss out of hand all proposed criteria of objectivity which would make it vacuous. But even then the range of possibilities is considerable; and we have no option but to canvass them in turn. 'Is history objective?' is a question to which one can only give the not very satisfactory answer 'It all depends on how high you set your standards.'

Criterion One (the Cartesian or mathematico-deductive): *An objective inquiry either (a) deduces its conclusions from self-evident axioms or (b) unfolds them from essences or definitions.*

It has sometimes been held, as by the Hegelians, that history consists in the gradual revelation of a plan, or an Idea; on this view, it might seem, the historian could satisfy the Cartesian criterion. But the conception of a plan, as Hegel explicitly says, emerges within a philosophy of history, in which history is made the starting-point for philosophical reflection. It cannot be so used as to obviate the need for historical investigation, enabling it to be replaced by logical analysis. 'History itself', writes Hegel in his *Lectures on the Philosophy of History*, 'must be taken as it is; we have to proceed historically, empirically ... only the study of world history can show that it has proceeded rationally.' Hegel's most distinguished historical disciple, Ranke, sought his inspiration in the archives of Venice; if he was convinced that it was 'the hand of God' which he there sought to disclose, the fact remains that history disclosed God, not God history.

We can safely conclude, then, that if the 'objectivity' of a form of inquiry depends upon the possibility of deducing its content *a priori*, history must abandon all claims to objectivity. In this respect, however, it is in excellent company: company which includes at least all that scientific activity which Mr. Toulmin describes, interestingly enough from our present point of view, as 'natural history'.

Criterion Two (Mach's criterion): *An objective inquiry is one which begins from data which are literally such, i.e. which nakedly confront us.*

This ideal at once stirred the ambitions and disturbed the dreams of nineteenth-century historians. Events flow around us: why should we not, by restricting ourselves to their description, achieve a history which is barely, but truly, a record?

We might assail this ideal on purely epistemological grounds; we might argue that there are no 'pure data' in the Machian sense of that phrase. But we should not, by so doing, seriously perturb the positivistically minded historian. The philosophical difficulty in nominating data which are strictly such has never interested the historian; he leaves anxiety on that point, we might say, to the physicist. For him it is enough if his 'data' are equal in status to the observations and experiments of the natural scientists; quite sensibly, he feels that if their work is not objective, the word ceases to have any methodological significance. His ideal-in-theory may be a science composed out of Machian data; his ideal-in-practice, the ideal to which he hopes to conform or despairs of realizing, transforms 'bare data' into observations, with no niggardliness, even then, in the use of the word 'observation'.

Thus he is not made uneasy by the objection that since the events which concern him are *past*, they cannot be data, but must always be inferences or reconstructions. For since the simplest of experiments and observations takes time, the restriction of 'data' to the 'immediately present'—presuming one can make some sense of that phrase—would carry with it the consequence that science knows nothing of data, either. And the historian's ideal, as we said, is natural science, not an epistemologist's Utopia.

For that reason, another objection has been taken more seriously. The natural scientist, it is argued, can always pass beyond the recorded facts to the facts themselves, and this direct reference to the facts is the essence of objectivity; the scientist confronts the world as it nakedly is, whereas the historian sees it, always, through the medium of someone else's testimony—a testimony he can never by the nature of the case penetrate beyond, because the events the testimony describes are gone for ever. If a scientist doubts the testimony of some other scientist that when hydrochloric acid is poured on to zinc, hydrogen is produced, he can repeat the experiment for himself; if a historian doubts Ben Jonson's testimony about Shakespeare's character, he has no way of examining that character for himself—the most he can do is to set Jonson's testimony against somebody else's. Thus the historian cannot hope to achieve objectivity.

Criterion Three: An objective inquiry is a direct examination of the world which does not rely upon testimony.

One may note, in the first place, that there is implicit in this way of looking at the matter a curious kind of methodological solipsism. The contrast 'other people's testimony'—'the facts' presumes that what *we* observe is a fact, whereas the best that other people can do is to 'express an opinion'. It is perhaps worth remembering that what *we* call 'our observations' are from the point of view of other people 'our testimony'.

Even historians are not exempt from a vulgar preference for what 'they can see with their own eyes'. Sir Henry Lambert, for example, suggests in his *The Nature of History* that the evidence that the Jameson raid took place is superior to the evidence that Napoleon was defeated at the Battle of Waterloo, because there are still people alive who took part in Jameson's raid. This, it seems to me, is an obvious error: the historian is in a much better position to know that Napoleon was defeated at Waterloo than any participant in the battle could be. He can take a wider view of the situation than is accessible to any participant. Furthermore, if men are sometimes deceived by testimony, they are no less capable of deceiving themselves in the actual situation; indeed, this, rather than the risk of lying, is the principal reason for regarding their testimony with suspicion. There are some points of detail, of course, on which the evidence of a participant—who could be cross-examined— might happen to be useful, but these are of minor consequence. Historians do not in fact go in search of 'old soldiers'.

A second point is that what is called 'observation' is always to a considerable measure dependent upon testimony; we never can put ourselves in such a situation that we are relying on nothing except 'pure observation'. If we say that we have 'observed for ourselves' that hydrochloric acid acts on zinc to produce hydrogen, this observation, of course, depends on someone's testimony that what confront us in this case are hydrochloric acid, zinc, and hydrogen; and if we wish to question any part of this testimony, we can do so only by depending upon some other testimony. So there can be nothing 'non-objective' about making use of testimony—unless 'objective' is vacuous—although this does not mean, of course, that any *particular* testimony is exempt from critical examination.

A third point is that considerable areas of physical science, in their reliance upon testimony, are in exactly the same position as history. Astronomy and seismology will serve as examples. One might, however, argue thus: the testimony on which the scientist has to rely is the careful recording of a fact by a trained observer; the historian, on the other hand, begins with chronicles, i.e. with testimonies composed by somebody who had an axe to grind. 'The so-called "sources" of history', wrote Popper in *The Open Society*, 'only record such facts as appeared sufficiently interesting to record, so that sources will contain only facts that fit in with a preconceived theory.'

Now, of course, the historian does occasionally find himself in a situation in which he has no 'sources' at his disposal except chronicles or, in the worst case, except *a* chronicle. But even then the historian is not quite at the mercy of the chronicler; he has his ways of testing chronicle accounts, and he can discover important facts from them which the chronicler had no intention whatever of recording. Medieval lives of saints, for example, are invaluable to the historian for the light they throw on the life of the Middle Ages, a life which the chronicler certainly would not have bothered deliberately to record. Furthermore, the greater part of the historian's sources, at least since Ranke's time, no chronicler compiled. They are, let us say, lists of tax-collections, drawn up by careful and certainly unimaginative bureaucrats for purposes quite temporary and official—not at all for the greater glory of the Emperor. Or the sources may be archaeological, rather than written documents—and rubbish-tips were not constructed to deceive the archaeologist. In short, the historian is not in the position of having to rely wholly on the propaganda of partisans.

It does not seem to me, then, that such a statement as 'Peter Pipkin paid twopence rent' need fear any comparison against 'this gas is oxygen'; or that it is possible to maintain, against history's objectivity, that it has no way of getting access to the facts. But one feature of the 'Peter Pipkin' statement deserves some little attention; it contains the phrase 'paid rent', and this is a phrase which refers to a set of rights and duties which are not precisely defined. Such 'open texture' is characteristic of statements of historians, and is sometimes alleged against history's objectivity.

Thus M. E. Hulme in his *History and its Neighbours* maintains that historical facts, in sharp distinction from scientific facts, are 'highly subjective'; taking as an example such a historical statement as that 'Lincoln is a great man' he argues that different historians have such different conceptions of 'a great man', that there is no objectivity in the fact the statement asserts. On this showing, I suppose, a science proceeds objectively *only if its statements contain no expressions except those which 'mean the same' for all observers*. Let us call this *Criterion Four*. In its extreme form, we can, I think, dismiss it on the familiar ground that it makes objectivity vacuous. As has emerged very clearly from the chequered history of logical positivism, no language can be so constructed as to make misunderstanding impossible—to guarantee that everyone will have the same conception of the terms it employs. But it is characteristic of science that it uses expressions we can bring to 'the test', i.e. allowing that there is always the risk of misunderstanding, we can be given explanations which will enable us to see how to criticize statements the scientist makes. History could certainly not be conducted objectively if its statements were not criticizable. And no doubt some historians make statements which are not in this sense 'objectively testable'—statements about 'the German spirit', for example. It will, I should say, be a sign of a good historian, that he avoids *ex parte* assertions like 'Lincoln was a great man', unless this is meant as a summary way of referring to a number of characteristics to which he has drawn attention; or that he makes it clear to us how, if at all, 'paying rent' differs from what we now understand by that same expression. So far as we can safely talk about degrees of open texture, I think we should have to admit that historical statements are 'more open' than chemical statements; but this does not entitle us to dismiss them as 'subjective'.

Suppose, however, it be admitted that there are historical facts; it it might still be argued that history is incurably subjective because it is bound to *impose a pattern* on the facts. History consists not in the simple accumulation of facts but in telling some sort of connected story, and the choice of the pattern, so it is sometimes suggested, can only be a matter of arbitrary decision. We can take the implicit criterion in two different ways: as maintaining that the pattern is an arbitrary *construction*, or that it is an arbitrary *selection*.

Criterion Five: An inquiry is objective only if it keeps to atomic facts.

At this point, the argument is reminiscent of the British empiricist view that all relations are 'the work of the mind'. We can see this in the well-known textbook by Langlois and Seignobos, *Introduction to the Study of History*. 'Historical construction', they write, 'has to be performed with an incoherent mass of minute facts, with detail-knowledge reduced as it were to a powder.' If history really begins with an 'incoherent mass', then certainly it would be reasonable to conclude that a coherent history book is a merely personal construction: there would be no way whatever of checking the pattern it suggests. But Langlois and Seignobos break down this simple-minded empiricism when they go on to suggest that there are links and connections between these atomic facts. This is clearly so: indeed, as we have already suggested, to say that someone is 'paying rent' is already to have become conscious of a system of rights and duties. Relations and connections are ingredient within the simplest facts; they are not somehow imposed upon facts which are quite devoid of them. There is no *a priori* reason, then, for maintaining that order is imposed, as distinct from discovered. Let us turn then, rather, to:

Criterion Six: An inquiry is objective only if it does not select from within its material.

Here, for example, is L. B. Namier in *Avenues of History*:

The function of the historian is akin to that of the painter and not of the photographic camera; to discover and set forth, to single out and stress that which is the nature of the thing and not to reproduce indiscriminately all that meets the eye.... History is therefore necessarily subjective and individual, conditioned by the interest and the vision of the historian.

The historian regards certain facts as unimportant and others as important; in thus distinguishing them, so Namier is saying, he demonstrates that his inquiries are rooted in subjectivity. This complaint goes back to Descartes:

Even the most accurate of histories [he wrote in his *Discourse on Method* (Pt. I)], if they do not wholly misrepresent or exaggerate the value of things in order to render them more worthy of being read, at last omit in them all the circumstances which are basest and least notable; and from that fact it follows that what is retained is not portrayed as it really is.

On the face of it, this is a queer criterion, because every form of inquiry is selective. Nothing is more irritating to the botanist or to the geologist than the presumption that every flower or every stone is of equal interest to him. A physicist is interested only in such physical operations as bear upon a problem he is investigating; a historian, similarly, will refer only to those facts which in some way bear upon the story he is telling.

The difficulty, however, lies in this conception of 'bearing upon'. We are accustomed, in discussing physical science, to talk in terms of problem, hyopthesis, testing; if anybody asks us which facts are relevant, we shall say 'those which assist us to test the hypothesis'. Of course, we can overlook, or can unscrupulously ignore, relevant facts, but at least we have a relatively secure—and objective—test of relevance. Is there a comparable test of relevance in history?

Our discussion of this point is complicated by the tendency of a great many historians to speak as if description as such, description for its own sake, were their object—as if an ideal history would be one which described every social action which has ever taken place on the surface of the earth. Recognizing that it is not their object to discover general laws, and anxious, not unnaturally, to distinguish their work from that of the 'interpreters' or 'philosophers' of history, historians have concluded that their attention must be directed towards the *complete* description, in all its particularity, of a world which interests the sociologist, by comparison, only as exhibiting this or that social law. Then, since from this point of view one fact is as good as another, the historian lies open to the charge that the selectivity which is forced upon him is purely arbitrary; he has left himself with no way of distinguishing between what is important and what is unimportant, except in terms of arbitrary preference.

Historians write books, for example, with what seems to me to be preposterous titles—titles like *The History of England*. Then the critics complain: 'He says he is writing about the history of England, and yet he doesn't mention the Romantic Revival, or the institution of joint-stock companies, or the invention of the triple-expansion engine, or the publication of Newton's *Principia*.' And they allege these omissions as proof that the historian has a prejudice against literature, or against commerce, or science, or whatever else he fails to discuss. Since no historian can discuss everything, it is an easy step to the conclusion that history is irredeemably subjective.

The fact of the matter is that there is no such subject as *The History of England*: a book which purports to be a history of England is either a collection of fragments—like Trevelyan's *Social History* which, to borrow a metaphor from Butterfield, is a set of lantern-slides, not a moving picture—or else it tacitly confines itself to a more specific problem, say to the changes which have taken place in the distribution of sovereignty. Very often, the historian does not seem to know *what* he is doing; his instinct leads him to select a single problem for consideration, and yet he feels uneasily that since he is purporting to write about the 'History of England', he ought to say something about its literature, or its social life. So a good book is marred by perfunctory and irrelevant chapters; and the historian cannot defend himself against the charge of arbitrariness, since his selection is not determined by the structure of the work he has undertaken. History books, indeed, ought commonly to be more, not less, selective than they are; greater selectivity would be a step *towards* objectivity, not away from it. What the historian calls 'general history' is a fraud—resting for its plausibility upon the metaphysical notion that there is something called 'the whole community' which moves in the manner of a single man.

If this point be granted, the question still arises: how exactly is the historian to choose among his material? The determining factor, I have suggested, must be the nature of the problem from which he sets out, just as it is in the case of the physical scientist. There is, however, an important difference in the character of his problems; historical problems are more like a certain type of problem in applied science than they are like problems in pure science. This is a consequence of the fact that the historian is interested in what happens in a particular situation on a particular occasion; just as an engineer may have to ask himself: 'why did *that* aeroplane collapse?' so the historian asks: 'why did *that* monarchy collapse?' Furthermore, again like the engineer, he may, usually does, solve his problem by constructing a model. The engineer builds a scale model of the aeroplane, places it in what he takes to have been its environment on the fatal occasion, and shows it collapsing. What he shows can also be said, but only in a highly detailed form; 'aeroplanes with that sort of structure, with that length of span, etc., will not stand up to a wind of more than a certain force'. Similarly the historian constructs a narrative model of, say, the collapse of the monarchy in France—one which draws attention, he hopes, to the strains and stresses which were relevant to that collapse; then we see its collapse taking place. He may comment as well, bidding us pay special attention to this or that point in his narrative, as an engineer may comment on what is happening to his model aeroplane or (more irritatingly) a novelist on the development of his characters. Yet, at least in an important type of historical writing, the model, the narrative, is the central thing; and a 'relevant' fact is one which can be employed in the construction of a model. 'The last word of the historian', as Butterfield writes in *The Whig Interpretation of History*, 'is not some firm general statement: it is a detailed piece of research.'

The engineer, however, can test his model: if he puts the right stress on it, it collapses. What, if anything, corresponds, in history, to this testing process? Unless there is *some* test, it would seem, one model is as good as another; history, therefore, would fail to satisfy a familiar criterion for objectivity. Here, it might be said, is the crux of the matter: let it be granted that there are historical facts, let it be granted that these facts are 'important' or 'unimportant' in relation to a particular reconstruction, even then history fails to be objective because there are no grounds on which one historical reconstruction can rationally be preferred to another.

Criterion Seven: A branch of inquiry is objective only if it contains a method of deciding between conflicting hypotheses.

That history does not satisfy this criterion is persuasively argued by Popper in *The Open Society*. Popper's criticism amounts to this: the hypotheses of history are *ad hoc* hypotheses, and we are free to choose as we like between *ad hoc* hypotheses. In contrast, the hypotheses of science are designed to apply to situations other than those which suggested them; in this way, the facts compel us to choose between them. We accept the hypothesis which leads us to expect, as other hypotheses do not, certain changes to take place which we then observe to occur. In history, however, all the relevant facts are already before us when we construct our hypothesis. Thus in choosing between hypotheses, the historian is not, as the physicist is, *constrained* by the facts, and in this difference the subjectivity of history resides.

In making this contrast, Popper is certainly exaggerating, I should say, the degree to which the physicist is constrained by his experiments. At the same time he is pointing to a real difficulty, even if it is perhaps not quite so serious as he imagines. I can illustrate the character of the difficulty most clearly by drawing on my own experience. Some little time ago, I wrote a book which purported to be an interpretation of Hume's philosophy.[1] One reviewer addressed me somewhat as follows: 'a possible interpretation, but other interpretations are equally possible'. How is one to reply? Obviously, this is a case where Popper's difficulty

---

[1] Of course, writing an interpretation is not the same thing as writing a history book. I do not wish at the moment to consider more precisely in what an interpretation consists. But the general point I am making, I trust, applies to history books and to interpretations alike.

is at its most acute. I can produce as evidence nothing except passages in Hume's writings; I can do nothing which corresponds to predicting an as yet unobserved colour-shift in Mercury.

Yet at the same time my inquiry, as I conduct it, is not *ad hoc*. Why? Because what happens is something like this: an interpretation is suggested by certain passages in Hume; that interpretation is then confirmed by passages I had not previously so much as noticed, which the proposed interpretation serves to illuminate. Or I discover that passages which I previously could not understand now make good sense.

In the completed book, however, I lay all my cards on the table. All the passages are quoted as if they had equal confirmatory value. That explains why the interpretation has an *ad hoc* air. If a reader is convinced by my interpretation, this will be because he has himself been puzzled by passages in Hume, and my interpretation solves his puzzle for him. If, on the other hand, he approaches the book 'cold', with no problems of his own, it is bound to strike him as being at best ingenious, at worst wholly factitious.

The historian is very often in the position in which I found myself; it is not surprising, therefore, that to the outside observer his work has an *ad hoc* appearance, even if, as I have suggested, that appearance is distinctly misleading. Not infrequently, however, his position is a good deal more favourable. A hypothesis occurs to him, say, about the origins of the Peasants' Revolt; that hypothesis, were it true, would involve a revision of accepted views about population shifts after the Black Death; some ingenious inquirer discovers a quite new way of determining just what did happen to the population during those crucial years. He may, for example, light on the accounts of a medieval quarry whose stones were used exclusively for tombstones. Thus the historian's hypothesis is confirmed, at what seemed to be the weakest point, by evidence which was not at the disposal of its framer. The most that can be said against history, then, is that there is *sometimes* no known way of deciding between conflicting historical hypotheses; this difficulty is not peculiar to history and ought not to be alleged against its objectivity.

The question we have been considering, it should be observed, is substantially identical with one that has a more familiar ring about it: whether, as it is said, history employs a 'correspondence' or a 'coherence' theory of truth. For this amounts to asking whether there is any test of a historical hypothesis except that it 'makes sense', i.e. that the historian has constructed a plausible story. I have been suggesting that there often is such a test: we can look and see whether the hypothesis 'corresponds with the facts'—if we like to use that mode of expression—as they are dug up by the archaeologist or by the archive-ransacker. In ordinary life, if somebody gives us an account of what happened in a committee, we may believe him without further investigation—because the story has a familiar pattern—or else we may look for independent evidence. If we were asked whether we employed a coherence or a correspondence criterion of truth, we should look blank, as would the historian, quite rightly. Like the rest of us, he has various ways of testing his hypotheses, or his reconstructions, none of them committing him to a 'criterion of truth'.

So far, then, we have been arguing that the historian proceeds scientifically—in the sense that he puts forward hypotheses, or constructs narratives, which are subject to the constraint of facts. Yet, we may wonder, if this is so, how does it happen that historical works differ so notably one from another? The extent of this difference is perhaps the most popular of all grounds for denying the objectivity of history. Let us set out the implicit criterion thus:

Criterion Eight: In objective inquiries, conclusions are reached which are universally acceptable.

Compare, for example, Mr. Walsh in his *Philosophy of History*:

The main presuppositions of the thinking of physics [he writes] are shared by all physicists and to think scientifically is to think in accordance with them. And this is at any rate one of the things that gives general validity to the conclusions of physicists; they do not depend to any important extent on the personal idiosyncrasies or private feelings of those who reach them, but are reached by a process in which complete abstraction is made from them. (P. 96.)

In this statement there is, I should say, more than a little exaggeration, a relic of the calculating-machine theory of science. The personal idiosyncrasies and private feelings of natural scientists are much more powerful agents both of discovery and of confusion than Mr. Walsh allows. One does not doff an idiosyncrasy as easily as one dons a white coat. But we could put his point thus (this might be described as the ideal-in-practice of 'absolute impartiality'): physical scientists have developed regular ways of tackling scientific problems and of testing proposed solutions to them. Not to accept these methods is to be 'prejudiced', 'biased', 'unscientific'.

One may well ask, however, whether the situation within history is so very different. There are generally accepted ways—involving a considerable level of expertness—of showing that a certain document (e.g.

the *Donation of Constantine*) is a forgery, or that another (e.g. the *Kings of Rome*) is unreliable. If a man would not now be described as a 'physicist' who made assertions about physical operations without supporting them by experiment or calculation, so equally a man is 'no historian' who writes about past events without paying any attention to documentary evidence.

So much must be said; and yet the cases of history and natural science do not seem to be quite parallel. One distinguishes a Roman Catholic from a Protestant historian whereas one does not refer to the religion of a physicist; it seems sensible to talk about the Marxist interpretation of the French Revolution but not about the Marxist interpretation of the Doppler effect. Nor does this difficulty entirely vanish even after a distinction is made between history and the interpretation of history; it is not just that the French Revolution is used by the Marxists to illustrate some particular sociological thesis and by other philosophers of history to illustrate a *different* thesis. The Marxist model of the events which took place will be incompatible at certain points with the model constructed by non-Marxists. Yet is not the same true, or could it not be true, of natural science? A footnote in Mr. Walsh's book gives us pause: 'I am assuming', he says, 'that "Soviet biology" and "bourgeois physics" are non-existent.' This we read with a smile of agreement, but should we? Imagine a situation in which there were Marxist universities in our midst, as there are Roman Catholic schools; the physics taught at these universities would certainly differ, in important respects, from the physics taught at non-Marxist universities. Would we then deny that physics is objective?

Furthermore, to make the contrast one between history and physics is certainly misleading; the identification of science and physics is a perpetual source of philosophical confusion. A peculiarity of physics —deriving not from its form as a branch of inquiry but from the nature of its subject-matter—is that the conclusions at which it arrives do not generally touch upon the non-theoretical interests of human beings. A physicist can come to recognize that Boyle's law is not universally applicable without concluding that he must abandon going to church, or voting Conservative, or acting despotically as a father. The situation is quite different in psychology and sociology, and is somewhat different even in biology. Let us suppose that Freud's argument in *Totem and Taboo* were scientifically impregnable; could we contemplate a situation in which it was accepted by Roman Catholics? There is an insignificant band of flat-earthers, a much larger group which refuses to accept the evolutionary theory of human origins—the difference is a matter of degree, only, if we pass on to psychology, to sociology, to history.

What ought to surprise and gratify us is the extent to which the spirit of objectivity has won its triumphs. Roman Catholic and Protestant accounts of the Reformation, considered as a story about social institutions, come more and more into conformity. If the test of objectivity is that there are regular ways of settling issues, by the use of which men of whatever party can be brought to see what actually happened, then I do not see how one can doubt the objectivity of history. But if we are satisfied with nothing less than the production of histories which all men the least rational will accept as final, then that would be a greater victory for the scientific spirit than we have any reason to expect. Such unanimity, however, is not to be found in any branch of human inquiry. Once again, if we press the criterion of objectivity too hard, it applies to no form of inquiry; slacken it slightly and history edges its way in with the rest.

One must emphasize, also, that very many of the differences which undoubtedly exist between, say, various histories of the French Revolution do not proceed from genuine differences of opinion, or oppositions in policy. The historian, I said, attempts to construct a narrative-model. Now for one thing there are models on different scales; the smaller the scale, the more we shall be told and the less we shall be shown. That is what makes school textbooks so impossibly dull and so misleading, too, in their judgements. As Hegel puts this point: 'A history of this kind ... must give up the individual presentation of reality, and abridge itself by means of abstraction....' In so doing, we may argue, it quite falsifies the character of historical inquiry. Textbooks in elementary science, however, are no less dull and no less misleading. Differences between history books derive in part from differences in the extent to which they simplify.

Secondly, although we talk happily enough about 'the French Revolution', or 'the English Civil War', obviously these descriptive phrases refer to extremely complex and diversified states of affairs. The 'French Revolution', for example, was at once the collapse of the monarchy and the collapse of the feudal economic system. The name 'French Revolution' is a convenient abbreviation for a complex of historical changes, any one of which can set for us a historical problem. Thus two history books, one of which emphasizes the importance, for any understanding of the French Revolution, of the separation between monarchy and people, and the other of which emphasizes the economic obstacles encountered by the rising bourgeoisie, need not really be in conflict with one another; each has as its subject a different aspect of the Revolution. Of course, if there were some single cause from which all the events of the French Revolution flowed, then certainly we should have to choose between the luxury of the court and the rise of the middle classes; we should have to say that one of these was the true cause and the other was not.

Professor Gallie has recently argued in *Mind* ('Explanations in History and the Genetic Sciences', April 1955) that the task of the historian is to draw attention to those *necessary* conditions which we might otherwise overlook, and that he quite misconceives the limits of his just ambitions if he tries to nominate *sufficient* conditions. This doctrine, for all its attractiveness, would be difficult to accept as it stands; for necessary conditions are endless—even necessary conditions we could easily overlook. It was a necessary condition of Gladstone's becoming Prime Minister that at the age of seven he took his mother's advice and changed his wet clothes; but scarcely a matter for the historian's consideration. What can, however, be said is that in the excitement of discovering a particular type of necessary condition, the historian is sometimes led into asserting that it is both necessary and sufficient—as happens also in a great many other cases, say in the germ theory of disease. Or again, a condition which is necessary and sufficient for the explanation of a certain phase, or a certain aspect, of a historical complex is wrongly supposed to be sufficient and necessary for other phases or other aspects, as if we could deduce from the economic origins of the French Revolution why the Goddess of Reason was worshipped. Once we recognize the complexity of historical changes, and the multitude of different problems they raise, we can hope to avoid the more gratuitous cases of this particular error.

One can understand, also, why each generation rewrites its history books; a point sometimes urged in proof of history's incurable subjectivity. The explanation, often enough, is that men come to be interested in quite new aspects of past events; we look differently at the French Revolution now we have experienced the Russian Revolution, with a new interest in the way in which it passed into a dictatorship. In that sense, all history is contemporary history: our contemporary interests determine what we select for consideration from the past—as, for example, the working out of a propositional calculus, or of a modal logic, may cause us to examine from a new point of view the medieval doctrine of 'consequences'. But nothing of importance about the nature and status of historical inquiry follows from this fact.

What is our final conclusion about the 'placing' of history among forms of human activity? Well, one can see why there have been arguments about its relation both to literature and to science. If we mean by 'science' the attempt to find out what really happens, then history is a science. It demands the same kind of dedication, the same ruthlessness, the same passion for exactness, as physics. That is all I have been trying to show. If, however, we mean by science the search for general theories, then history is not science; indeed, in so far as it tries to show us something through a particularized pattern of action, it stands closer to the novel and the drama than it does to physics. It differs from literature, however, in two important respects: human society, not individual entanglements, provides it with its themes—and, more important for our present purposes, it is both sensible and necessary to ask whether its narrative 'really happened like that'. It is *history*, neither literature nor science, but sharing some of the properties of both. Its very existence, indeed, helps to bring home to us the connection and the distinction between these two forms of human endeavour.

IX

HISTORICAL INEVITABILITY

SIR ISAIAH BERLIN

THE notion that history obeys law, whether natural or supernatural, that every event of human life is an element in a necessary pattern, has deep metaphysical origins: infatuation with the natural sciences feeds this stream, but is not its sole nor, indeed, its principal source. In the first place, there is the teleological outlook whose roots reach back to the beginnings of human thought. It occurs in many versions, but what is common to them all is the belief that men, and all living creatures and perhaps inanimate things as well, not merely are as they are, but have functions and pursue purposes. These purposes are either imposed upon them by a creator who has made every person and thing to serve each a specific goal; or else these purposes are not, indeed, imposed by a creator but are, as it were, internal to their possessors, so that every entity has a 'nature' and pursues a specific goal which is 'natural' to it, and the measure of its perfection consists in the degree to which it fulfils it. Evil, vice, imperfection, all the various forms of chaos and error, are, on this view, forms of frustration, impeded efforts to reach such goals, failures due either to misfortune which puts obstacles in the path of self-fulfilment, or to misdirected effort to fulfil some goal not 'natural' to the entity in question.

In this cosmology the world of men (and, in some versions, the entire universe) is a single all-inclusive hierarchy; so that to explain why each ingredient of it is as, and where, and when it is, and does what it does, is *eo ipso* to say what its goal is, how far it successfully fulfils it, and what are the relations of co-ordination and subordination between the goals of the various goal-pursuing entities in the harmonious pyramid which they collectively form. If this is a true picture of reality, then historical explanation, like every other form of explanation, must consist, above all, in the attribution to individuals, groups, nations, species, of their proper place in the universal pattern. To know the 'cosmic' place of a thing or a person is to say what it is and does, and at the same time why it should be and do as it is and does. Hence to be

From *Four Essays on Liberty* by Isaiah Berlin (London: Oxford University Press, 1969), pp. 51–81. Reprinted by permission of the publishers.

and to have value, to exist and to have a function (and to fulfil it less or more successfully) are one and the same. The pattern, and it alone, brings into being, and causes to pass away, and confers purpose, that is to say, value and meaning, on all there is. To understand is to perceive patterns. To offer historical explanations is not merely to describe a succession of events, but to make it intelligible; to make intelligible is to reveal the basic pattern; not one of several possible patterns, but the one unique plan which, by being as it is, fulfils only one particular purpose, and consequently is revealed as fitting in a specifiable fashion within the single 'cosmic' over-all schema which is the goal of the universe, the goal in virtue of which alone it is a universe at all, and not a chaos of unrelated bits and pieces. The more thoroughly the nature of this purpose is understood, and with it the patterns it entails in the various forms of human activity, the more explanatory or illuminating —the 'deeper'—the activity of the historian will be. Unless an event, or the character of an individual, or the activity of this or that institution or group or historical personage, is explained as a necessary consequence of its place in the pattern (and the larger, that is, the more comprehensive the schema, the more likely it is to be the true one), no explanation—and therefore no historical account—is being provided. The more inevitable an event or an action or a character can be exhibited as being, the better it has been understood, the profounder the researcher's insight, the nearer we are to the one embracing, ultimate truth.

This attitude is profoundly anti-empirical. We attribute purposes to all things and persons not because we have evidence for this hypothesis; for if there were a question of evidence for it, there could in principle be evidence against it; and then some things and events might turn out to have no purpose and therefore, in the sense used above, be incapable of being fitted into the pattern, that is, of being explained at all; but this cannot be, and is rejected in advance, *a priori*. We are plainly dealing not with an empirical theory but with a metaphysical attitude which takes for granted that to explain a thing—to describe it as it 'truly' is—even to define it more than verbally, that is, superficially—is to discover its purpose. Everything is in principle explicable, for everything has a purpose, although our minds may be too feeble or too distraught to discover in any given case what this purpose is. On such a view to say of things or persons that they exist is to say that they pursue goals; to say that they exist or are real, yet literally lack a purpose, whether imposed from outside or 'inherent' or 'innate', is to say something not false, but literally self-contradictory and therefore meaningless. Teleology is not a theory, or a hypothesis, but a category or a framework in terms of which everything is, or should be, conceived and described. The influence of this attitude on the writing of history from the epic of Gilgamesh to those enjoyable games of patience which Professor Arnold Toynbee plays with the past and future of mankind —and plays with exhilarating skill and imagination—is too familiar to need emphasis. It enters, however unconsciously, into the thought and language of those who speak of the 'rise' and 'fall' of states or movements or classes or individuals as if they obeyed some irresistible rhythm, a rising or falling wave of some cosmic river, an ebb or tide in human affairs, subject to natural or supernatural laws; as if discoverable regularities had been imposed on individuals or 'super-individuals' by a Manifest Destiny, as if the notion of life as a play were more than a vivid metaphor.[1] To those who use this figure history is a piece—or succession of pieces—comical or tragical, a libretto whose heroes and villains, winners and losers, speak their lines and suffer their fate in accordance with the text conceived in terms of them but not by them; for otherwise nothing could be rightly conceived as tragical or comical; no pattern—no rules—no explanation. Historians, journalists, ordinary men speak in these terms; they have become part and parcel of ordinary speech. Yet to take such metaphors and turns of phrase literally; to believe that such patterns are not invented but intuitively discovered or discerned, that they are not only some among many possible tunes which the same sounds can be made to yield to the

---

[1] I do not, of course, wish to imply that metaphors and figures of speech can be dispensed with in ordinary utterance, still less in the sciences; only that the danger of illicit 'reification'—the mistaking of words for things, metaphors for realities—is even greater in this sphere than is usually supposed. The most notorious cases are, of course, those of the State or the Nation, the quasi-personification of which has rightly made philosophers and even plain men uneasy or indignant for over a century. But many other words and usages offer similar dangers. Historical movements exist, and we must be allowed to call them so. Collective acts do occur; societies do rise, flourish, decay, die. Patterns, 'atmospheres', complex interrelationships of men or cultures are what they are, and cannot be analysed away into atomic constituents. Nevertheless, to take such expressions so literally that it becomes natural and normal to attribute to them causal properties, active powers, transcendent properties, demands for human sacrifice, is to be fatally deceived by myths. 'Rhythms' in history occur, but it is a sinister symptom of one's condition to speak of them as 'inexorable'. Cultures possess patterns, and ages spirits; but to explain human actions as their 'inevitable' consequences or expressions is to be a victim of misuse of words. There is no formula which guarantees a successful escape from either the Scylla of populating the world with imaginary powers and dominions, or the Charybdis of reducing everything to the verifiable behaviour of identifiable men and women in precisely denotable places and times. One can do no more than point to the existence of these perils; one must navigate between them as best one can.

musical ear, but are in some sense unique; to think that there exists *the* pattern, *the* basic rhythm of history—something which both creates and justifies all that there is—that is to take the game too seriously, to see in it a key to reality. Certainly it is to commit oneself to the view that the notion of individual responsibility is, 'in the end', an illusion. No effort, however ingenious, to reinterpret that much-tormented expression will, within a teleological system, restore its normal meaning to the notion of free choice. The puppets may be conscious and identify themselves happily with the inevitable process in which they play their parts; but it remains inevitable, and they remain marionettes.

Teleology is not, of course, the only metaphysics of history; side by side with it there has persisted a distinction of appearance and reality even more celebrated but of a somewhat different kind. For the teleological thinker all apparent disorder, inexplicable disaster, gratuitous suffering, unintelligible concatenations of random events, are due not to the nature of things but to our failure to discover their purpose. Everything that seems useless, discordant, mean, ugly, vicious, distorted, is needed, if we but knew it, for the harmony of the whole which only the Creator of the world, or the world itself (if it could become wholly aware of itself and its goals), can know. Total failure is excluded *a priori,* for at a 'deeper' level all processes will always be seen to culminate in success; and since there must always exist a level 'deeper' than that of any given insight, there is in principle no empirical test of what constitutes 'ultimate' success or failure. Teleology is a form of faith capable of neither confirmation nor refutation by any kind of experience; the notions of evidence, proof, probability, and so on, are wholly inapplicable to it.

But there is a second, no less time-honoured view according to which it is not goals, less or more dimly discerned, which explain and justify whatever happens, but a timeless, permanent, transcendent reality, 'above', or 'outside', or 'beyond'; which is as it is for ever, in perfect, inevitable, self-explaining harmony. Each element of it is necessitated to be what it is by its relations to the other elements and to the whole. If the world does not appear to manifest this, if we do not see actual events and persons as connected with each other by those relations of logical necessity which would make it inconceivable that anything could be other than it is, that is due solely to the failure of our own vision. We are blinded by ignorance, stupidity, passion, and the task of explanation in science or in history is the attempt to show the chaos of appearances as an imperfect reflection of the perfect order of reality, so that once more everything falls into its proper place. Explanation is the discovery of the 'underlying' pattern. The ideal is now not a distant prospect beckoning all things and persons towards self-realization, but a self-consistent, eternal, ultimate 'structure of reality', compresent 'timelessly', as it were, with the confused world of the senses which it casts as a distorted image or a feeble shadow, and of which it is at once the origin, the cause, the explanation, and the justification. The relation of this reality to the world of appearances forms the subject-matter of all the departments of true philosophy—of ethics, aesthetics, logic, of the philosophy of history and of law and of politics, according to the 'aspect' of the basic relation that is selected for attention. But under all its various names—form and matter, the one and the many, ends and means, subject and object, order and chaos, change and rest, the perfect and the imperfect, the natural and the artificial, nature and mind—the central issue, that of Reality and Appearance, remains one and the same. To understand truly is to understand it and it alone. It plays the part which the notion of function and purpose plays in teleology. It alone at once explains and justifies.

Finally there is the influence of the natural sciences. At first this seems a paradox: scientific method is surely the very negation of metaphysical speculation. But historically the one is closely interwoven with the other, and, in the field of which I speak, shows important affinities with it, namely, the notion that all that exists is necessarily an object in material nature, and therefore susceptible to explanation by scientific laws. If Newton was able in principle to explain every movement of every particular constituent of physical nature in terms of a small number of laws of great generality, is it not reasonable to suppose that psychological events, which constitute the conscious and unconscious lives of individuals, as well as social facts—the internal relationships and activities and 'experiences' of societies—could be explained by the use of similar methods? It is true that we seem to know a good deal less about the subject-matter of psychology and sociology than about the facts dealt with by physics or chemistry; but is there any objection in principle to the view that a sufficiently scrupulous and imaginative investigation of human beings might, one day, reveal laws capable of yielding predictions as powerful and as precise as those which are now possible in the natural sciences? If psychology and sociology ever attain to their proper stature—and why should they not?—we shall have laws enabling us, at least in theory (for it might still be difficult in practice), to predict (or reconstruct) every detail in the lives of every single human being in the future, present, and past. If this is (as surely it is) the theoretical ideal of such sciences as psychology, sociology, and anthropology, historical explanations will, if they are successful, simply consist in the application of the laws—the established hypotheses—of these sciences to specific individual situations. There will perhaps be 'pure' psychology, sociology, history, i.e. the principles themselves: and there will be their 'application': there will come into being social mathematics, social physics, social engineering, the 'physiology' of every feeling and attitude and inclination, as precise and powerful and useful as their originals in the natural sciences. And indeed this is the very phraseology and the ideal of eighteenth-century rationalists like d'Holbach and d'Alembert and Condorcet. The metaphysicians are victims of a delusion; nothing in nature is transcendent, nothing purposive; everything is measurable; the day will dawn when, in answer to all the painful problems now besetting us, we shall be able to say with Condorcet, 'Calculemus', and return the answers clearly, exactly, and conclusively.

What all these concepts—metaphysical and scientific alike—have in common (despite their even vaster differences) is the notion that to explain is to subsume under general formulae, to represent as examples of laws which cover an infinite number of instances; so that with knowledge of all the relevant laws, and of a sufficient range of relevant facts, it will be possible to tell not merely what happens, but also why; for, if the laws have been correctly established, to describe something is, in effect, to assert that it cannot happen otherwise. The question 'why?' for teleologists means 'in pursuit of what unalterable goal?'; for the non-teleological metaphysical 'realists' it means 'determined unalterably by what ultimate pattern?'; and for the upholders of the Comtean ideals of social statics and dynamics it means 'resulting from what causes?'—actual causes which are as they are, whether they might have been otherwise or not. The inevitability of historical processes, of trends, of 'rises' and 'falls', is merely *de facto* for those who believe that the universe obeys only 'natural laws' which make it what it is; it is *de jure* as well—the justification as well as the explanation—for those who see such uniformity as not merely something given, brute fact, something unchangeable and unquestionable, but as patterns, plans, purposes, ideals, as thoughts in the mind of a rational Deity or Universal Reason, as goals, as aesthetic, self-fulfilling wholes, as metaphysical rationales, theological other-worldly justifications, as theodicies, which satisfy the craving to know not merely why the world exists, but why it is worthy of existence; and why it is this particular world that exists, rather than some other, or no world at all; the solution being provided in terms of values which are either somehow 'embedded' in the facts themselves or 'determine' them from some 'transcendent' height or depth. All these theories are, in one sense or another, forms of determinism, whether they be theological, metaphysical, mechanistic, religious, aesthetic, or scientific. And one common characteristic of all such outlooks is the implication that the individual's freedom of choice (at any rate here, below) is ultimately an illusion, that the notion that human beings could have chosen otherwise than they did usually rests upon ignorance of facts; with the consequence that any assertion that they should have acted thus or thus, might have avoided this or that, and deserve (and not merely elicit or respond to) praise or blame, approval or condemnation, rests upon the presupposition that some area, at any rate, of their lives is not totally determined by laws, whether metaphysical or theological or expressing the generalized probabilities of the sciences. And this assumption, it is then maintained, is patently false. The advance of knowledge constantly brings new areas of experience under the sway of laws which make systematic inference and prediction possible. Hence we can, if we seek to be rational, praise and condemn, warn and encourage, advocate justice or self-interest, forgive, condone, make resolutions, issue orders, feel justified remorse, only to the degree to which we remain ignorant of the true nature of the world. The more we know, the farther the area of human freedom, and consequently of responsibility, is narrowed. For the omniscient being, who sees why nothing can be otherwise than as it is, the notions of responsibility or guilt, of right and wrong, are necessarily empty; they are a mere measure of ignorance, of adolescent illusion; and the perception of this is the first sign of moral and intellectual maturity.

This doctrine has taken several forms. There are those who believe that moral judgements are groundless because we know too much, and there are those who believe that they are unjustified because we know too little. And again, among the former there are those whose determinism is optimistic and benevolent, and those whose determinism is pessimistic, or else confident of a happy ending yet at the same time indignantly or sardonically malevolent. Some look to history for salvation; others for justice; for vengeance; for annihilation. Among the optimistic are the confident rationalists, in particular the heralds and prophets (from Bacon to modern social theorists) of the natural sciences and of material progress, who maintain that vice and suffering are in the end always the product of ignorance. The foundation of their faith is the conviction that it is possible to find out what all men at all times truly want; and also what they can do and what is for ever beyond their power; and, in the light of this, to invent, discover, and adapt means to realizable ends. Weakness and misery, folly and vice, moral and intellectual defects are due to maladjustment. To understand the nature of things is (at the very least) to know what you (and others who, if they are human, will be like you) truly want, and how to get it. All that is bad is due to ignorance of ends or of means; to attain to knowledge of both is the purpose and function of the sciences. The sciences will advance; true ends as well as efficient means will be discovered; knowledge will increase, men will know more, and therefore be wiser and better and happier. Condorcet, whose *Esquisse* is the simplest and most moving statement of this belief, has no doubt that happiness, scientific knowledge, virtue, and liberty are bound as 'by an indissoluble chain', while stupidity, vice, injustice, and unhappiness are forms of a disease which the advance of science will eliminate for ever; for we are made what we are by natural causes; and when we understand them, this alone will suffice to bring us into harmony with 'Nature'. Praise and blame are functions of ignorance; we are what we are, like stones and trees, like bees and beavers, and if it is irrational to blame or demand justice from things or animals, climates or soils or wild beasts when they cause us pain, it is no less irrational to blame the no less determined characters or acts of men. We can regret—and deplore and expose—the depth of human cruelty, injustice, and stupidity, and comfort ourselves with the certainty that with the rapid progress of our new empirical knowledge this will soon pass away like an evil dream; for progress and education, if not inevitable, are at any rate highly probable. The belief in the possibility (or probability) of happiness as the product of rational organization unites all the benevolent sages of modern times, from the metaphysicians of the Italian Renaissance to the evolutionary thinkers of the German *Aufklärung*, from the radicals and utilitarians of pre-revolutionary France to the science-worshipping visionaries of the nineteenth and twentieth centuries. It is the heart of all the utopias from Bacon and Campanella, to Lessing and Condorcet, Saint-Simon and Cabet, Fourier and Owen, culminating in the bureaucratic fantasies of Auguste Comte, with his fanatically tidy world of human beings joyfully engaged in fulfilling their functions, each within his own rigorously defined province, in the rationally ordered, totally unalterable hierarchy of the perfect society. These are the benevolent humanitarian prophets—our own age has known not a few of them, from Jules Verne and H. G. Wells and Anatole France and Bernard Shaw to their unnumbered American disciples—generously disposed towards all mankind, genuinely seeking to rescue every living being from its burden of ignorance, sorrow, poverty, and humiliating dependence on others.

The other variant of this attitude is a good deal less amiable in tone and in feeling. When Hegel, and after him Marx, describe historical processes, they too assume that human beings and their societies are part and parcel of a wider nature, which Hegel regards as spiritual, and Marx as material, in character. Great social forces are at work of which only the acutest and most gifted individuals are ever aware; the ordinary run of men are blind in varying degrees to that which truly shapes their lives, worship fetishes and invent childish mythologies, which they dignify with the title of views or theories in order to explain the world in which they live. From time to time the real forces—impersonal and irresistible—which truly govern the world develop to a point where a new historical advance is 'due'. Then (as both Hegel and Marx notoriously believed) the crucial moments of advance are reached; these take the form of violent, cataclysmic leaps, destructive revolutions which, often with fire and sword, establish a new order upon the ruins of the old. Inevitably, the foolish, obsolete, purblind, home-made philosophies of the denizens of the old establishment are knocked over and swept away together with their possessors. For Hegel, and for a good many others, though by no means all, among the philosophers and poets of the Romantic movement, history is a perpetual struggle of vast spiritual forces embodied now in institutions—churches, races, civilizations, empires, national states—now in individuals of more than human stature—'world-historical figures'—of bold and ruthless genius, towering over, and contemptuous of, their puny contemporaries. For Marx, the struggle is a fight between socially conditioned, organized groups—classes shaped by the struggle for subsistence and survival and consequently for the control of power. There is a sardonic note (inaudible only to their most benevolent and single-hearted followers) in the words of both these thinkers as they contemplate the discomfiture and destruction of the philistines, the ordinary men and women caught in one of the decisive moments of history. Both Hegel and Marx conjure up an image of peaceful and foolish human beings, largely unaware of the part they play in history, building their homes, with touching hope and simplicity, upon the green slopes of what seems to them a peaceful mountain side, trusting in the permanence of their particular way of life, their own economic, social, and political order, treating their own values as if they were eternal standards, living, working, fighting without any awareness of the cosmic processes of which their lives are but a passing stage. But the mountain is no ordinary mountain; it is a volcano; and when (as the philosopher always knew that it would) the inevitable eruption comes, their homes and their elaborately tended institutions and their ideals and their ways of life and values will be blown out of existence in the cataclysm which marks the leap from the 'lower' to a 'higher' stage. When this point is reached, the two great prophets of destruction are in their element; they enter into their inheritance; they survey the conflagration with a defiant, almost Byronic, irony and disdain. To be wise is to understand the direction in which the world is inexorably moving, to identify oneself with the rising power which ushers in the new world. Marx—and it is part of his attraction to those of a similar emotional cast—identifies himself exultantly, in his way no less passionately than Nietzsche or Bakunin, with the great force which in its very destructiveness is creative, and is greeted with bewilderment and horror only by those whose values are hopelessly subjective, who listen to their consciences, their feelings, or to what their nurses or teachers tell them, without realizing the glories of life in a world which moves from explosion to explosion to fulfil the great cosmic design. When history takes her revenge—and every *enragé* prophet in the nineteenth century looks to her to avenge him against those he hates most—the mean, pathetic, ludicrous, stifling human ant-hills will be justly pulverized; justly, because what is just and unjust, good and bad, is determined by the goal towards which all creation is tending. Whatever is on the side of victorious reason is just and wise; whatever is on the other side, on the side of the world that is doomed to destruction by the working of the forces of reason, is rightly called foolish, ignorant, subjective, arbitrary, blind; and, if it goes so far as to try to resist the forces that are destined to supplant it, then it—that is to say, the fools and knaves and mediocrities who constitute it—is rightly called retrograde, wicked, obscurantist, perversely hostile to the deepest interests of mankind.

Different though the tone of these forms of determinism may be—whether scientific, humanitarian, and optimistic, or furious, apocalyptic, and exultant—they agree in this: that the world has a direction and is governed by laws, and that the direction and the laws can in some degree be discovered by employing the proper techniques of investigation: and moreover that the working of these laws can only be grasped by those who realize that the lives, characters, and acts of individuals, both mental and physical, are governed by the larger 'wholes' to which they belong, and that it is the independent evolution of these 'wholes' that constitutes the so-called 'forces' in terms of whose direction truly 'scientific' (or 'philosophic') history must be formulated. To find the explanation of why given individuals, or groups of them, act or think or feel in one way rather than another, one must first seek to understand the structure, the state of development and the direction of such 'wholes', as for example, the social, economic, political, religious institutions to which such individuals belong; once that is known, the behaviour of the individuals (or the most characteristic among them) should become almost logically deducible, and does not constitute a separate problem. Ideas about the identity of these large entities or forces, and their functions, differ from theorist to theorist. Race, colour, church, nation, class; climate, irrigation, technology, geo-political situation; civilization, social structure, the Human Spirit, the Collective Unconscious, to take some of these concepts at random, have all played their parts in theologico-historical systems as the protagonists upon the stage of history. They are represented as the real forces of which individuals are ingredients, at once constitutive, and the most articulate expressions, of this or that phase of them. Those who are more clearly and deeply aware than others of the part which they play, whether willingly or not, to that degree play it more boldly and effectively; these are the natural leaders. Others, led by their own petty personal concerns into ignoring or forgetting that they are parts of a continuous or convulsive pattern of change, are deluded into assuming that (or, at any rate, into acting as if) they and their fellows are stabilized at some fixed level for ever.

What the variants of either of these attitudes entail, like all forms of genuine determinism, is the elimination of the notion of individual responsibility. It is, after all, natural enough for men, whether for practical reasons or because they are given to reflection, to ask who or what is responsible for this or that state of affairs which they view with satisfaction or anxiety, enthusiasm or horror. If the history of the world is due to the operation of identifiable forces other than, and little affected by, free human wills and free choices (whether these occur or not), then the proper explanation of what happens must be given in terms of the evolution of such forces. And there is then a tendency to say that not individuals, but these larger entities, are ultimately 'responsible'. I live at a particular moment of time in the spiritual and social and economic circumstances into which I have been cast: how then can I help choosing and acting as I do? The values in terms of which I conduct my life are the values of my class, or race, or church, or civilization, or are part and parcel of my 'station'—my position in the 'social structure'. Nobody denies that it would be stupid as well as cruel to blame me for not being taller than I am, or to regard the colour of my hair or the qualities of my intellect or heart as being due principally to my own free choice; these attributes are as they are through no decision of mine. If I extend this category without limit, then whatever is, is necessary and inevitable. This unlimited extension of necessity, on any of the views described above, becomes intrinsic to the explanation of everything. To blame and praise, consider possible alternative courses of action, accuse or defend historical figures for acting as they do or did, becomes an absurd activity. Admiration and contempt for this or that individual may indeed continue, but it becomes akin to aesthetic judgement. We can eulogize or denounce, feel love or hatred, satisfaction and shame, but we can neither blame nor justify. Alexander, Caesar, Attila, Mohammed, Cromwell, Hitler are like floods and earthquakes, sunsets, oceans, mountains; we may admire or fear them, welcome or curse them, but to denounce or extol their acts is (ultimately) as sensible as addressing sermons to a tree (as Frederick the Great pointed out with his customary pungency in the course of his attack on d'Holbach's *System of Nature*).[2]

---

[2] Determinism is, of course, not identical with fatalism, which is only one, and not the most plausible, species of the vast determinist genus. The majority of determinists seem to maintain that such distinctions as those between voluntary and involuntary behaviour, or between acts and mechanical movements or states, or what a man is and what he is not accountable for, and therefore the very notion of a moral agent, depend on what is or could be affected by individual choice, effort, or decision. They hold that I normally praise or blame a man only if, and because, I think that, what occurred was (or might at any rate in part be) caused by his choice or the absence of it; and should not praise or blame him if his choices, efforts, etc., were, conspicuously unable to affect the result that I applaud or deplore; and that this is compatible with the most rigorous determinism, since choice, effort, etc., are themselves causally inevitable consequences of identifiable spatio-temporal antecedents. This (in substance the classical 'dissolution' of the problem of free will by the British empiricists—Hobbes, Locke, Hume, and their modern followers Russell, Schlick, Ayer, Nowell-Smith, Hampshire, etc.) does not seem to me to solve the problem, but merely to push it a step further back. It may be that for legal or other purposes I may define responsibility, moral accountability, etc., on some such lines as these. But if I were convinced that although acts of choice, dispositional characteristics, etc., did affect what occurred, yet were themselves wholly determined by factors not within the individual's control (including his own motives and springs of action), I should certainly not regard him as morally praiseworthy or blameworthy. In such circumstances the concept of worth and desert, as these terms are now used, would become empty for me.

The same kind of objection seems to me to apply to the connected doctrine that free will is tantamount to capacity for being (causally) affected by praise, blame, persuasion, education, etc. Whether the causes that are held completely to determine human action are physical or psychical or of some other kind, and in whatever pattern or proportion they are deemed to occur, if they are truly causes —if their outcomes are thought to be as unalterable as, say, the effects of physical or physiological causes—this of itself seems to me to make the notion of a free choice between alternatives inapplicable. On this view 'I could have acted otherwise' is made to mean 'I could have acted otherwise if I had chosen', i.e. if there were no insuperable obstacle to hinder me (with the rider that my choice may well be

To assess degress of their responsibility, to attribute this or that consequence to their free decision, to set them up as examples or deterrents, to seek to derive lessons from their lives, becomes senseless. We can feel ashamed of our acts or of our states of mind, or of theirs, as a hunchback may be ashamed of his hump; but we cannot feel remorse: for that entails the belief that we not only could have acted otherwise, but also could have freely chosen to do so. These men were what they were; and so are we. They acted as they acted; and so do we. Their behaviour can be explained in terms of whatever fundamental category is to be used, whereby history is reducible to a natural science or a metaphysical or theological schema. So much we can do for them, and, to a more limited degree, for ourselves and our contemporaries. This is all that can be done.

Yet we are adjured, oddly enough, by tough-minded determinists in the very name of the scientific status of the subject, to avoid bias; regular appeals are made to historians to refrain from sitting in judgement, to remain objective, not to read the values of the present into the past, or of the West into the East; not to admire or condemn ancient Romans for being like or unlike modern Americans; not to denounce the Middle Ages because they failed to practise toleration as it was conceived by Voltaire, nor applaud the Gracchi because we are shocked by the social injustices of our time, or criticize Cicero because of our own experience

---

affected by praise, social disapproval, etc.; but if my choice is itself the result of antecedent causes, I am, in the relevant sense, not free. Freedom to act depends not on absence of only this or that set of fatal obstacles to action—physical or biological, let us say—while other obstacles, e.g. psychological ones—character, habits, 'compulsive' motives, etc.—are present; it requires a situation in which no sum total of such causal factors wholly determines the result—in which there remains some area, however narrow, within which choice is not completely determined. This is the minimal sense of 'can' in this context. Kant's argument that where there is no freedom there is no obligation, where there is no independence of causes there is no responsibility and therefore no desert, and consequently no occasion for praise or reproach, carries conviction. If I can correctly say 'I cannot help choosing thus or thus', I am not free. To say that among the factors which determine the situation are my own character, habits, decisions, choices, etc.— which is, of course, conspicuously true—does not alter the case, or render me, in the only relevant sense, free. The feeling of those who have recognized free will as a genuine issue, and were not deceived by the latest efforts to interpret it away, turns out, as so often in the case of major problems which have plagued thoughtful men in every generation, to be sound as against philosophers armed with some all-conquering simple methods of sweeping troublesome questions out of sight. Dr. Johnson, as in other matters affecting common-sense notions, here, too, seems to have been guided by a sound linguistic sense. It does not, of course, follow that any of the analyses so far provided of the relevant senses of 'can', 'freedom', 'uncaused', etc. is satisfactory. To cut the knot, as Dr. Johnson did, is not to untie it.

of lawyers in politics. What are we to make of such exhortations, or of the perpetual pleas to use our imagination or our powers of sympathy or of understanding in order to avoid the injustice that springs from an insufficient grasp of the aims and codes and customs of cultures distant from us in time or space? What meaning has this, save on the assumption that to give moral praise and blame, to seek to be just, is not totally irrational, that human beings deserve justice as stocks or stones do not, and that therefore we must seek to be fair, and not praise and blame arbitrarily, or mistakenly, through ignorance, or prejudice, or lack of imagination? Yet once we transfer responsibility for what happens from the backs of individuals to the causal or teleological operation of institutions or cultures or psychical or physical factors, what can be meant by calling upon our sympathy or sense of history, or sighing after the ideal of total impartiality, which may not indeed be fully attainable, but to which some come nearer than others? Few are accused of biased accounts of geological changes or lack of intuitive sympathy in describing the effect of the Italian climate upon the agriculture of ancient Rome. To this it may be answered that even if history, like natural science, is satisfaction of curiosity about unalterable processes—merely disfigured by the intrusion of moral judgements—we shall attain a less adequate grasp of even the bare facts unless we have some degree of imaginative insight into ways of life alien, or little known, to us. This is doubtless true; but it does not penetrate to the heart of the objection brought against historians who are accused of prejudice or of colouring their accounts too strongly. It may be (and has doubtless often been said) that Gibbon or Macaulay or Treitschke or the late Mr. Belloc fail to reproduce the facts as we suspect them to have been. To say this is, of course, to accuse the writers of serious inadequacy as historians; but that is not the main gravamen of the charge. It is rather that they are in some sense not merely inaccurate or superficial or incomplete, but that they are unjust; that they are seeking to secure our approval for one side, and, in order to achieve this, unfairly denigrate the other; that in dealing with one side they cite evidence and use methods of inference or presentation which, for no good reason, they deny to the other; and that their motive for doing this derives from their conviction of how men should be, and what they should do; and sometimes also that these convictions spring from views which (judged in terms of the ordinary standards and scales of value which prevail in the societies to which they and we belong) are too narrow; or irrational or inapplicable to the historical period in question; and that because of this they have suppressed or distorted the true facts, as true facts are conceived by the educated society of their, or our, time. We complain, that is to say, not merely of suppression or distortion, but of propagandist aims to which we think this may be due; and to speak of propaganda at all, let alone assume that it can be dangerously effective, is to imply that the notion of injustice is not inoperative, that marks for conduct are, and can properly be, awarded; it is in effect to say that I must either seek not to praise or blame at all, or, if I cannot avoid doing so because I am a human being and my views are inevitably shot through with moral assessments, I should seek to do so justly, with detachment, on the evidence, not blaming men for failing to do the impossible, and not praising them for it either. And this, in its turn, entails belief in individual responsibility—at any rate some degree of it. How great a degree—how wide the realm of possibility—of alternatives freely choosable—will depend on one's reading of nature and history; but it will never be nothing at all. And yet it is this, it seems to me, that is virtually denied by those historians and sociologists, steeped in metaphysical or scientific determinism, who think it right to say that in (what they are fond of calling) 'the last analysis', everything—or so much of it as makes no difference—boils down to the effects of class, or race, or civilization, or social structure. Such thinkers seem to me committed to the belief that although we may not be able to plot the exact curve of each individual life with the data at our disposal and the laws we claim to have discovered, yet, in principle, if we were omniscient, we could do so; and that consequently even that minimum residue of value judgement which no amount of conscious self-discipline and self-effacement can wholly eliminate, which colours and is part of our very choice of historical material, of our emphasis, however tentative, upon some events and persons as being more important or interesting or unusual than others, must be either the result of our own 'ineluctable' conditioning, or else the fruit of our own incurable vanity and ignorance; and in either case remains in practice unavoidable—the price of our human status, part of the imperfection of man; and must be accepted only because it literally cannot be rejected, because men and their outlooks are what they are, and men judge as they do; because they are finite, and forget, or cannot face, the fact that they are so. This stern conclusion is not, of course, actually accepted by any working historian, or any human being in his non-theoretical moments; even though, paradoxically enough, the arguments by which we are led to such untenable conclusions, by stressing how much narrower is the area of human freedom, and therefore of responsibility, than it was believed to be during the ages of scientific ignorance, have taught many admirable lessons in restraint and humility. But to maintain that, since men are 'determined', history, by which I mean the activity of historians, cannot, strictly speaking, ever be just or unjust but only true or false, wise or stupid, is to expound a noble fallacy, and one that can seldom, if ever, have been acted upon. For its theoretical acceptance, however half-hearted, has led to the drawing of exceedingly civilized consequences, and checked much traditional cruelty and injustice.

The proposition that everything that we do and suffer is part of a fixed pattern—that Laplace's observer (supplied with adequate knowledge of facts and laws) could at any moment of historical time describe correctly every past and future event including those of the 'inner' life, that is, human thoughts, feelings, acts, etc.—has often been entertained, and very different implications have been drawn from it; belief in its truth has dismayed some and inspired others. But whether or not determinism is true or even coherent, it seems clear that acceptance of it does not in fact colour the ordinary thoughts of the majority of human beings, including historians, nor even those of natural scientists outside the laboratory. For if it did, the language of the believers would reflect this fact, and be different from that of the rest of us. There is a class of expressions which we constantly use (and can scarcely do without) like 'you should not (or need not) have done this'; 'need you have made this terrible mistake?'; 'I could do it, but I would rather not'; 'why did the King of Ruritania abdicate? Because, unlike the King of Abyssinia, he lacked the strength of will to resist'; '*must* the Commander-in-Chief be quite so stupid?' Expressions of this type plainly involve the notion of more than the merely logical possibility of the realization of alternatives other than those which were in fact realized, namely of differences between situations in which individuals can be reasonably regarded as being responsible for their acts, and those in which they can not. For no one will wish to deny that we do often argue about the best among the possible courses of action open to human beings in the present and past and future, in fiction and in dreams; that historians (and detectives and judges and juries) do attempt to establish, as well as they are able, what these possibilities are; that the ways in which these lines are drawn mark the frontiers between reliable and unreliable history; that what is called realism (as opposed to fancy or ignorance of life or utopian dreams) consists precisely in the placing of what occurred (or might occur) in the context of what could have happened (or could happen) and in the demarcation of this from what could not; that this is what (as I think Sir Lewis Namier once suggested) the sense of history, in the end, comes to; that upon this capacity historical (as well as legal) justice depends; that it alone makes it possible to speak of criticism, or praise and blame, as just or deserved or absurd or unfair; and that this is the sole and obvious reason why accidents, *force majeure*—being unavoidable—are necessarily outside the category of responsibility and consequently beyond the bounds of criticism, of the attribution of praise and blame The difference between the expected and the exceptional, the difficult and the easy, the normal and the perverse, rests upon the drawing of these same lines. All this seems too self-evident to argue. It seems superfluous to add that all the discussions of historians about whether a given policy could or could not have been prevented, and what view should therefore be taken of the acts and characters of the actors, are intelligible only on the assumption of the reality of human choices. If determinism were a valid theory of human behaviour, these distinctions would be as inappropriate as the attribution of moral responsibility to the planetary system or the tissues of a living cell. These categories permeate all that we think and feel so pervasively and universally that to think them away, and conceive what and how we should be thinking, feeling, and talking without them, or in the framework of their opposites, psychologically greatly strains our capacity—is nearly, if not quite, as impracticable as, let us say, to pretend that we live in a world in which space, time, or number in the normal sense no longer exist. We may indeed always argue about specific situations, about whether a given occurrence is best explained as the inevitable effect of antecedent events beyond human control, or on the contrary as due to free human choice; free not merely in the sense that the case would have been altered if we had chosen—tried to act—differently; but that nothing prevented us from so choosing. It may well be that the growth of science and historical knowledge does in fact tend to show—make probable—that much of what was hitherto attributed to the acts of the unfettered wills of individuals can be satisfactorily explained only by the working of other, 'natural', impersonal factors; that we have, in our ignorance or vanity, extended the realm of human freedom much too far. Yet, the very meaning of such terms as 'cause' and 'inevitable' depends on the possibility of contrasting them with at least their imaginary opposites. These alternatives may be improbable; but they must at least be conceivable, if only for the purpose of contrasting them with causal necessities and law-observing uniformities; unless we attach some meaning to the notion of free acts, i.e. acts not wholly determined by antecedent events or by the nature and 'dispositional characteristics' of either persons or things, it is difficult to see why we come to distinguish acts to which responsibility is attached from mere segments in a physical, or psychical, or psycho-physical causal chain of events—a distinction signified (even if all particular applications of it are mistaken) by the cluster of expressions which deal with open alternatives and free choices. Yet it is this distinction that underlies our normal attribution of values, in particular the notion that praise and blame can ever be justly (not merely usefully or effectively) given. If the determinist hypothesis were true, and adequately accounted for the actual world, there is a clear sense in which, despite all the extraordinary casuistry which has been brought to avoid this conclusion, the notion of human responsibility, as ordinarily understood, would no longer apply to any actual, but only to imaginary or conceivable, states of affairs. I do not here wish to say that determinism is necessarily false, only that we neither speak nor think as if it could be true, and that it is difficult, and perhaps beyond our normal powers, to conceive what our picture of the world would be if we seriously believed it; so that to speak, as some theorists of history (and scientists with a philosophical bent) tend to do, as if one might (in life and not only in the study) accept the determinist hypothesis, and yet to continue to think and speak much as we do at present, is to breed intellectual confusion. If the belief in freedom— which rests on the assumption that human beings do occasionally choose, and that their choices are not wholly accounted for by the kind of causal explanations which are accepted in, say, physics or biology— if this is a necessary illusion, it is so deep and so pervasive that it is not felt as such.[3] No doubt we can try to convince ourselves that we are systematically deluded;[4] but unless we attempt to think that the implications of this possibility, and alter our modes of thought and speech to allow for it accordingly, this hypothesis remains hollow; that is, we find it impracticable even to entertain it seriously, if our behaviour is to be

---

[3] What can and what cannot be done by particular agents in specific circumstances is an empirical question, properly settled, like all such questions, by an appeal to experience. If all acts were causally determined by antecedent conditions which were themselves similarly determined, and so on *ad infinitum*, such investigations would rest on an illusion. As rational beings we should, in that case, make an effort to disillusion ourselves—to cast off the spell of appearances; but we should surely fail. The delusion, if it is one, belongs to the order of what Kant called 'empirically real' and 'transcendentally ideal'. To try to place ourselves outside the categories which govern our empirical ('real') experience is what he regarded as an unintelligible plan of action. This thesis is surely valid, and can be stated without the paraphernalia of the Kantian system.

[4] This desperate effort to remain at once within and without the engulfing dream, to say the unsayable, is irresistible to German metaphysicians of a certain type: e.g. Schopenhauer and Vaihinger.

taken as evidence of what we can and what we cannot bring ourselves to believe or suppose not merely in theory, but in practice. My submission is that to make a serious attempt to adapt our thoughts and words to the hypothesis of determinism is a fearful task, as things are now, and have been within recorded history. The changes involved are very radical; our moral and psychological categories are, in the end, more flexible than our physical ones, but not much more so; it is not much easier to begin to think out in real terms, to which behaviour and speech would correspond, what the universe of the genuine determinist would be like, than to think out, with the minimum of indispensable concrete detail (i.e. begin to imagine) what it would be like to be in a timeless world, or one with a seventeen-dimensional space. Let those who doubt this try for themselves; the symbols with which we think will hardly lend themselves to the experiment; they, in their turn, are too deeply involved in our normal view of the world, allowing for every difference of period and clime and culture, to be capable of so violent a break. We can, of course, work out the logical implications of any set of internally consistent premises—logic and mathematics will do any work that is required of them—but this is a very different thing from knowing how the result would look 'in practice', what the concrete innovations are; and, since history is not a deductive science (and even sociology becomes progressively less intelligible as it loses touch with its empirical foundations), such hypotheses, being abstract models, pure and unapplied, will be of little use to students of human life. Hence the ancient controversy between free will and determinism, while it remains a genuine problem for theologians and philosophers, need not trouble the thoughts of those whose concern is with empirical matters—the actual lives of human beings in the space and time of normal experience. For practising historians determinism is not, and need not be, a serious issue.

Yet, inapplicable as it may be as a theory of human action, specific forms of the deterministic hypothesis have played an arresting, if limited, role in altering our views of human responsibility. The irrelevance of the general hypothesis to historical studies must not blind us to its importance as a specific corrective to ignorance, prejudice, dogmatism, and fantasy on the part of those who judge the behaviour of others. For it is plainly a good thing that we should be reminded by social scientists that the scope of human choice is a good deal more limited than we used to suppose; that the evidence at our disposal shows that many of the acts too often assumed to be within the individual's control are not so—that man is an object in (scientifically predictable) nature to a larger degree than has at times been supposed, that human beings more often than not act as they do because of characteristics due to heredity or physical or social environment or education, or biological or physical characteristics or the interplay of these factors with each other and with the obscurer factors loosely called psychical characteristics; and that the resultant habits of thought, feeling, and expression are[5] as capable of being classified and made subject to hypotheses and systematic laws as the behaviour of material objects. And this certainly alters our ideas about the limits of freedom and responsibility. If we are told that a given case of stealing is due to kleptomania, we protest that the appropriate treatment is not punishment but a remedy for a disease; and similarly, if a destructive act or a vicious character is ascribed to a specific psychological or social cause, we decide, if we are convinced that the explanation is valid, that the agent is not responsible for his acts and consequently deserves therapeutic rather than penal treatment. It is salutary to be reminded of the narrowness of the field within which we can begin to claim to be free; and some would claim that such knowledge is still increasing, and the field still contracting. Where the frontier between freedom and causal laws is to be determined is a crucial practical issue; knowledge of it is a powerful and indispensable antidote to ignorance and irrationality, and offers us new types of explanation—historical, psychological, sociological, biological—which previous generations have lacked. What we cannot alter, or cannot alter as much as we had supposed, cannot be used as evidence for or against us as free moral agents; it can cause us to feel pride, shame, regret, interest, but not remorse; it can be admired, envied, deplored, enjoyed, feared, wondered at, but not (save in some quasi-aesthetic sense) praised or condemned; our tendency to indignation is curbed, we desist from passing judgement. '*Je ne propose rien, je ne suppose rien, je n'impose rien ... j'expose,*' said a French writer proudly, and such *exposition* meant for him the treatment of all events as causal or statistical phenomena, as scientific material to the exclusion of moral judgement. Historians of this persuasion, anxious to avoid all personal, above all, all moral, judgements, tend to emphasize the immense predominance of impersonal factors in history, of the physical media in which life is lived, the power of geographical, psychological, social factors which are not, at any rate consciously, man-made, and often beyond human control. This does tend to check our arrogance, to induce humility by forcing us to admit that our own outlook and scales of value are neither permanent nor universally accepted, that the over-confident, too com-

---

[5] At least in principle.

placent, moral classifications of past historians and of their societies sprang all too obviously from specific historical conditions, specific forms of ignorance or vainglory, or from particular temperamental traits in the historian (or moralist), or from other causes and circumstances which, from our vantage point, we perceive to belong to their own place and time, and to have given rise to interpretations which later seem idiosyncratic, smug, shallow, unjust, and often grotesque in the light of our own standards of accuracy or objectivity. And, what is even more important, such a line of approach throws doubt upon all attempts to establish a definitive line between the individual's free choice and his natural or social necessitation, and does this by bringing to light the egregious blunders of some of those who tried to solve this or that problem in the past, and made mistakes of fact which now, all too plainly, seem due to their (unalterable) *milieu*, or character, or interests. And this tends to make us ask whether the same might not be equally true of us and our own historical judgements; and so, by suggesting that every generation is 'subjectively' conditioned by its own psychological peculiarities, leads us to wonder whether it might not be best to avoid all moral judgement, all ascription of responsibility, might not be safest to confine ourselves to impersonal terms, and leave whatever cannot be said in such terms altogether unsaid. Have we learned nothing from the intolerable moral dogmatism and the mechanical classifications of those historians and moralists and politicians whose views are now so dated, so obsolete, and so justly discredited? And, indeed, who are we to make such a parade of our personal opinions, to give such importance to what are no more than symptoms of our own ephemeral outlook? And what right, in any case, have we to sit in judgement on our fellows whose moral codes are the products of their specific historical environments, as our own are of ours? Is it not better to analyse, to describe, to present the events, and then withdraw and let them 'speak for themselves', refraining from the intolerable presumption of awarding marks, meting out justice, dividing the sheep from the goats according to our own personal criteria, as if these were eternal and not, as in fact they are, neither more nor less valid than those of others with other interests, in other conditions?

Such advice to us (in itself salutary enough) to retain a certain scepticism about our own powers of judgement, especially to beware of ascribing too much authority to our own moral views, comes to us, as you may recollect, from at least two quarters; from those who think that we know too much, and from those who think we know too little. We know now, say the former, that we are as we are, and our moral and intellectual criteria are what they are, in virtue of the evolving historical situation. Let me once more remind you of their varieties. Some among them, who feel sure that the natural sciences will in the end account for everything, explain our behaviour in terms of natural causes. Others, who accept a more metaphysical interpretation of the world, explain it by speaking of invisible powers and dominions, nations, races, cultures; the spirit of the age, the 'workings', overt and occult, of 'the Classical Spirit', 'the Renaissance', 'the Medieval Mind', 'the French Revolution', 'the Twentieth Century', conceived as impersonal entities, at once patterns and realities, in terms of whose 'structure' or 'purpose' their elements and expressions—men and institutions—must behave as they do. Yet still others speak in terms of some teleological procession, or hierarchy, whereby each man, country, institution, culture, age, fulfil their part in some cosmic drama, and are what they are in virtue of the part cast for them, but not by them, by the divine Dramatist Himself. From this it is not far to the views of those who say that History is wiser than we, that its purposes are unfathomable to us, that we, or some among us, are but the means, the instruments, the manifestations, worthy or unworthy, of some vast all-embracing schema of eternal human progress, or of the German Spirit, or of the Proletariat, or of post-Christian civilization, or of Faustian man, or of Manifest Destiny, or of the American Century, or of some other myth or mystery or abstraction. To know all is to understand all; it is to know why things are and must be as they are; therefore the more we know the more absurd we must think those who suppose that things could have been otherwise, and so fall into the irrational temptation to praise or blame. *Tout comprendre, c'est tout pardonner* is transformed into a mere truism. Any form of moral censure—the accusing finger of historians or publicists or politicians, and indeed the agonies of the private conscience, too—tends, so far as possible, to be explained away as one or other sophisticated version of primitive taboos or psychical tensions or conflicts, now appearing as moral consciousness, now as some other sanction, growing out of, and battening upon, that ignorance which alone generates fallacious beliefs in free will and uncaused choice, doomed to disappear in the growing light of scientific or metaphysical truth. Or, again, we find that the adherents of a sociological or historical or anthropological metaphysics tend to interpret the sense of mission and dedication, the voice of duty, all forms of inner compulsion of this type, as being an expression within each individual's conscious life of the 'vast impersonal forces' which control it, and which speak 'in us', 'through us', 'to us', for their own inscrutable purposes. To hear is then literally to obey—to be drawn towards the true goal of our 'real' self, or its 'natural' or 'rational' development—that to which we are called in virtue of belonging to this or that class, or nation, or race, or church, or station in society, or tradition, or age, or character. The explanation, and in some sense the weight of responsibility, for all human action is (at times with ill-concealed relief) transferred to the broad backs of these vast impersonal forces—institutions or historic trends—better made to bear such burdens than a feeble thinking reed like man —a creature that, with a megalomania scarcely appropriate to his physical and moral frailty, claims, as he too often does, to be responsible for the workings of Nature or of the Spirit; and flown with his importance, praises and blames, worships and tortures, murders and immortalizes other creatures like himself for conceiving, willing, or executing policies for which neither he nor they can be remotely responsible; as if flies were to sit in solemn judgement upon each other for causing the revolutions of the sun or the changes of the seasons which affect their lives. But no sooner do we acquire adequate insight into the 'inexorable' and 'inevitable' parts played by all things animate and inanimate in the cosmic process, than we are freed from the sense of personal endeavour. Our sense of guilt and of sin, our pangs of remorse and self-condemnation, are automatically dissolved; the tension, the fear of failure and frustration, disappear as we become aware of the elements of a larger 'organic whole' of which we are variously described as limbs or members, or reflections, or emanations, or finite expressions; our sense of freedom and independence, our belief in an area, however circumscribed, in which we can choose to act as we please, falls from us; in its place we are provided with a sense of a membership in an ordered system, each with a unique position sacred to oneself alone. We are soldiers in an army, and no longer suffer the pains and penalties of solitude; the army is on the march, our goals are set for us, not chosen by us; doubts are stilled by authority. The growth of knowledge brings with it relief from moral burdens, for if powers beyond and above us are at work, it is wild presumption to claim responsibility for their activity or blame ourselves for failing in it. Original sin is thus transferred to an impersonal plane, and acts hitherto regarded as wicked or unjustifiable are seen in a more 'objective' fashion—in a larger context—as part of the process of history which, being responsible for providing us with our scale of values, must not therefore itself be judged in terms of it; and viewed in this new light they turn out no longer wicked but right and good because necessitated by the whole. This is a doctrine which lies at the heart equally of scientific attempts to explain moral sentiments as psychological or sociological 'residues' or the like, and of the metaphysical vision for which whatever is— 'truly' is—is good. To understand all is to see that nothing could be otherwise than as it is; that all blame, indignation, protest is mere complaint about what seems discordant, about elements which do not seem to fit, about the absence of an intellectually or spiritually satisfying pattern. But this is always only evidence of failure on the part of the observer, of his blindness and ignorance; it can never be an objective assessment of reality, for in reality everything necessarily fits, nothing is superfluous, nothing amiss, every ingredient is 'justified' in being where it is by the demands of the transcendent whole; and all sense of guilt, injustice, ugliness, all resistance or condemnation, is mere proof of (at times unavoidable) lack of vision, misunderstanding, subjective aberration. Vice, pain, folly, maladjustment, all come from failure to understand, from failure, in Mr. E. M. Forster's celebrated phrase, 'to connect'. This is the sermon preached to us by great and noble thinkers of very different outlooks, by Spinoza and Godwin, by Tolstoy and Comte, by mystics and rationalists, theologians and scientific materialists, metaphysicians and dogmatic empiricists, American sociologists, Russian Marxists, and German historicists alike. Thus Godwin (and he speaks for many humane and civilized persons) tells us that to understand a human act we must always avoid applying general principles but examine each case in its full individual detail. When we scrupulously examine the texture and pattern of this or that life, we shall not, in our haste and blindness seek to condemn or to punish; for we shall see why this or that man was caused to act in this or that manner by ignorance or poverty or some other moral or intellectual or physical defect, as (Godwin optimistically supposes) we can always see, if we arm ourselves with sufficient patience, knowledge, and sympathy, and we shall then blame him no more that we should an object in nature; and since it is axiomatic that we cannot both act upon our knowledge, and yet regret the result, we can and shall in the end succeed in making men good, just, happy, and wise. So, too, Condorcet and Henri de Saint-Simon, and their disciple, Auguste Comte, starting from the opposite conviction, namely that men are not unique and in need, each one of them, of individual treatment, but, no less than inhabitants of the animal, vegetable, and mineral kingdom, belong to types and obey general laws, maintain no less stoutly that once these laws have been discovered (and therefore applied) this will by itself lead to universal felicity. And this conviction has since been echoed by many idealistic liberals and rationalists, technocrats, positivists, and believers in the scientific organization of society; and in very different keys by theocrats, neo-medieval romantics, authoritarians, and political mystics of various kinds. This, too, is in substance the morality preached if not by Marx, then by most of the disciples of Engels and Plekhanov, by Prussian nationalist historians, by Spengler, and by many another thinker who believes that there is a pattern which he has seen but others have not seen, or at least not so clearly seen, and that by this vision men may be saved. Know and you will not be lost. What it is that we must know differs from thinker to thinker, differs as views of the nature of the world differ. Know the laws of the universe, animate and inanimate, or the principles of growth, or of evolution, or of the rise and fall of civilizations, or the goals towards which all creation tends, or the stages of the Idea, or something less tangible still. Know, in the sense of identifying yourself with it, realizing your oneness with it, for, do what you may, you cannot escape from the laws to which you are subject, of whatever kind they may be, 'mechanistic', 'vitalistic', causal, pur-posive, imposed, transcendent, immanent, or the 'myriad' impalpable strands which bind you to the past—to your land and to the dead, as Barrès declared; to the *milieu*, the race, and the moment, as Taine as-serted; to Burke's great society of the dead and living, who have made you what you are; so that the truth in which you believe, the values in terms of which you judge, from the profoundest principles to the most trivial whims, are part and parcel of the historical continuum to which you belong. Tradition or blood or class or human nature or progress or humanity; the *Zeitgeist* or the social structure or the laws of history, or the true ends of life; know these—be true to them—and you will be free. From Zeno to Spinoza, from the Gnostics to Leibniz, from Thomas Hobbes to Lenin and Freud, the battle-cry has been essentially the same; the object of knowledge and the methods of discovery have often been violently opposed, but that reality is knowable, and that knowledge and only knowledge liberates and absolute knowledge liberates absolutely—that is common to many doctrines which are so large and valuable a part of Western civilization. To understand is to explain and to explain is to justify. The notion of individual freedom is a delusion. The further we are from omniscience, the wider our notion of our freedom and responsibility and guilt, products of ignorance and fear which populate the unknown with terrifying fictions. Personal freedom is a noble delusion and has had its social value; society might have crumbled without it; it is a necessary instrument—one of the greatest devices of 'the cunning' of Reason or of History, or of whatever other cosmic force we may be invited to worship. But a delusion however noble, useful, metaphysically justified, historically indispensable, is still a delusion. And so individual responsibility and the perception of the difference between right and wrong choices, between avoidable evil and misfortune, are mere symptoms, evidences of vanity, of our imperfect adjustment, of human inability to face the truth. The more we know, the greater the relief from the burden of choice; we forgive others for what they cannot avoid being, and by the same token we forgive ourselves. In ages in which the choices seem peculiarly agonizing, when strongly held ideals cannot be reconciled and collisions cannot be averted, such doctrines seem peculiarly comforting. We escape moral dilemmas by denying their reality; and, by directing our gaze towards the greater wholes, we make them responsible in our place. All we lose is an illusion, and with it the painful and superfluous emotions of guilt and remorse. Freedom notoriously involves responsibility, and it is for many spirits a source of welcome relief to lose the burden of both, not by some ignoble act of surrender, but by daring to contemplate in a calm spirit things as they must be; for this is to be truly philosophical. Thereby we reduce history to a kind of physics; as well blame the galaxy or gamma-rays as Genghis Khan or Hitler. 'To know all is to forgive all' turns out to be, in Professor Ayer's striking phrase (used in another context) nothing but a dramatized tautology.

DETERMINISM IN HISTORY

ERNEST NAGEL

SOME thirty years ago a historian of some eminence examined the apparently decisive influence exercised by a number of famous persons upon such important historical occurrences as the Protestant Reformation in England, the American Revolution, and the development of parliamentary government. He then assessed the supposedly critical role which the decisions and actions of these men played in bringing about those events, generalized his findings, and concluded as follows:

These great changes seem to have come about with a certain inevitableness; there seems to have been an independent trend of events, some inexorable necessity controlling the progress of human affairs.... Examined closely, weighed and measured carefully, set in true perspective, the personal, the casual, the individual influences in history sink in significance and the great cyclical forces loom up. Events come of themselves, so to speak; that is, they come so consistently and unavoidably as to rule out as causes not only physical phenomena but voluntary human action. So arises the conception of *law in history*. History, the great course of human affairs, has not been the result of voluntary efforts on the part of individuals or groups of individuals, much less chance; but has been subject to law. (Edward P. Cheney, *Law in History and Other Essays*, New York, 1927, p. 7.)

The view expressed in this quotation is a variant of a conception of human affairs that is familiar and continues to be widely held. It is a conception that has sometimes been advanced as ancillary to a theodicy; sometimes to a romantic philosophy of cosmic organicism; sometimes to an ostensibly 'scientific' theory of civilization which finds the causes of human progress or decline in the operations of impersonal factors such as geography, race, or economic organization. Despite important differences between them, these various doctrines of historical inevitability share a common premiss: the impotence of deliberate human action, whether individual or concerted, to alter the course of human history, since historical changes are allegedly the products of deep-lying forces which conform to fixed, though perhaps not always known, patterns of development.

It is not my aim here to discuss this doctrine of historical inevitability.

From *Philosophy and Phenomenological Research*, 20, 3 (1960), 291–317. Reprinted by permission of the author and the editor of the Journal.

That doctrine has not lacked effective critics, and in recent years it has been subjected to severe scrutiny by numerous historians and philosophers. I would like to say in passing, however, that I agree with its critics in holding it to be untenable. In some of its variant forms the doctrine can indeed be shown to have no empirical content, since in those versions notions are employed such that no conceivable empirical evidence can ever be relevant for evaluating the doctrine as true or false. But even when it is formulated as a factually verifiable statement, the available evidence supports neither the thesis that all human events illustrate a unitary, transculturally invariant law of development, nor the thesis that individual or concerted human effort never operates as a decisive factor in the transformations of society. In asserting all this I am, of course, not denying that in many historical situations individual choice and effort may count for little or nothing. On the contrary, I want to affirm explicitly that frequently there are ascertainable limits to human power, whether individual or collective, for directing the course of historical changes—limits that may be set by facts of physics and geography, by biological endowment, by modes of economic production and available technological skills, by tradition and political organization, by human stupidity and ignorance, as well as by various antecedent historical occurrences.

On the other hand, many recent critics of historical inevitability have not stopped with denying the manifestly exaggerated claims of this doctrine. They have gone on to challenge what they believe is the basic assumption underlying that doctrine, an assumption to which that doctrine is supposedly but an easy corollary. More specifically, a growing number of thinkers has been claiming that what is really at the bottom of beliefs in historical inevitability is the very notion that human events generally occur only under determinate and determining conditions. Many writers have in consequence argued that a thoroughgoing determinism is incompatible with the established facts of history as well as with a genuinely significant imputation to human beings of responsibility for their choices and actions. In the eyes of many, furthermore, it is this deterministic assumption which is ultimately behind current attempts at extending behaviouristic (or more generally, naturalistic) methods of inquiry into the study of human affairs; and the undeniable crudities which have sometimes accompanied the use of such methods, have been therefore cited as the unavoidable fruits of the deterministic assumption itself. Accordingly, a number of critics of historical inevitability have also trained their fire on the putative deterministic premise of much current psychological and social research;

they have challenged the worth of such research in effect because of its allegedly disruptive effects on vital beliefs in human freedom and in the validity of any judgement ascribing responsibility to individual persons for any of their actions.

It would not be difficult to suggest plausible explanations, psychological and sociological, based on the events of the past few decades, for the current intellectual hostility towards the assumption of a thoroughgoing determinism in human history. It is not my aim, however, to propose such explanations. I wish, instead, to examine the major arguments as I have encountered them which have been advanced in criticism of determinism, and to indicate where they seem to be mistaken. I hope thereby to show that critics of historical inevitability who have argued for either a radical or a qualified indeterminism in human affairs, have rejected one extreme position only to adopt another one no less extreme and dubious.

I

I must, however, first state briefly what is to be understood by 'determinism', and also indicate summarily what I believe to be the cognitive status of the general assumption of determinism.

There are writers, like the Dutch historian Pieter Geyl, who construe it as the doctrine 'according to which we are helplessly caught in the grip of a movement proceeding from all that has gone before' (Pieter Geyl, *Debates with Historians*, New York, 1956, p. 236). But if we adopt such a definition, and take strictly the phrase 'helplessly caught' or its equivalents, we are committed from the outset not only to identifying determinism with a particular and even mistaken interpretation of historical processes. We are also committed to a formulation that makes the issue of determinism, as discussed traditionally as well as currently, of doubtful relevance to the analysis of most branches of knowledge. I think, however, that this issue is not foreign to such analyses; and it is therefore desirable to formulate the doctrine in a manner that does not preclude its pertinence to extensive areas of scientific inquiry.

Let me sketch a definition of 'determinism' in terms of an example that is generally familiar, relatively simple, and commonly regarded as a deterministic one. I borrow the example from a discussion of a physio-chemical system by the late physiologist, Lawrence J. Henderson (*Pareto's General Sociology*, Cambridge, Mass., 1937, Ch. 3). The system consists of a mixture of soda-water, whisky, and ice, contained in a sealed vacuum bottle. We assume for the sake of simplicity that no air is present in the bottle, or at any rate that if air is present it can be ignored. We also assume that the mixture is completely isolated from other systems, for example, from sources of heat in the environment, from the influence of electric and gravitational fields, and so on. It is of great importance to note, moreover, that the sole characteristics of the system which are of concern are its so-called thermodynamical ones, and that any other traits which the system may exhibit fall outside of this discussion. In particular, the factors (or 'variables') to which attention is here directed include the following: the *number of components* of the system (the components here are water, alcohol, and carbon dioxide); the *phases* or types of aggregation in which the components occur (i.e. whether they occur in a solid, liquid, or gaseous phase); the *concentrations* of the components in each phase; the *temperature* of the mixture; its *pressure* on the walls of the container; and so on. Now it is well known that under the stipulated conditions, and for a given temperature and pressure, each component will occur in the various phases with definite concentrations; and conversely, if the concentrations are fixed, the temperature and pressure will have a unique set of values. Thus, if the pressure of the mixture were increased (for example, by pressing down the stopper of the bottle), the concentration of water in the gaseous phase would be reduced, and its concentration in the liquid phase would be increased; and analogously for a change in temperature. It is therefore evident that the variables of the system which are under consideration stand to each other in definite relations of interdependence. Accordingly, I propose to say that the value of a variable at any given time is 'determined' by the values of the other variables at that time.

But we can go one step further, and indicate what is to be understood by saying that the system as a whole is a deterministic one. Suppose that at some initial time, the system is in a definite *state*—i.e. the variables of the system have certain fixed values; suppose that because of a change induced in one or more of those values at that time, the system moves into another state after an interval of time t; and suppose, finally, that the system is brought back in some way to its initial state, that the same changes are induced in the variables as before, and that after the same interval of time t the system again is in the second state. If, now, the system behaves in this manner, no matter what state is taken to be the initial state and no matter what interval of time t is specified for the duration of its development into the second state, then the system will be said to be a deterministic one in respect to the indicated class of characteristics of variables. It is evident that if a deterministic system is in a definite state at a given time, the occurrence of that state at that time is determined—in the sense that the necessary and sufficient condition for the occurrence of that state at that time is that the system was in a certain state at a certain previous time. Moreover, if a variable of the system has a certain value at a given time, that value can be said to be determined by the state of the system at any prior time—that is to say, the necessary and sufficient condition for that variable of the system having that value at that time is that the system was in some definite state at some prior time.

This skeletal account of what is to be understood by a deterministic system can be generalized and made more precise. In particular, it can be extended to include systems whose characteristics are not (and perhaps cannot be) represented by numerically measurable variables. It can also be broadened so as to cover systems whose 'macroscopic' or 'molar' characteristics may be said to be determined by the structures and characteristics of certain 'microscopic' constituents of those systems—as in the case of the thermal properties of a gas being contingent on the occurrence of certain relations between the molecules of the gas. Space is lacking, however, for presenting a more generalized and technically more adequate definition of determinism, though enough has been said to suggest how such an analysis would proceed.

But there are several points in this account to which special attention must be directed. In the first place, it is immediately clear that when determinism is understood in the above sense, the assumption that a system is deterministic does *not* entail that the states of the system are *predictable*—whether from prior states of the system or from the states of the microscopic parts of the system. Accordingly, a system may be a deterministic one, though we may not know that it is such; and it is a mistake to identify, as some influential philosophers seem to have done, the meaning of 'determinism' with the possibility of prediction with unlimited accuracy. On the other hand, both our practical and theoretical interests are directed towards discovering certain regularities in the operations of various systems, with a view to formulating laws or rules that may enable us to predict (or retrodict) the occurrences of events and their characteristics. Indeed, we have been remarkably successful, in the case of many systems, in constructing theories which are instrumental to highly precise predictions of many varieties of events. Moreover, we can rarely be certain in formulating such laws that all the necessary and sufficient conditions for the occurrence of events and processes have been enumerated. Nevertheless, most of our practical interests, and even some of our theoretical ones, are satisfied if we succeed in stating only some of the necessary conditions whose own existence is relatively impermanent or sporadic, provided that 'other things are equal' and provided that when those conditions do become actualized (perhaps because we are able to control their occurrence) the events in question are also realized.

In the second place, it will also be clear that while a given system may be deterministic with respect to one set of properties, it need not necessarily be deterministic with respect to some other set. Moreover, while the occurrence of a given set of properties exhibited by one system may not be determined by a prescribed class of characteristics also exhibited by that system, the occurrence of those properties may be determined by other characteristics manifested in some other system. Accordingly, should we have reason to believe that a given system is not deterministic in respect to a specified set of properties, at least two alternatives are in principle open to us. We may have evidence to show that the system is not an isolated one; and we may therefore either make allowances for the disturbing influences which play upon it from the 'outside', or enlarge the system so that it is taken to be part of a more *inclusive* deterministic system. The other alternative is to attribute the apparent indeterminism of the system to an incomplete or incorrect analysis of the system itself. We may then, for example, come to regard it as made up of a differently specified set of parts or processes, and so perhaps discover that the macroscopic states of the system are determined by certain of its microscopic states.

In the third place, determinism in its most general form appears to be the claim that for every set of characteristics which may occur at any time, there is some system that is deterministic in respect to those occurrences. Now it is easy to see that determinism so construed has not been conclusively established, nor can it be conclusively refuted by the outcome of any empirical investigation. It has not been conclusively established, since there are perhaps an endless number of classes of events for which we do not yet know the determining conditions; and it is at least logically possible that for some of those classes of events no determining conditions in fact exist. On the other hand, determinism cannot be definitely disproved, since our failure to discover the determining conditions for some event (or type of event) does not prove that there are in fact no such conditions. In my view, therefore, a doctrine of universal determinism can be defended only partly on the ground that it is a correct generalized description of the world as we actually know it; and its operative role in inquiry seems to me to be that of a guiding principle, which formulates in a comprehensive fashion one of the major objectives of positive science.

It is worth noting, however, that determinism functions most effectively as a regulative principle, when the highly generalized formulation suggested above is replaced by a more specific one—one which stipulates more or less definitely what sort of characteristics are to be looked into in our search for the determining conditions of various types of events. For example, in the Laplacian version of determinism, the determining conditions for all occurrences are taken to be the positions and momenta of mass-particles, together with certain dynamic relations (classically called 'forces') between the latter. It is a familiar fact that the Laplacian notion of determinism was for a time a fruitful guiding principle for an extensive class of investigations, although its fertility eventually became exhausted, and by the end of the nineteenth century physical scientists adopted other special forms of deterministic assumption. No comparably fruitful specializations of this assumption have been proposed in the psychological and social sciences—although in these areas of study particular forms of determinism have also led to important findings, for example, those which have directed attention to such determining factors as heredity, attitudes acquired by training, repetition of exposure to stimuli, modes of economic production, or social stratification and social mobility.

Although such specializations of the deterministic assumption may have only a limited range of adequacy, enough has been said to make clear that the inadequacies of these special forms do not constitute a definite disproof of the general deterministic principle. Nor do I believe, though I cannot here advance any supporting arguments, and despite the almost unanimous opinion of contemporary physicists to the contrary, that current developments in quantum theory have established the untenability of a universal determinism as a generalized regulative principle.

These considerations, though somewhat abstract and initially remote from my theme, have a direct bearing on current objections to the use of deterministic assumptions in the study of human history. What, then, are the arguments which have led so many recent thinkers to reject such assumptions? I shall examine the main reasons that have been advanced for such rejection under the following convenient heads: (1) the argument from the non-existence of so-called 'necessary laws of development' in human history; (2) the argument from the unpredictability and inexplicability of human events; (3) the argument from the emergence of novelties in human affairs; (4) the argument from the occurrence of chance events in human history; and (5) the argument from the incompatibility of determinism with the reality of human freedom and with the attribution of moral responsibility.

II

The first argument can be quickly dismissed. It is directed primarily against those grandiose philosophies of history, whether religious or secular in orientation, which claim to find either a definite pattern of development in the apparently chaotic story of the entire human race, or at any rate a fixed order of change repeatedly exhibited by each human society or civilization. On this view, accordingly, every human act has a definite place in an unalterable or timeless structure of changes, and each society must necessarily pass through a definite series of antecedent changes before it can achieve a subsequent stage. Moreover, though human individuals are the ostensible agents which bring about the movement of history, in most of these philosophies human actions are at best only the 'instruments' through which certain 'forces', operating and evolving in conformity with fixed laws, become manifest.

Philosophies of history of this type often possess the fascination of great dramatic literature; and few of their readers would be willing to deny the remarkable imaginative powers and amazing erudition that frequently go into their construction. As I have already indicated, however, the historical evidence, when such evidence is at all relevant for judging such philosophies, is overwhelmingly negative; and like most of their current critics I feel safe in rejecting them as false.

But does it follow from the falsity of the doctrine of historical inevitability that there are no causal connections in history, and that determinism in history is a myth? Those recent critics of the doctrine who believe that it does follow, offer no explicit grounds for their claim, and appear to base their contention on what I think is an extraordinarily narrow conception of what a deterministic system must be like. For they appear to assume that astronomy supplies the typical example of such a system; and they tacitly suppose that since human history does not exhibit the stability and the regular periodicity of the solar system, historical events cannot possibly be elements in a deterministic system. In point of fact, however, some of the familiar features of the solar system are not representative of most deterministic systems. For the relatively unchanging periodicity of planetary motions, for example, is contingent upon the continued relative isolation of the system from the influence of other bodies in remote regions of space, as well as from the effects of various changes within the system (such as chemical or biological ones) that are formally excluded from the province of celestial mechanics—a circumstance which is rarely encountered in connection with most deterministic systems even in the natural sciences. Thus, a straw flying in the wind exhibits no such familiar regularities as do the planets, not because we have reason to believe that the motion of the straw is not determined by definite dynamic properties, but because some of these determining factors are undergoing rapid (and indeed unknown) variations. The crucial point to note is that while a given system may fail to exhibit some special pattern of regular behaviour, it may nevertheless manifest a more complex, because less uniform, pattern of changes; and it also may happen that certain apparently random changes in parts of the system depend on variable factors located in other parts of the system. Accordingly, even if there are no laws of historical development, as claimed by proponents of historical inevitability, it may still be the case, for example, that the rise of the towns in tenth-century northern Europe was determined at least in part by the Mohammedan interruption of the Mediterranean trade, that the decline of Spanish power in the seventeenth century was in part the consequence of Spanish economic and colonial policy, or that a necessary condition for the entrance of the United States into the First World War was the adoption by Germany of an unrestricted submarine warfare. In short, the argument against determinism from the non-existence of historical laws of development, does not achieve its objective.

III

Critics of determinism in history place much weight on the essential inexplicability and unpredictability of historical events. This argument is frequently coupled with a strong emphasis on the 'creative novelties' which emerge from human actions and which constitute at least part of the ground for the alleged unpredictability of historical changes; but I shall postpone discussing this latter point. Even so, there are several dimensions to the present argument, and I shall consider them in turn.

1. Let me first quickly dispose of an argument, repeatedly used by Charles Beard, to support the conclusion that historical occurrences are basically inexplicable. In substance, the argument claims that all attempts at an explanation of what happens in human history lead to an endless regress, since even if we succeed in discovering the conditions for the

occurrence of an event, the occurrence of those conditions will need to be explained in terms of the occurrence of another set of antecedent conditions, and so on without limit. (Thus Beard declared: 'A search for the causes of America's entry into the [First World War] leads into the causes of the war, into all the history that lies beyond 1914, and into the very nature of the universe of which history is a part; that is, unless we arbitrarily decide to cut the web and begin at some point that pleases us.' *The Discussion of Human Affairs*, New York, 1936, p. 79; cf. also pp. 68 ff.)

Such an objection to the possibility of explanation, however, is absurd. If it were sound, no explanations for the occurrence of events could be achieved, neither in the social nor in the natural sciences. But the retort to it is obvious. Although C may be the cause or a determining condition for B, where B is a condition for the occurrence of A, B is none the less a determining factor for A; and in stating the determinants for B, we are answering a different question from the one we are seeking to resolve when we ask for the determinants of A. In brief, an explanation can be completely satisfactory, even though in offering it we are assuming something which has not in turn been also explained.

2. There is another issue, largely verbal, which will also require only brief attention. It has already been mentioned that a number of recent writers have identified the meaning of 'determined' as the possibility of making predictions with unlimited precision. Moreover, according to current quantum theory there are definite theoretical limits to the degree of precision with which subatomic processes can be predicted. These writers have therefore concluded that the general deterministic assumption must be judged as either false or as inapplicable to a large class of occurrences. (Cf., for example, Moritz Schlick, 'Die Kausalität i.d. gegenwärtigen Physik', *Gesammelte Aufsätze*, pp. 73–4.)

Is it plausible, however, to equate except by fiat the meanings of the words 'determined' and 'predictable'? It is customary in this connection to distinguish two senses of 'predictable' or its opposite 'unpredictable'. In one sense, an event is unpredictable if, because of the state of our knowledge and our technology at a given time, the event cannot be foretold at all, or only with some degree of precision. In the second sense of the word, an event is *theoretically* unpredictable if the assumption that its occurrence can be calculated in advance, either at all or with unlimited precision, is incompatible with some accepted theory of science. In neither of these senses, however, is 'unpredictable' synonymous with 'undetermined' (or 'predictable' with 'determined')—at any rate not when 'determined' has the meaning I have suggested for it. For on that meaning the occurrence of solar eclipses, for example, may be determined, despite the fact that some primitive tribes lack the knowledge for anticipating them, and despite the fact that the ancient Babylonians were able to predict them with far less precision than we can. Moreover, even though quantum theory places an upper bound on the precision with which subatomic processes are predictable, it surely is not nonsense to hold, as Planck, Einstein, and De Broglie have in fact held whether correctly or mistakenly, that an alternative theory may eventually be constructed which will not impose such theoretical limits on precise predictions in that domain. Accordingly, the verbal gambit which stipulates the synonymy of 'determined' and 'predictable' does not dispose of the issue raised by critics of the assumption of determinism in human history.

3. Let us turn to more substantive problems related to the predictability of human events. Are such events utterly unpredictable in fact? It would be just silly to maintain that the whole of the human future is predictable by us, or that our present information suffices for retrodicting every event in the human past. But it would also be absurd to hold that we are completely incompetent to do any of these things with reasonable assurance of being correct. It is banal to note that our personal relations with other men, our political arrangements and social institutions, our transportation schedules, and our administration of justice, could not be what they are, unless fairly safe inferences were possible about the human past and future. As I write this line, we cannot predict with certainty who will be the next president of the United States. But if we take for granted current American attitudes towards domestic and foreign powers, and also take into account the present alignment of the world powers, we do have good grounds for confidence that there will be a presidential election this year, that neither major political party will nominate a Communist sympathizer, and that the successful candidate will be neither a woman nor a Negro. These various predictions are indefinite in certain ways, for they do not foretell the future in a manner to exclude all conceivable alternatives but one. Nevertheless, they *do* exclude an enormous number of logical possibilities for the coming year; and they do point up the fact that though the human beings who will participate in those coming events may have a considerable range of free choice in their actions, their actual choices and actions will fall within certain limits. The obvious import of all this is that not everything which is logically possible is also historically possible during a given period and for a given society

of men; and the equally obvious interpretation of this fact is that there are determining conditions for both what has happened as well as what will happen in human history.

4. It is nevertheless pertinent to ask why even our subsequent historical explanations of past human events, to say nothing of our forecasts of future ones, are almost invariably imprecise and incomplete. For our accounts of past occurrences, whether these be individual or collective acts, rarely if ever explain the exact details of what did happen, and succeed in exhibiting only the grounds which make *probable* the occurrence of a more or less vaguely (or precisely) formulated characteristic.

It will be helpful to recall the ideal logical structure of an explanation. That structure is usually described as that of a formally valid deductive argument, whose conclusion is a statement formulating the event to be explained, and whose premisses contain one or more statements of universal laws (expressing some assumed invariable connections of attributes or relations), as well as relevant singular statements that specify the initial and boundary conditions for applying those laws to the case at hand.

This logical structure can be amply illustrated by examples of explanation in many areas of inquiry, especially when what is being explained is some *law* (rather than some particular *event*) on the basis of other laws or theories. But it is notorious that the explanations encountered in the study of human affairs do not conform strictly to this pattern; and it is at least a debatable question whether that pattern is fully embodied in explanations of concrete, individual occurrences even in the natural sciences—except perhaps in rare cases (as in the case of events occurring under carefully controlled laboratory conditions). The deductive structure of explanation thus appears to represent what may at best be a limiting or ideal case in historical study. I proceed to mention several reasons, most of them perhaps quite familiar, why this is so.

a. As just noted, an explanation of a particular event ideally includes among its premisses the set of initial and boundary conditions for the application of assumed universal laws; and in specifying those conditions, the explanation states the sufficient conditions for the occurrence of the event. But even if we knew all the relevant laws pertaining to the traits of an event under study, we are rarely if ever in the position in historical investigations to specify more than a fraction of the initial conditions for the application of those laws. Because of our ignorance of many if not of most of these initial data, we can therefore state only some of the *necessary* conditions for historical occurrences. For this reason alone, accordingly, explanations in history do not have the structure of a straightforward deductive argument.

Nevertheless, this circumstance hardly constitutes evidence against determinism in history; on the contrary, it testifies to the dependence of events on the occurrence of other contingencies additional to those we can usually identify. Indeed, explanations of particular happenings in the natural sciences face difficulties essentially comparable to those encountered in historical inquiry. These difficulties are often concealed even in physics, by the tacit assumption of a *ceteris paribus* clause, where the 'other things' which are supposedly 'constant' are frequently unknown or are only hazarded. For example, the path traversed by a bullet can be explained with the help of the Newtonian theory of mechanics and gravitation. That explanation may explicitly mention such items as the muzzle-velocity of the projectile or the resistance of the air; but it will not mention the position of the earth in relation to our own and other galactic systems. The explanation ignores this latter fact, because on the theory which it employs the mass of the bullet is constant, and independent not only of the velocity of the body but also of its distances from other bodies. However, as Mach pointed out in his critique of Newtonian theory, it may well be that the inertia of a body is a function of its distance from all other bodies in the universe. This observation, baptized as 'Mach's Principle', receives serious attention in current physical cosmology, though the possibility which it notes apparently was never considered prior to Mach. One important difference between explanations of particular events in the natural and social sciences thus seems to be that while in the former we frequently have no good reasons for supposing that the conditions we mention for the occurrence of an event are not sufficient, in the latter we are usually acutely aware that the conditions we cite are only necessary.

b. There is, however, a further point about explanations in history that is perhaps even more important. In the ideal pattern of explanation, the generalizations included in the premises are assumed to be strictly universal in form. But in historical studies the generalizations we tacitly invoke are rarely if ever plausible if they are asserted with strict universality; they are credible only if they are construed as formulating statistical regularities. Moreover, the characterizations employed in those generalizations are usually vague; and if they are defined at all, in order to introduce greater precision into our account of things, they are made more definite only in some quasi-statistical manner. In consequence, in applying such generalizations to particular occurrences, there may be considerable uncertainty whether the given occurrence properly falls under these generalizations. Accordingly, and quite apart from the question whether we can specify all the requisite initial conditions for the application of assumed laws, the statement asserting the occurrence of the event to be explained does not follow *deductively* from the premisses; that statement stands to the explanatory premisses which we can assert with a measure of warrant, only in some relation of probability.

The point is important enough to merit an illustration. At the time of his death Henry VIII's official style read essentially as follows: By the Grace of God, King of England, Ireland, and France, Defender of the Faith and Only Supreme Head of the Church of England and Ireland. But when Elizabeth succeeded to the throne in 1558, eleven years later, she proclaimed herself: By the Grace of God, Queen of England, Ireland, and France, Defender of the Faith, etc., and she was the first English sovereign to *etceterate* herself in an unabbreviated official title. Why did she do so? F. W. Maitland, the legal historian, offered an explanation. He produced evidence to show that the introduction of the 'et cetera' was not a slip, but was a deliberate act which sought to conceal her plans, for the time being at least, concerning the difficult Roman question. Maitland in effect argued that because the alignment of political forces both at home and abroad was unsettled, and because a clear stand by her on the future relation of the English Church to Rome was fraught with grave perils no matter how she decided, she won for herself freedom of action by employing a style in which her eventual decision on this issue was ambiguously stated.

Now an examination of Maitland's discussion shows beyond doubt that the event he sought to explain does indeed logically follow from the explanatory premisses, provided these include an assumption essentially as follows: Whenever anyone acquires a position of great political power, is faced with an issue fraught with peril, but is required to announce immediately a policy, then such a person will make a statement that is momentarily non-committal. However, such an assumption, if asserted universally, is clearly false; and it is plausible only if it is construed as holding either for the most part or in some appreciable fraction of cases. But if this emended generalization is adopted, the fact to be explained no longer follows strictly from the premisses. Furthermore, even in the emended form the generalization makes use of the notion of a policy decision involving uncertain dangers; and it is clear that this notion is a vague one. Indeed, though we might conceivably agree that a policy is dangerous to a maximal degree only if it possess a certain set of specified traits, we would ordinarily classify a policy as dangerous even if it possessed only some undetermined fraction of those traits. In subsuming the decision which Elizabeth was required to make under the heading 'being fraught with peril', we are thus characterizing it in an essentially statistical fashion; and we may be therefore not at all sure that the generalization, even in its emended form, is actually applicable to the case under discussion.

5. There is accordingly little doubt that typical explanations in history are in an obvious sense incomplete, since they specify what is at best only some of the necessary conditions for the occurrence of events. But before commenting on the import of this point for the issue of determinism, let us consider one further crucial issue: Granted that we have not succeeded in discovering strictly universal laws which would account completely for historical events, and which would indicate the sufficient conditions for their occurrence, are there reasons of principle for our failure, or are there reasons for believing that our failures may be only temporary?

An adequate answer to these questions must take into account the frequently neglected though familiar point that in providing explanations for historical events, historians usually operate on certain typical (and often conventionally set) levels of analysis—despite the possibility that causal determinants for those events may be found on various other levels of analysis. Historians are in the main habitually interested in accounting for the occurrence of only a somewhat limited class of traits; and they normally also seek to explain them in terms of a comparably restricted set of traits characterizing events. Thus, Maitland was concerned with explaining the *ambiguity* occurring in Elizabeth's title; and he evidently did not set himself the task of explaining her use of the *specific* locution 'et cetera', rather than some other form of ambiguity. Nor was he interested in explaining the occurrence of Elizabeth's particular facial expression or the amount of her blood pressure, which were also parts or phases of the event in which she conceived the ambiguous locution. Furthermore, Maitland explained her adoption of an ambiguous title in terms of Elizabeth's political intelligence and the alignment of politically powerful groups. It evidently did not occur to him to account for the ambiguous form of her title in terms of such factors as the details of her individual psychology or her particular physiological constitution. These things did not occur to him, not necessarily because they were known by him to be irrelevant to the facts under inquiry, but most likely because their consideration belongs to a level of analysis that normally falls outside the range of the historian's interests, and outside the scope of the historian's competence.

For convenience of reference, and for lack of better labels, let me call those phases of historical occurrences to which historians usually pay attention the 'common-sense molar characteristics' of events; and let me refer to other characteristics of events which may be of possible causal relevance to their occurrence as 'analytic molecular characteristics'. I hasten to add that I realize this distinction to be a loose one, and that I know no way of sharpening it. Nevertheless, the distinction is a serviceable one, and permits me to state briefly why, as I see it, the actual explanations of human affairs will most likely continue to specify only some of the necessary conditions for the occurrence of events.

The point is that our customary formulations of common-sense molar characteristics are not only vague; they also cover an indefinite number of *specific variant forms* of such characteristics, which have never been exhaustively codified and catalogued in some systematic fashion. In consequence, only a statistical concomitance between common-sense molar traits can be reasonably expected. It is as if a physicist, after recognizing a gross distinction between metals and non-metals, were to investigate the electrical conductivity of different objects without distinguishing further between different kinds of metals. Would it be surprising, in the light of what we know, if the generalizations he would then obtain about the variation of conductivity with, say, the temperature of metal objects, would be only statistical in form? Would we not agree that on such a level of analysis nothing more could be expected, and that to obtain more exact relations of dependence the physicist must refine his distinctions, and perhaps even undertake a detailed molecular analysis of his materials? On the other hand, the explanations which the historian usually offers for historical occurrences are in large measure controlled by those interests we all normally have in human affairs—interests which in a broad sense are practical, even if they are sometimes disinterested. I venture the opinion that if someone were to succeed in stating the sufficient conditions for Elizabeth's proclamation of her ambiguous title, but explained that occurrence in terms of analytic molecular characteristics—which included mention of, say, her detailed biological and genetic traits, the condition of her neural synapses, and the specific physical stimuli supplied by her environment— we would all turn away from such an account as not being the sort of history to which we are accustomed or in which we are interested. Accordingly, I see no genuine prospect for explanations in human history which will indeed state the necessary and sufficient conditions for the traits of events in which we are actually interested.

But it would certainly be unwarranted to conclude from all this that common-sense molar characteristics do not have determinate conditions for their occurrence. For it is conceivable that those conditions may need to be specified, at least in part, in terms of some analytic molecular characteristics. We are admittedly ignorant of just what the full complement of those conditions is; and even if there are in fact such conditions, it is possible that we shall never discover the complete set. On the other hand, the existence of sufficient conditions on some analytical molecular level of analysis cannot be excluded *a priori*. I therefore conclude that neither the *de facto* incomplete form of historical explanations, nor the restricted scope of our actual predictions of human events, is cogent evidence against determinism in history.

IV

I now turn to the argument which offers as ground for the rejection of determinism the production in the human scene of new ideas, novel modes of behaviour, and unprecedented works of imagination and skill, and which attributes the unpredictability of human actions in part at least to the 'creative advance of nature' manifested in the life of man.

The issues raised by this argument are identical with those associated with the doctrine of emergence; and I have time to discuss them only summarily. Two forms of this doctrine must be distinguished. The first form, which for convenience will be called 'the doctrine of emergent levels', is atemporal. It maintains that many complex systems exhibit traits and modes of action which cannot be explained or predicted in terms of the properties that the component parts of those systems possess when not members of these systems. The second form of the doctrine commonly known as 'emergent evolution', is a temporal or historical thesis. It asserts that novel forms of organization appear in time, new traits are exhibited, and types of activities are manifested which did not previously exist, and which cannot be understood in terms of what had preceded them. I shall now argue that both versions of the doctrine of emergence are fully compatible with determinism.

Consider first a standard illustration for the thesis of emergent levels: the water molecule, many of whose traits are allegedly not predictable from the properties of its component hydrogen and oxygen atoms—that is, predictable neither from the properties of these atoms when they exist uncombined with other atoms, nor from the properties they possess in other chemical unions. Such formulations of illustrative examples are misleading, as could easily be shown. For the alleged 'unpredictability' of emergent traits is not absolute, but is always relative to a particular theory that is adopted for the components of the systems exhibiting those emergent traits. For example, many properties of water are indeed emergents, relative to Dalton's theory of the atom; but some of these very properties are predictable, and hence not emergents, relative to the current quantum theory of atomic structure. But waiving this point, what do such examples of emergent levels really show? Do they establish the untenability of determinism? On the contrary, they clearly testify to the fact that, for example, certain distinctive properties of water come into existence only when hydrogen and oxygen atoms combine in a certain definite manner. More generally, the evidence seems to be overwhelming that even in those cases in which we cannot deduce the properties of complex wholes from the properties of their components, those complexes and their various traits come into existence or continue to exist only under determinate conditions.

The import of the doctrine of emergent evolution is essentially no different. There are various analytical and empirical difficulties which must be surmounted, before many specific claims of the doctrine can be regarded as established. For example, criteria must be stated for judging whether two traits are 'really' the same or different, as a preliminary to the empirical question whether one of them is temporally novel; indications must be given of the sort of evidence that is to be deemed relevant for supporting the frequently voiced claim that laws of nature themselves undergo change; and our present knowledge of the past must in many cases be enormously enlarged, if we are to assert with warrant that certain traits of events are temporally unprecedented. But despite such difficulties, no one can seriously question the main thesis that human beings are perennial sources of temporal novelties.

It must also be admitted that the emergence of many of these novelties could not have been predicted in advance. No one could have predicted the invention of the telephone prior to the work of Faraday and Henry; and no one could have predicted that Faraday was to make the scientific discoveries he did make. Nevertheless, there is nothing mysterious about the impossibility of such predictions, and the impossibility can indeed be shown to be a matter of formal logic. For to predict an event, the traits of that event must be formulated in a statement; and unless the predicates describing those traits occur in the premisses of the predictive argument, that statement can follow from the premisses neither deductively nor with any significant measure of probability. However, if some trait of an event is radically novel (and hence not definable in terms of previously existing traits), there will be no antecedently known regularities (or laws) connecting the former with the latter. In consequence, the predicate describing such a novel trait will not occur in any premises from which a predictive inference could be made. In short, our inability to predict a radically novel future is simply the consequence of a logical truism.

On the other hand, once a novel characteristic or novel object has come into existence, we are in the position to inquire, and often do inquire, into the conditions upon which the occurrence of that novelty is contingent. We may not always succeed in discovering those conditions, and we may perhaps never succeed in doing so in many cases. But we do not always fail entirely, nor is it just unintelligible to pursue such a quest.

Let me cite two examples of recent inquiries in this connection, though neither of them is especially favourable for my case. The sociology of science seeks, among other things, to ascertain the social conditions which are favourable to successful scientific research, as well as to the general acceptance of scientific discoveries. Its findings are thus far relatively meagre; and given the level of analysis upon which its inquiries operate, it is hardly surprising that no sufficient conditions have yet been found for the occurrence or acceptance of a great scientific achievement. These inquiries have nevertheless established some things; for example, that a measure of free discussion and communication is a minimal requirement for progress in science, or that there are various necessary conditions, individual and social, for the occurrence of scientific innovations and their subsequent acceptance. Again, there has been some study of the psychology of creative thinking, directed to specifying the circumstances under which mathematicians, composers, and other inventive minds have achieved their creative successes. Here again the findings are slight. Certainly nothing has yet been discovered which would explain such remarkable feats as Mozart's writing of *The Magic Flute* or Newton's deduction of the Keplerian laws from gravitation theory; and it may well be that much more will have to be known about the genetic and physiological constitution of individual men, as well as about the effects of various types of environmental stimuli, before we can hope to account for even lesser achievements. But my point is that these diverse attempts at pushing back the frontiers of our ignorance are not inherently absurd, and that no antecedent limits can be fixed as to how far they may be pushed back. But the assumption of determinism in effect simply codifies our general objective as inquirers, to make those frontiers recede. To abandon that assumption would be tantamount to setting prescribed limits to inquiry itself.

V

The next argument against determinism I wish to consider is based on the claim that there is a fortuitous or chance element in history. But the word 'chance' is far from univocal in the writings of historians and philosophers, and several of its more prominent senses must be distinguished.

In the first place, the word is frequently used to signify the absence of a pervasive and unified 'design, plan, and order in human affairs', and in effect to deny that each historical event is relevantly related to every other. Those who employ 'chance' in this sense, clearly intend to controvert those philosophies of history already mentioned, which descry in the apparently chaotic happenings of the human scene the impress of some timeless Reason, or a unitary pattern of cumulative development. So used, the word obviously does not denote any agency or instrumentality that brings events into being, and in this sense it has no explanatory value whatsoever. On the other hand, it is also evident that on this meaning of 'chance', the affirmation of chance happenings does not entail the denial of causal determinants for historical events, nor does such affirmation imply the futility of all inquiry into the conditions upon which specific historical occurrences may be contingent.

In the second place, 'chance is sometimes equated with 'the unexpected and the unforeseen', where what is unforeseen may be a purely physical event or the social consequence of an action deliberately undertaken. Thus, the shift in the winds which contributed to the destruction of the Spanish Armada was apparently not anticipated by the Spaniards when they set sail for England. The disappearance of slave economy in the United States, which seemed to many Southern landowners to be part of the permanent social order, was not foreseen by most of them even as late as 1859. And few if any of those who contributed to the development of the internal combustion engine or to the production of moderately priced automobiles, envisaged in advance the enormous changes which resulted from these innovations in modes of urban and rural living, in individual and public morals, or in domestic politics and foreign relations. More generally, none of us can fully anticipate the unintended consequences of our choices and actions; and we are frequently inclined to label any striking departure from what is expected to happen normally as an 'accident'. However, 'chance' in this sense is on the face of it but a name for our *de facto* ignorance. Clearly, the tenability of determinism is not being challenged when an event is designated as a 'chance' occurrence in this meaning of the word.

In the third place, an event is often said to occur by chance if, to use a familiar formula, it occurs at the 'intersection of two or more independent causal series'. It is in this meaning of 'chance' or 'accident' that Bismarck is reported to have once remarked, after reflecting on the role of accident in ruining the plans of wise men, that there is a special providence for drunkards, fools, and the United States. For example, the military situation in 1781 during the American Revolutionary War made it imperative for Cornwallis to retreat from Yorktown. The disposition of the superior American and French forces prevented him from moving his troops by land, and he sought to escape by water. He did in fact transport some of his men across the York River, when a storm arose making the passage of the rest impossible—so that he was eventually compelled to surrender and in effect thereby to terminate the war. Commenting on these events, a recent historian remarks that 'the atmospheric conditions that brought on the storm and the military conditions that caused Cornwallis's army to retreat were the products of altogether separate chains of causes and effects' (Oscar Handlin, *Chance or Destiny*, p. 192). Cornwallis's surrender is thus credited to chance, since it occurred at the juncture of two independent causal sequences—one of which was the chain of events that terminated in the distribution of the British and Franco-American forces, while the other was the different sequence which terminated in the storm. The two sequences themselves are said to be 'independent', because no elements in either determined any elements in the other; and accordingly, the events in no one of the series determined the conjuncture consisting in the defeat of Cornwallis.

This notion of chance, as is well known, has an ancient lineage; and despite the unclarities that surround the metaphoric phrase 'independent causal chains', it directs attention to the important if obvious point that while the occurrence of one phase of an event may be determined by one set of conditions, the latter may not suffice to determine some more inclusive phase of the event. But does it follow that an event which is the juncture of two independent causal lines is not determined at all? Does it even follow, as some writers have asserted, that the juncture 'cannot be predicted from the laws determining any or all of the series?' These are patently gratuitous claims. For let us assume that an event is a 'chance' occurrence in the present sense of the word—i.e. it occurs at the juncture of several independent causal chains; then it is quite plain that the event *does* occur under the *determinate* conditions which are mentioned when the causal chains are specified at whose 'intersection' the event lies. Moreover, it is surely a mistake to maintain that the point of juncture is *necessarily* unpredictable from the laws of 'any or all the series', even if the detailed outcome of the juncture may not be predictable in *some* cases. A billiard ball moving along a certain line under the impact of a blow from a cue, can certainly be predicted to collide with a steel ball travelling in the opposite direction along that line because of the presence of a strong magnet. More generally, and indeed more precisely, a statement asserting the occurrence of some event may not be deducible from either of two sets of premisses; nevertheless, that statement may be deducible (and the event it describes predictable) from the logical conjunction of those sets of premisses. Accordingly, to be a chance event in this sense of the word, is relative to the explanatory premisses that happen to be adopted; and the characterization of an event as a chance occurrence is thus based on a purely logical distinction. But surely nothing in this distinction is prejudicial to the adequacy of the deterministic assumption.

There is one remaining sense of 'chance' I want to note. According to it, an event happens by chance, if there are absolutely no determining conditions for its occurrence. *If* there are such events (or traits of events), they are not merely unexpected and unforeseen, but are *inherently* unforeseeable; and their occurrence could not be explained, even *after* they had happened, no matter how extensive our knowledge may become. It is, however, at best an unsettled question whether there *are* such chance events—and I venture this opinion despite the well-known rumour that it has been affirmatively settled by modern physics. For as I have already argued, such a question cannot, in the nature of the case, be answered definitively, since even repeated failure to find any causal conditions for some type of event can always be construed as evidence for human stupidity. Would we not ordinarily interpret a competent historian's readiness to label as 'chance event' (in the present sense of the word) an occurrence which he is unable to explain, as simply an expression of his weariness or despair? On the other hand, if there are indeed chance events in this meaning of the word, there certainly is a definite limit to what can be explained. But since we cannot be sure for which specific events this limit is in force, we cannot be certain in connection with any of them that we really have an impregnable excuse for stopping our inquiries into their determinants.

VI

The final argument I must consider consists in the claim that imputation of genuine responsibility to human beings for any of their actions, is incompatible with a thoroughgoing determinism. I turn to this issue with a measure of dislike, for I would prefer not to stir up what ought to be dead ashes. If I nevertheless propose to discuss it, it is because the issue has been recently revived, not only by writers who make a career out of muddying clear waters, but also by sensitive thinkers of great acumen.

I shall take for my main text the recent book by Mr. Isaiah Berlin on *Historical Inevitability* (London and New York, 1954).[1] This book is primarily a critique, and in my opinion a devastating critique, of philosophies of history which view the changes in human life as the unfolding of an inevitable destiny, and which therefore deny that human effort is of any avail in altering the ultimate course of events. However, Mr. Berlin also maintains that such philosophies are but the direct products of a consistent application of the deterministic assumption to human affairs. He therefore believes there are sufficient reasons for rejecting determinism, partly because it leads to such untenable philosophies of history, and partly because of several further difficulties he adduces. I shall ignore the former of these considerations, for I have already tried to show that determinism does not entail any doctrine of historical inevitability; and it is with Mr. Berlin's two additional arguments against determinism that I shall deal.

1. Berlin takes his point of departure from the commonplace that an individual is morally responsible for an act he performs, only if the individual has not been coerced into doing it, and only if he has elected to do it of his own free volition. Accordingly, if a man is genuinely responsible for some act of his, he *could* have acted differently had his choice been different. So much perhaps everyone will be willing to grant. However, Mr. Berlin appears to hold that on the deterministic assumption (which he construes to deny that there are any areas of human life which cannot be exhaustively determined by law), the individual *could not* have chosen differently from the way he in fact did choose; he could not have done so, presumably because his choice at

---

[1] See this volume, pp. 161–86. (It should be noted that the work referred to was subsequently revised by the author for inclusion in his book *Four Essays on Liberty* (1969). The revisions in question do not affect the substance of the argument: none the less there are certain minor discrepancies between the passages quoted by Professor Nagel from the original text and the corresponding passages in the extract from the revised text which is reprinted here. Ed.)

the time he made it was determined by circumstances over which he had no control—circumstances such as his biological heritage, his character as formed by his previous actions, and the like. Mr. Berlin therefore maintains that on the deterministic premiss, the supposition that a man could have chosen otherwise than he in fact did, is ultimately an illusion, resting on an ignorance of the facts. In consequence, Berlin concludes that determinism entails the elimination of individual responsibility, since it is not a man's *free* choice, but the conditions which determine his choice, that must be taken to explain a man's action. So Berlin declares:

Nobody denies that it would be stupid as well as cruel to blame me for not being taller than I am, or to regard the colour of my hair or the qualities of my intellect or heart as being due principally to my own free choice; these attributes are as they are through no decision of mine. If I extend this category without limit, then whatever is, is necessary and inevitable.... To blame and praise, consider possible alternative courses of action, damn or congratulate historical figures for acting as they do or did, becomes an absurd activity. (P. 26.)

And he adds:

If I were convinced that although choices did affect what occurred, yet they were themselves wholly determined by factors not within the individual's control (including his own motives and springs of action), I should certainly not regard him as morally praiseworthy or blameworthy. (Pp. 26–7, footnote.)

I have two comments to make on this.

a. In the first place, it is difficult to obtain a clear idea of the notion of the human self with which Mr. Berlin operates. For one his view, the human self is apparently not only to be distinguished from the human body, but also from any of the choices an individual makes—in so far as a choice is dependent on a man's dispositions, motives, and springs of action.

Now no doubt, when I deliberate and finally seem to choose between alternatives, I am usually not aware that the choice may be the expression of a set of more or less stable dispositions, more transient impulses, and the like—any more than I am usually aware of my heartbeat or of the organ which produces it. But should I become aware of these things, as I sometimes am aware, does my choice or my heart cease to be mine? If I understand Mr. Berlin, he requires me to answer in the negative, though for no obviously good reason. On the contrary, he appears to have an irresolvable puzzle on his hands of how to identify the human self—a puzzle that arises from his so construing the nature of that self, that any trait or action which stands in relations of causal dependence to anything whatever, is automatically cut off from being a genuine phase of the self. It is as if a physicist in analysing the performance of a baseball, and noting that the shape, the surface quality, and the elastic properties of the ball are partly determinative of its behaviour when it is struck by a bat, were to declare that these traits do not properly belong to the ball, but are as much external to it as the impulse imparted by the bat. Just how and where the boundaries of the individual human self are drawn, may vary with different contexts of self-identification, and there may even be important cultural differences in this respect. But however they are drawn, they must not be so drawn that nothing finally can be identified as the self. They must not be so drawn that an insoluble puzzle is made of the fact that we conceive ourselves to be acting freely (i.e. without external constraints), even though we may recognize that some of our choices are the products of our dispositions, our past actions, and our present impulses.

b. This brings me to my second comment. Mr. Berlin's argument seems to be unwittingly patterned on the model used so typically by Eddington—namely, that since physics analyses common-sense objects like tables into a large number of rapidly moving minute particles, with relatively large distances between them, it is therefore illusory to regard tables as hard solids with continuous surfaces. This argument is fallacious, as has often been noted, and involves among other things a confusion of types or categories. In any event, it does not follow that because terms like 'solid', 'hard', and 'continuous' are not applicable in their ordinary senses to a cloud of molecules, they are therefore not correctly applicable to macroscopic objects like tables.

But Mr. Berlin's argument suffers from a similar flaw. For it is a similar mistake to claim that men cannot be genuinely responsible for any of their acts, just because there are conditions inherent in the biological and psychological structure of the human body, under which such responsibility is manifested. Now it is an empirical fact, as well attested as any, that men often do deliberate and decide between alternatives; and whatever we have discovered, or may in the future discover, about the conditions under which men deliberate and choose, cannot be taken, on pain of a fatal incoherence, as evidence for *denying* that such deliberative choices *do* occur.

On the other hand, the imputation of responsiblity is an empirically controllable matter, and we may be mistaken in some of the imputations we make. We may discover, for example, that an individual continues to be a petty thief, despite our best efforts to educate him by way of praise and blame, rewards and punishments, and despite his own apparently serious attempts to mend his ways. We may then conclude that the individual suffers from a mild derangement and cannot control certain of his acts. In such a case, the imputation of responsibility to that individual for those acts would be misplaced. But the fact nevertheless remains that the distinction between acts over which a man does have control and those over which he does not, is not thereby impugned —even if we should discover that there are conditions under which the capacity for such control is manifested and acquired. In short, an individual is correctly characterized as a responsible moral agent, if he behaves in the manner in which a normal moral agent behaves; and he is correctly characterized in this way, even if all the conditions which make it possible for him to function as a moral agent at some given time are not within his control on that occasion.

2. But Mr. Berlin has one further argument against determinism, upon which he apparently sets great store. He claims that irrespective of the truth of determinism, belief in it does not colour the ordinary thoughts of the majority of men. If it did, so he argues, the language we employ in making moral distinctions and in expressing moral suasions would not be what it actually is. For this language in its customary meaning tacitly assumes that men are free to choose and to act *differently* from the way they *actually* choose and act. But if determinism were sound and we really believed in it, Mr. Berlin therefore concludes, our ordinary moral distinctions would not be applicable to anything, and our moral experience would be unintelligible.

Mr. Berlin puts his case as follows:

If determinism were a valid theory of human behaviour, these distinctions [like 'you should not (or need not) have done this', and 'I could do it, but I would rather not', which plainly involve the notion of more than the merely logical possibility of the realization of alternatives other than those which were in fact realized, namely of differences between situations in which individuals can be reasonably regarded as being responsible for their acts, and those in which they cannot] would be as inappropriate as the attribution of moral responsibility to the planetary system or the tissues of a living cell.... Unless we attach some meaning to the notion of free acts, i.e. acts not wholly determined by antecedent events or by the nature and 'dispositional characteristics' of either persons or things, it is difficult to see how we come to distinguish acts to which responsibility is attached from mere segments in a physical, psychical, or psycho-physical causal chain of events.... If the determinist hypothesis were true, and adequately accounted for the actual world, there is a clear sense in which (despite all the extraordinary casuistry which has been employed to avoid this conclusion) the notion of human responsibility, as ordinarily understood would no longer apply to any actual, but only imaginary or conceivable, states of affairs. . . . To speak, as some theorists of history (and scientists with a philosophical bent) tend to do, as if one might accept the determinist hypothesis, and yet to continue to think and speak much as we do at present, is to breed intellectual confusion. (Pp. 32–3.)

I have already examined those parts of this critique which, as I see it, thoroughly confound the notion of 'free acts' with that of 'undetermined acts'; and my readers must decide where the real intellectual confusion is to be found. But I do want to consider whether, as Mr. Berlin claims, a consistent determinist cannot employ ordinary moral discourse in its customary meanings.

a. Is this claim to be decided on the basis of straightforward empirical evidence, as Berlin sometimes hints it ought to be? If so, then although no statistical data are available and the available information is doubtless not conclusive, the evidence we do have does not appear to support his contention. The language of many devout religious believers, to say nothing of philosophers like Spinoza, provides some ground for maintaining that many men find no psychological obstacles to making normal moral appraisals, despite their explicit and apparently whole-hearted adherence to a thoroughgoing determinism. I cite one instance out of a large number that could be mentioned. As is well known, Bishop Bossuet composed his *Discourse on Universal History* with the intent to offer guidance to the Dauphin on the proper conduct of a royal prince. In it, however, he maintained that

. . . the long concatenation of particular causes which make and undo empires depends on the decrees of Divine Providence. High up in His heavens God holds the reins of all kingdoms. He has every heart in His hand. Sometimes He restrains passions, sometimes He leaves them free, and thus agitates mankind. By this means God carries out his redoubtable judgements according to ever infallible rules. He it is who prepares results through the most distant causes, and who strikes vast blows whose repercussion is so widespread. Thus it is that God reigns over all nations. (*Discourse on Universal History*, Part XIV, Chap. 8; quoted by Renier, G. J., *History: Its Purpose and Method*, p. 264.)

The relevant question to ask at this point is not whether Bossuet was sound in his claims, nor whether he was correct in holding that the reconciliation of human freedom with the operation of a Divine Providence is a transcendent mystery. The relevant question is whether Bossuet did in fact subscribe to a Providential (and therefore deterministic) conception of history, and yet employ ordinary moral language to express familiar moral distinctions. There seems to me little doubt that the answer is clearly affirmative, contrary to Mr. Berlin's assumption that the answer ought to be negative.

b. Let us suppose, however, that Mr. Berlin is right in claiming that if we really did come to believe in a thoroughgoing determinism, the meanings of our moral discourse would be altered. But just what would this assumed fact establish? There are indeed comparable cases in other domains of thought in which, because of the influence of new theoretical ideas the meanings of older but surviving locutions have to some extent been revised. Thus, most educated men today accept the heliocentric theory of planetary motions, but continue to use the language of the sun rising and setting; and it is safe to suppose that they do not associate with such locutions the precise meanings those expressions doubtless had when the Ptolemaic theory was dominant. Nevertheless, some of the distinctions which this older language codified are not without foundation even today, for in many contexts of observation and analysis it is not incorrect to describe the facts by saying that the sun rises in the east and sinks in the west; and we have learned to use this language so as to express these distinctions, without committing ourselves to a number of others that depend on an acceptance of a geocentric theory of the heavens.

Analogously, however, should the majority of men accept the deterministic assumptions—perhaps because all human acts had in fact been discovered to have determinate conditions for their occurrence—the difference would not thereby be wiped out between those acts which we now describe in our current language as freely chosen and those acts which are not, between those traits of character and personality over which an individual manifestly has control and those over which he has not. When the assumed shifts in linguistic meanings are completed, moreover, it still will be the case that certain types of acts will be affected by praise and blame, that men will continue to be able to control and modify by suitable discipline some of their impulses but not others, that some men will be able by making the effort to improve certain of their performances while other men will not be able to do so, and so on. To deny this, and to maintain the contrary, is to suppose that men would be transformed, by a mere change in theoretical belief, into creatures radically different from what they were prior to that alteration in belief; and such a supposition is hardly credible. But if such a supposition *is* rejected, our ordinary moral language with its associated customary meanings will survive at least partially a general acceptance of the deterministic assumption. Belief in determinism is therefore not incompatible, either psychologically or logically, with the normal use of moral discourse or with the significant imputation of moral responsibility. The alleged incompatibility can be established, so it seems to me, only if the question-begging premiss is introduced that our making moral distinctions at all entails disbelief in determinism.

Let me say in conclusion what I have already asserted earlier. I do not believe that determinism is a demonstrable thesis, and I think that if it is construed as a statement about a categorical feature of everything whatsoever is may even be false. I have spent much time in this paper defending it against various types of criticism because, were those criticisms mistakenly accepted as sound, there would be a strong likelihood that premature limits would be set on the possible scope of scientific inquiry. For on my construction of determinism, it is in effect a regulative principle which formulates the general objective of science as a search for explanations—as a quest for ascertaining the conditions upon which the occurrence of events is contingent. I do not wish to disguise the fact that the dogmatic adoption of various *special* forms of the deterministic principle has often hindered the advance of knowledge, or that much iniquitous social practice and much doubtful social theory have been defended in the name of *particular* versions of determinism. Nevertheless, to abandon the deterministic principle itself, is to withdraw from the enterprise of science. And I do not believe that however acute is our awareness of the rich variety of human experience, and however sensitive our concern for the fuller development of human individuality, our best interests will be served by stopping objective inquiry into the various conditions which determine the existence of human traits and actions, and by thus shutting the door to the progressive liberation from illusion that can come from the achievement of such knowledge.

NOTES ON THE CONTRIBUTORS

R. G. COLLINGWOOD, who died in 1943, had been Wayneflete Professor of Metaphysical Philosophy at Oxford since 1935. Among his many publications are *The Idea of History* (1945) and—for he was also a historian—*Roman Britain and the English Settlements* (with J. L. N. Myres, 1936).

PETER WINCH is Professor of Philosophy at King's College, London. His publications include *The Idea of a Social Science* (1958) and *Ethics and Action* (1972).

MAURICE MANDELBAUM is a professor at Johns Hopkins University, Baltimore. Among his many publications are *The Problem of Historical Knowledge* (1938) and *History, Man and Reason* (1971).

WILLIAM DRAY is chairman of the Philosophy Department of Trent University in Canada. His publications include *Laws and Explanation in History* (1957) and *Philosophy of History* (1954).

CARL G. HEMPEL has been a professor at Princeton University since 1955. He is the author of many influential papers, and of *Fundamentals of Concept Formation in Empirical Science* (1952) and *Aspects of Scientific Explanation* (1965).

QUENTIN SKINNER is a lecturer in history at Cambridge and a Fellow of Christ's College.

W. H. WALSH has been Professor of Logic and Metaphysics at Edinburgh since 1960. Among his publications are *Reason and Experience* (1947), *Introduction to Philosophy of History* (1951), and *Hegelian Ethics* (1969).

JOHN PASSMORE is Professor of Philosophy at the Australian National University. His books include *A Hundred Years of Philosophy* (1957) and *The Perfectibility of Man* (1970).

SIR ISAIAH BERLIN is President of Wolfson College, Oxford, and until 1967 was Chichele Professor of Social and Political Theory. Among his publications are *The Hedgehog and the Fox* (1953), *Karl Marx* (rev. edn., 1963), and *Four Essays on Liberty* (1969).

ERNEST NAGEL was until recently John Dewey Professor of Philosophy at Columbia University in New York. Among his major publications are *Logic without Metaphysics* (1956) and *The Structure of Science* (1961).

BIBLIOGRAPHY

I. BOOKS

ARON, RAYMOND, *Introduction to the Philosophy of History*, trans. G. J. Irwin (London: Weidenfeld and Nicolson, 1961)

BERLIN, ISAIAH, *Four Essays on Liberty* (London: Oxford University Press, 1969)

CARR, E. H., *What is History?* (New York: Alfred A. Knopf, 1962)

COLLINGWOOD, R. G., *The Idea of History* (Oxford: Clarendon Press, 1946)

CROCE, BENEDETTO, *History: Its Theory and Practice*, trans. D. Ainslee (New York: Harcourt, Brace and Co., 1921)

DANTO, ARTHUR C., *Analytical Philosophy of History* (Cambridge: Cambridge University Press, 1965)

DILTHEY, WILHELM, *Meaning in History*, ed. H. P. Rickman (London: Allen and Unwin, 1961)

DONAGAN, ALAN, *The Later Philosophy of R. G. Collingwood* (Oxford: Clarendon Press, 1962)

DRAY, WILLIAM, *Laws and Explanation in History* (Oxford: Oxford University Press, 1957)

——, *Philosophy of History* (Englewood Cliffs, N.J.: Prentice-Hall, 1964)

FISCHER, D. H., *Historians' Fallacies* (London: Routledge and Kegan Paul, 1971)

GALLIE, W. B., *Philosophy and the Historical Understanding* (London: Chatto and Windus, 1964)

GARDINER, PATRICK, *The Nature of Historical Explanation* (Oxford: Oxford University Press, 1952)

GEYL, PIETER, *Debates with Historians* (The Hague: Wolters and Nijhoff, 1955)

LOUCH, A. R., *Explanation and Human Action* (Oxford: Basil Blackwell, 1966)

LÖWITH, KARL, *Meaning in History* (Chicago: Chicago University Press, 1949)

MANDELBAUM, MAURICE, *The Problem of Historical Knowledge* (New York: Liveright Publishing Corporation, 1938)

MANUEL, FRANK E., *Shapes of Philosophical History* (London: Allen and Unwin, 1965)

MEILAND, J. W., *Scepticism and Historical Knowledge* (New York: Random House, 1965)

MINK, L. O., *Mind, History and Dialectic* (Bloomington: Indiana University Press, 1969)

NAGEL, ERNEST, *The Structure of Science* (London: Routledge and Kegan Paul, 1961)

OAKESHOTT, MICHAEL, *Experience and its Modes* (Cambridge: Cambridge University Press, 1933)

POPPER, K. R., *The Open Society and its Enemies* (London: Routledge and Kegan Paul, 1945)

POPPER, K. R., *The Poverty of Historicism* (London: Routledge and Kegan Paul, 1957)

RYAN, ALAN, *The Philosophy of the Social Sciences* (London: Macmillan, 1970)

STOVER, ROBERT, *The Nature of Historical Thinking* (Chapel Hill: University of North Carolina Press, 1967)

TAYLOR, CHARLES, *The Explanation of Behaviour* (London: Routledge and Kegan Paul, 1964)

WALSH, W. H., *Introduction to Philosophy of History* (London: Hutchinson, 1951)

WEBER, MAX, *The Methodology of the Social Sciences*, trans. E. A. Shils and H. A. Finch (Glencoe, Ill.: Free Press, 1949)

WHITE, MORTON, *Foundations of Historical Knowledge* (New York: Harper and Row, 1965)

WINCH, PETER, *The Idea of a Social Science* (London: Routledge and Kegan Paul, 1958)

WRIGHT, G. H. VON, *Explanation and Understanding* (London: Routledge and Kegan Paul, 1971)

II. ARTICLES

Explanation and Understanding

ATKINSON, R. F., 'Explanation in History', *Proceedings of the Aristotelian Society* (1971–2)

BAKER, A. J., 'Historical Explanation and Universal Propositions', *Australasian Journal of Philosophy* (1963)

BEER, SAMUEL H., 'Causal Explanation and Imaginative Re-enactment', *History and Theory* (1963)

BERLIN, ISAIAH, 'The Concept of Scientific History', *History and Theory* (1960); reprinted in *Philosophical Analysis and History*, ed. W. H. Dray (New York: Harper and Row, 1966)

CHURCHLAND, PAUL M., 'The Logical Character of Action-Explanations', *Philosophical Review* (1970)

DAVIDSON, D., 'Actions, Reasons and Causes', *Journal of Philosophy* (1963)

DONAGAN, ALAN, 'Explanation in History', *Mind* (1957); reprinted in *Theories of History*, ed. P. L. Gardiner (Glencoe, Ill.: Free Press, 1959)

——, 'Historical Explanation: The Popper–Hempel Model Reconsidered', *History and Theory* (1964); reprinted in *Philosophical Analysis and History*, ed. Dray

——, 'Alternative Historical Explanations and their Verification', *The Monist* (1969)

DRAY, WILLIAM, ' "Explaining What" in History', in *Theories of History,* ed. Gardiner

——, 'Singular Hypotheticals and Historical Explanation', in *Sociological Theory: Inquiries and Paradigms*, ed. L Gross (New York: Harper and Row, 1967)

GALLIE, W. B., 'Explanations in History and the Genetic Sciences', *Mind* (1955); reprinted in *Theories of History*, ed. Gardiner

GARDINER, PATRICK, 'Historical Understanding and the Empiricist Tradition', in *British Analytical Philosophy*, ed. B. Williams and A. Montefiore (London: Routledge and Kegan Paul, 1965)

HEMPEL, C. G., 'The Function of General Laws in History', *Journal of Philosophy* (1942); reprinted in *Theories of History*, ed. Gardiner

——, 'Explanation in Science and in History', in *Frontiers of Science and Philosophy*, ed. R. G. Colodny (Pittsburgh: University of Pittsburgh Press, 1962); reprinted in *Philosophical Analysis and History*, ed. Dray

——, 'Rational Action', in *Proceedings and Addresses of the American Philosophical Association*, vol. 35 (Yellow Springs, Ohio: Antioch Press, 1962)

JOYNT, C. B. and RESCHER, N., 'On Explanation in History', *Mind* (1959)

——, 'The Problem of Uniqueness in History', *History and Theory* (1961)

MACINTYRE, A. C., 'A Mistake about Causality in Social Science', in *Philosophy, Politics and Society* (2nd Ser.), ed. P. Laslett and W. G. Runciman (Oxford: Basil Blackwell, 1962)

MACIVER, A. M., 'The Character of a Historical Explanation', *Proceedings of the Aristotelian Society*, Supplementary Volume 21 (1947)

MARC-WOGAU, K., 'On Historical Explanation', *Theoria* (1962)

MINK, L. O., 'The Autonomy of Historical Understanding', *History and Theory* (1965); reprinted in *Philosophical Analysis and History*, ed. Dray

NOWELL-SMITH, P. H., 'Are Historical Events Unique?', *Proceedings of the Aristotelian Society* (1956–7)

PASSMORE, JOHN, 'Explanation in Everyday Life, in Science, and in History', *History and Theory* (1962)

POPPER, K. R., 'A Pluralist Approach to the Philosophy of History', in *Roads to Freedom: Essays in Honour of F. A. von Hayek,* ed. E. Streissler (London: Routledge and Kegan Paul, 1969)

SKINNER, QUENTIN, 'The Limits of Historical Explanations', *Philosophy* 1966)

——, 'Meaning and Understanding in the History of Ideas', *History and Theory* (1969)

SCRIVEN, MICHAEL, 'Truisms as the Grounds for Historical Explanations', in *Theories of History*, ed. Gardiner

——, 'Causes, Connections and Conditions in History', in *Philosophical Analysis and History*, ed. Dray

WALSH, W. H., 'Historical Causation', *Proceedings of the Aristotelian Society* (1962–3)

WATKINS, J. W. N., 'Ideal Types and Historical Explanation', *British Journal for the Philosophy of Science* (1952); reprinted in *Readings in the Philosophy of Science*, ed. H. Feigl and M. Brodbeck (New York: Appleton-Century-Crofts, 1953)

——, 'Imperfect Rationality', in *Explanation in the Behavioural Sciences*, ed. R. Burger and F. Cioffi (Cambridge: Cambridge University Press, 1970)

WHITE, MORTON, 'Historical Explanation', *Mind* (1943); reprinted in *Theories of History*, ed. Gardiner

WINCH, PETER, 'Understanding a Primitive Society', *American Philosophical Quarterly* (1964); reprinted in *Rationality*, ed. B. R. Wilson (Oxford: Basil Blackwell, 1970)

Structure and Narrative in Historiography

DANTO, ARTHUR C., 'Narrative Sentences', *History and Theory* (1962)

DRAY, WILLIAM, 'On the Nature and Role of Narrative in Historiography', *History and Theory* (1971)

ELY, R. G., GRUNER, ROLF, and DRAY, WILLIAM, 'Mandelbaum on Historical Narrative: A Discussion', *History and Theory* (1969)

FAIN, HASKELL, 'History as Science', *History and Theory* (1970)

GALLIE, W. B., 'The Historical Understanding', *History and Theory* (1963)

LOUCH, A. R., 'History as Narrative', *History and Theory* (1969)

MANDELBAUM, MAURICE, 'A Note on History as Narrative', *History and Theory* (1967)

OLAFSON, F. A., 'Narrative History and the Concept of Action', *History and Theory* (1970)

STALNAKER, R., 'Events, Periods and Institutions in Historians' Language', *History and Theory* (1967)

WHITE, MORTON, 'The Logic of Historical Narration', in *Philosophy and History: A Symposium*, ed. Sidney Hook (New York: New York University Press, 1963)

Objectivity and Evaluation

BEARD, Charles A., 'That Noble Dream', *American Historical Review* (1935); reprinted in *The Varieties of History*, ed. F. Stern (New York: Meridian Books, 1956)

BLAKE, C., 'Can History be Objective?', *Mind* (1955); reprinted in *Theories of History*, ed. Gardiner

BURY, J. B., 'The Science of History', in *Selected Essays of J. B. Bury*, ed. H. Temperley (Cambridge: Cambridge University Press, 1930)

DEWEY, JOHN, 'Historical Judgements', in *The Philosophy of History in our Time*, ed. H. Meyerhoff (New York: Doubleday Anchor Books, 1959)

DRAY, WILLIAM, 'Some Causal Accounts of the American Civil War', *Daedalus* (1962)

LEACH, JAMES, 'Historical Objectivity and Value Neutrality', *Inquiry* (1968)

LEVICH, MARVIN, 'Disagreement and Controversy in History', *History and Theory* (1962)

LOVEJOY, A. O., 'Present Standpoints and Past History', *Journal of Philosophy* (1939); reprinted in *The Philosophy of History in our Time*, ed. Meyerhoff

MANDELBAUM, MAURICE, 'Objectivism in History', in *Philosophy and History: A Symposium*, ed. Hook

MELDEN, A. I., 'Historical Objectivity, a "Noble Dream"?', *Journal of General Education* (1952)

NAGEL, ERNEST, 'Some Issues in the Logic of Historical Analysis', *Scientific Monthly* (1952); reprinted in *Theories of History*, ed. Gardiner

RITTER, GERHARD, 'Scientific History, Contemporary History and Political Science', *History and Theory* (1960)

STRAUSS, L., 'The Social Science of Max Weber', *Measure* (1951)

TAYLOR, CHARLES, 'Interpretation and the Sciences of Man', *Review of Metaphysics* (1971)

UNGER, RUDOLF, 'The Problem of Historical Objectivity: A Sketch of its Development to the Time of Hegel', *History and Theory* (1971)

WALSH, W. H., 'The Limits of Scientific History', in *Historical Studies III*, ed. James Hogan (London: Bowes and Bowes, 1961); reprinted in *Philosophical Analysis and History*, ed. Dray

WHITE, MORTON, 'Can History be Objective?', in *The Philosophy of History in our Time*, ed. Meyerhoff

History and Social Science

AYER, A. J., 'Man as a Subject for Science', *Auguste Comte Memorial Lecture* (London: Athlone Press, 1964); reprinted in *Philosophy, Politics and Society* (3rd Ser.), ed. P. Laslett and W. G. Runciman (Oxford: Basil Blackwell, 1967)

BRODBECK, MAY, 'Methodological Individualisms: Definitions and Reduction', *Philosophy of Science* (1958); reprinted in *Philosophical Analysis and History*, ed. Dray

DANTO, ARTHUR C., 'The Historical Individual', in *Philosophical Analysis and History*, ed. Dray

GARDINER, PATRICK, 'The Concept of Man as Presupposed by the Historical Studies', in *Royal Institute of Philosophy Lectures*, vol. 4, ed. G. N. A. Vesey (London: Macmillan, 1971)

GELLNER, ERNEST, 'Holism versus Individualism in History and Sociology', in *Theories of History*, ed. Gardiner

GOLDSTEIN, L. J., 'The Inadequacy of the Principle of Methodological Individualism', *Journal of Philosophy* (1956)

GRUNER, ROLF, 'Understanding in the Social Sciences and History', *Inquiry* (1967)

MANDELBAUM, MAURICE, 'Societal Facts', *British Journal of Sociology* (1955); reprinted in *Theories of History*, ed. Gardiner

——, 'Societal Laws', *British Journal for the Philosophy of Science* (1957); reprinted in *Philosophical Analysis and History*, ed. Dray

PASSMORE, JOHN, 'History and Sociology', *Australian Journal of Politics and History* (1958)

ROTENSTREICH, NATHAN, 'The Idea of Historical Progress and its Assumptions', *History and Theory* (1971)

SEN, A. K., 'Determinism and Historical Predictions', *Enquiry* (New Delhi, 1959)

WATKINS, J. W. N., 'Historical Explanation in the Social Sciences', *British Journal for the Philosophy of Science* (1957); reprinted in *Theories of History*, ed. Gardiner

INDEX OF NAMES

(not including authors mentioned only in the Bibliography)